CHILD CARE MANUAL FOR SOCIAL WORKERS

THIRD EDITION

BY

A. E. LEEDING, D.P.A., M.B.A.S.W.

One-time Children's Officer,
Warwickshire County Council

LONDON
BUTTERWORTHS
1976

ENGLAND:	BUTTERWORTH & CO. (PUBLISHERS) LTD. LONDON: 88 Kingsway, WC2B 6AB
AUSTRALIA:	BUTTERWORTHS PTY. LTD. SYDNEY: 586 Pacific Highway, Chatswood, NSW 2067 Also at Melbourne, Brisbane, Adelaide and Perth
CANADA:	BUTTERWORTH & CO. (CANADA) LTD. TORONTO: 2265 Midland Avenue, Scarborough M1P 4S1
NEW ZEALAND:	BUTTERWORTHS OF NEW ZEALAND LTD. WELLINGTON: 26/28 Waring Taylor Street, 1
SOUTH AFRICA:	BUTTERWORTH & CO. (SOUTH AFRICA) (PTY.) LTD. DURBAN: 152/154 Gale Street

SB 1276.FA. 2.77

©

A. E. LEEDING

1976

ISBN 0 406 27002 3

Printed in Great Britain by Cox & Wyman Ltd, London, Fakenham and Reading

SOCIAL WORKERS

TO MY WIFE
With gratitude
for many years of care

FOREWORD

A manual like this is indispensable, since social service responsibilities are constantly broadening while courses of social work
education often remain restricted to two years or even less of full-
time study.

Five years after the integration of local authority social services, we
recognise anew the significances of specific functions in the generic
social work service. Some people imagined, in the early flush of
enthusiasm, that to make a social worker responsible for everything
would enable him or her to do everything. The concept of social
work as a calling in which learning was a continuous process
tended to be merged with an idea that training was a one-off
operation which finished with the award of a certificate of qualification.

Alfred Leeding's manual brings to readers at all levels of expertise
the refined wisdom of decades of experience in the administration of
services to children within the framework of law. It helps social
workers and administrators to tread the delicate path between
community intervention and the privacy of family life. The year
1963 marked the end of more than half a century of calm development in the law and the services for children in disturbed families.
The successive statutes from Churchill's Children Act of 1908 to
Henry Brooke's Children and Young Persons Act of 1963 were agreed
measures, distilling the consensus of forward-looking public and
vocational opinion and enjoying the full spectrum of party political
support. From the publication, in 1965, of the White Paper *The
Child, the Family and The Young Offender* and, in 1968, the Seebohm
Report on *The Local Authority Personal Social Services* development
seems only to have come through conflict and division. It is no
wonder if some social workers have turned away from that part of
their task which is to refine their own skill in helping people, to
concentrate upon the equally important task of convincing the
public that both self-interest and humanity demand a larger share of
resources for the disadvantaged.

The Children and Young Persons Act, enacted but not implemented in 1969, was the brain child of a few visionaries in the
Home Office Children's Department, carried to the arid pages of the
statute book in the flushed excitement of a reforming parliament.
A study of this manual shows how good intentions were frustrated by

an alarming lack of understanding, and how concern switched from caring about people to caring about the less attractive pressures of public opinion. The punitive approved schools were notionally swept away to be replaced by therapeutic community homes. The objective of containing the child who was unmanageable in the community was replaced by the objective of selecting those disturbed children who were likely to respond to treatment. The local authority residential social worker is now left to manage the unmanageable and the social worker in the field and in the courts is left to face the anger of press, police, property owners and magistrates.

The backlash marked by the Children Act 1975, displays, one hopes, the limits of the pendulum's swing. Parents voluntarily entrusting their children to the care of local authorities or voluntary agencies must be warned that they risk losing their parental status for no other reason than that their inability to care for them has continued for three years. For shorter periods a tariff of delays may limit a parent's right to resume care of his child, who, if with foster parents, may after varying periods of time be the subject of an application to the court for custodianship or even for an adoption order against his wishes, and possibly against the wishes of the authority or agency to whose care the parent originally entrusted him. This measure is to be introduced, if at all, in stages, like its predecessors, as a study of Chapter 17 will show.

What the author has done for one facet of social services might well be followed by manuals concerned with the handicapped, the sick, the delinquent, the homeless and the elderly all of whom are equally in need of special consideration.

Kenneth Brill
Director of Social Services
London Borough of Barnet

January 1976

PREFACE

Since the second edition of this book appeared in 1971, Social Services Departments have been faced with the demands of new legislation and with the actual implementation of the Children and Young Persons Act 1969. Many of them have also had to deal with the administrative problems arising from local government re-organisation, and from the current emphasis on corporate management and planning within the new authorities.

The last few years have been a time of commotion, of discovery, of new concepts, and of questioning; but through all this the phrase "child care" has continued to carry a specific meaning; it identifies an area of social work which is still of the highest importance both to local government as a whole, and to the staff of Social Services Departments.

At a time when difficulties abound, it is significant that the public care of children should have aroused enough concern and controversy to lead to new legislation in the shape of the Children Act 1975. The text of this book takes into account those provisions which are effective from January 1976; Chapter 17 contains a summary of the remainder of the Act for reference as and when it is brought into operation. In the meantime, there is ample scope for improvement in the day-to-day use of existing legislation, as will be evident in the chapters dealing with current child-care practice.

I am indebted to the Gloucestershire County Council for permission to quote extensively from their Community Care Programme, to their County Treasurer, Mr J. V. Miller, for valuable help and advice in the writing of Chapter 1, and to their Director of Social Services, Mr H. D. Nichols, for his kindness in granting facilities for the writing of the book. My thanks are also due to many colleagues in the Social Services Department for their willing co-operation and assistance; they are not to blame for any errors I may have made.

Chalford Hill,   A.E.L.
Glos.
January 1976

CONTENTS

Chapter 1

RESPONSIBILITY FOR CHILD CARE: ENGLAND AND WALES

SUMMARY

CHILD CARE AS PART OF PERSONAL SOCIAL SERVICES

In general terms child care may be defined as a blend of legislation and practice which inspires the social care of children and young persons under the age of 18. It has a long history, but the modern concept developed after the Second World War, when the Curtis Committee[1] report was followed by the Children Act of 1948, which for the first time established a social service specifically for children who for various reasons were unable to live with their parents under normal home conditions. This service led inevitably but gradually to a concern for the families of such children. This concern was translated into the family based social service which was established in 1971, but this does not in any way diminish the importance of the service to children and young people, still known as "child care", though now forming an integral part of the personal social services, which are provided by a partnership between the Government, voluntary organisations and local authorities.

1. GOVERNMENT

For many years, both before and since 1948, successive governments have been initiating and sponsoring progressive legislation in the interests of children; all child-care functions in England are now carried out under the general oversight of the Secretary of State for Social Services, through the Department of Health and Social

Security and the staff of the Social Work Service based in London and at regional centres throughout the country. Child-care functions in Wales are under the general oversight of the Secretary of State for Wales who also has the support of a Social Work Service. (It should be noted that the functions of the police, the courts and the probation and after care service are still within the purview of the Secretary of State for Home Affairs.)

2. VOLUNTARY ORGANISATIONS

Child care was largely pioneered by voluntary organisations, many of which are still very much concerned in it and are making an increasing contribution to the service as a whole. Most of them are in membership of a National Council of Voluntary Child Care Organisations which enables them jointly to consider current problems and to co-operate in many and various ways. A voluntary organisation is defined in the Children Act of 1948 as "a body, the activities of which are carried on otherwise than for profit", but is not "a public or local authority". Clearly, such organisations have no obligation to exist, or to undertake child-care work at all. They are free to provide such services as they think necessary or desirable, and have already initiated new experimental schemes and carried out original research of benefit to the service. For these voluntary organisations, child care is still a specialist service, indeed the only specialist service for children in difficulties; as such, it is used to strengthen and support the more wide-ranging social services of local authorities.

Although these voluntary organisations are independent of both the Minister and local government, they are subject in some of their activities to the Regulations which apply to local authorities, for instance with regard to the boarding-out of children in their care; the advice of the Social Work Service of the Ministry is available to them in the same way as it is to local authorities.

3. LOCAL AUTHORITIES

The duty of implementing social service legislation falls mainly upon local authorities, and there are many statutory requirements which are binding upon them, but not on voluntary organisations. Since local government was re-organised in 1974, there have been seven different types of local authority ranging from parish councils (community councils in Wales) to metropolitan counties. Only four types of local authority have social service responsibility, however, these being the Common Council of the City of London, the London boroughs, the non-metropolitan counties and the metropolitan districts.[2] Of these, the last-named are "all-purpose" authorities, the others being "most-purpose" authorities which do not provide all services. No local authority has power to delegate social service functions to a council of a different type, though there are a number of services in which there is consultation and co-operation between the councils of non-metropolitan counties and non-metropolitan districts.

Since the personal social services depend so heavily upon local authorities, social workers who are employed in local government (and this now includes those working in hospitals) should have some general understanding of the way in which the affairs of a council are managed, even though they may feel that this subject is rather remote from their day-to-day work. Some understanding in broad outline may help to explain how decisions about the use of resources are likely to be made, and why it is that not all demands for a particular service will be met. The current serious anxieties about the lack of resources for all local authority services (including the social services) have stressed the importance of making the best possible use of the main resources of land, manpower and finance, so that the investment may be of the greatest ultimate benefit to the community as a whole.

a *Committee Structure*

A local authority consists of a number of people who have been elected by the public to form a council, and is therefore a corporate body. As such, it is ultimately responsible for all the decisions taken in its name, but because of the vast range of its responsibilities, it has traditionally operated through a number of separate committees (most of which were established by statute). Each of these has delegated to it certain powers for the day-to-day performance of the duties of the Council as a whole. As new functions have continued to be entrusted to local authorities, so they have been delegated to the most appropriate committee. In this way there has grown up a concept of a number of specialist committees with sole powers to deal with specific subjects; this has become an accepted part of local government but it has been strongly challenged in recent years.

The specialist concept has been strengthened by the fact that local authorities once had an obligation to appoint a number of specified chief officers—for instance, a clerk, a treasurer, a chief education officer, a director of social services and a surveyor. When such a chief officer has been appointed, it has been assumed that he should lead a department, even though departments as such have no legal recognition in local government, and only consist of the facilities and staff provided to assist the designated chief officer in his work. It has always been assumed that a chief officer reports not to the Council, but to the committee whose special functions he carries out.

These trends have led to a local government pattern of a number of separate committees, each served by a chief officer with his "department", having its own professional skills and expert knowledge, though these are confined to only one aspect of the Council's overall activities.

It has therefore been very difficult in the past for a local authority to achieve unity in its internal organisation, since instead of co-operation there has been competition for resources; the system has tended to make the committees' interests more important than those of the community they serve.

b *Corporate Management*

As this has been increasingly recognised, and as local government has spent greater sums of public money, it has become clear that a different approach is essential. If a local authority is to function effectively, it must adopt a corporate scheme of management so that it acts as one entity rather than as a group of loosely allied committees, each with its own chief officer, and each, quite understandably, seeking the maximum resources for its own activities or services. A local authority, unlike a business organisation, cannot demonstrate its effectiveness by the amount of profit it makes, but it must find some other way of measuring the effect of its growing expenditure; in the final analysis this must be done by assessing the impact of its services on the well-being of the community at large.

With this in mind, local authorities have recently devoted a great deal of attention to management techniques designed to promote a corporate, rather than a committee, approach. These techniques have different names, for instance, Planning Programming Budgeting, or Performance, Analysis, Review, and they may have somewhat different methods; but they all have the same purpose, that is, to decide what the overall objectives of the Council are, how they can best be met, and how they are in fact being served by the multifarious activities of the Council's staff in the exercise of statutory powers. These questions naturally give rise to consideration of preference and choice. Which is the best way of meeting this objective? Is proposal A more important than proposal B? Given present resources, what is the Council's order of priority?

Clearly, this management approach cuts across the traditional pattern of entirely separate committees and specialist chief officers. Its implementation has many effects, of which two are mentioned here:

i Chief Officers under the leadership of the Chief Executive are grouped into a management team, and *in that capacity* consider the interests and performance of the Council as a whole, rather than merely representing their own service responsibilities.

ii Committees work more closely to a central Policy and Resources Committee which, as its name implies, first agrees upon the Council's overall objectives and is then responsible to the Council as a whole for the best use of its resources of land, manpower and finance.

From these two innovations many others flow: the importance of research, the pooling of statistical and other information, uniform policies for staff recruitment and training, and methods of reviewing the actual performance of the Council in moving towards the objectives recommended by the Policy and Resources Committee and adopted by the Council.

c *The Local Government Act 1972*

This kind of thinking was going on in a number of the former local authorities before re-organisation and it was realised that the formation of new authorities under the Local Government Act 1972 would present a great opportunity for radically changing the traditional patterns. The Secretary of State for the Environment, together with the then local authority associations, set up a Study Group in May 1971 and in 1972 received its report, entitled *The New Local Authorities: management and structure* (usually known as Bains Report). This contained a number of recommendations which were fitted into the framework of the Local Government Act 1972, operative from 1 April 1974.

As a result of this Act, local authorities now have wider discretion with regard to the appointment of specified committees and designated chief officers, but, contrary to the Bains recommendations, are still required to appoint a *Social Services Committee* and a *Director of Social Services*. The import of the Act, however, is to give authorities greater freedom in the management of their internal affairs and there is much to encourage the adoption of the corporate approach even though a "special" committee and chief officer must be appointed for social service functions.

d *Standing Orders*

All local authorities make rules, known as Standing Orders, governing the conduct of the Council's affairs, and specially such matters as the appointment of Committees, delegation to them, and to officers, of the Council's powers, procedure at meetings, and the making of Financial Regulations. The Standing Orders are the instrument by which the Council sets out the ways in which it operates within the overall authority of the Local Government Act.

e *Committee Procedure*

The committee procedure in any local authority is a matter for the authority to determine and may, therefore, take different forms. Many local authorities have adopted the recommendations of the first Maud Report with the result that sub-committees have been greatly reduced in number or abolished altogether. In these authorities, day-to-day decisions are taken by the permanent staff of the departments, within a system of delegation. The Committee itself may meet only quarterly, and confine itself to the discussion of policies and principles, including the use of resources allocated to it by the Council. In such authorities, it is unlikely that social workers will attend the meetings of the Committee unless there is some matter of policy arising in connection with a particular case.

In other authorities, where sub-committees exist, they are usually concerned with a section of the Committee's work, such as the administration of homes, and may receive detailed reports from members of staff who are directly involved with the matters to be discussed or, they may have oversight of a service within a part of the Council's geographical area.

Officers of the authority are not members of the Committee or of sub-committees; they have the duty of tendering advice to the members and reporting on subjects of interest or concern. Officers cannot therefore vote, or speak to a motion, though they may be asked to give their views on any item on the agenda. Under the Local Government Act 1972, authorities have wide powers for the delegation of responsibility from the Council to committees and from committees to sub-committees or to officers.

f *Finance*

One of the central functions of a local authority is the approval of an annual budget, by which money is allocated to the various services and objectives. Like any other budget, it is made up of income and expenditure.

Income is derived partly from miscellaneous sources, including the charges made for some of its services, but mainly from the rates levied upon householders, and from the Government Rate Support Grant. This grant amounts at present to over 60% of total income and should in theory enable an authority to make its own decisions about the services it will provide. The government grant is calculated annually and is based on a "needs" element, a "resources" element, and a "domestic" element. It takes into account a number of population factors, such as the number of school children, the number of people receiving personal social services, and population growth and distribution. While there are a few services which receive a specific amount of grant, the police service for instance, the grant is made primarily in respect of an authority's total services and is not earmarked for particular purposes.

Expenditure can only be properly incurred under the various statutes which lay duties on the Council, and must be kept within the budget, once approved. All expenditure must be certified by the appropriate Chief Officer, and is subject to the authority's Financial Regulations, to internal audit, and to the annual audit of the Government Auditor.

4. OTHER BODIES AND ORGANISATIONS

Although the responsibility of an actual social service for children is shared between the government, voluntary organisations and local authorities, there are other important institutions and bodies which have important relevant powers or duties.

a The courts, which exist independently of both central and local government, are called upon to make decisions affecting the welfare of minors. At the highest level, the Family Division of the High Court has inherent power to make a minor a ward of the Court itself and having done so may exercise general supervision of his upbringing and of his parent or guardian. This court, together with County Courts and Magistrates' Courts have the power and duty to consider the welfare of children in divorce, custody, guardianship, adoption and matrimonial proceedings, and may in certain circumstances make appropriate orders for custody, care and control. Juvenile courts have a duty to consider the welfare of children and young persons who appear before them in either criminal or civil proceedings.

b The National Health Service, through Area Health Authorities, is responsible for the physical and mental care of all children, and there are many situations in which social and medical care are complementary to each other.

c The education service has general responsibility for the education of children of compulsory school age, and is involved in educational services both for those under the age of 5 and over the age of 16. Here again social factors for some children are of great importance, so that a watertight division between care and education becomes impossible.

d The Department of Social Security is concerned with the provision of adequate maintenance allowances for families or households and in this way directly contributes to the welfare of large numbers of children, especially those who are sometimes in voluntary or statutory care for short periods because of family circumstances.

In addition, there are many organisations which have no statutory powers or duties but which exist to further the interests of all children, or of some special group of them. These organisations are far too numerous to mention, but an exception must be made in the case of the National Children's Bureau because of its concern for every aspect of the care of children, and because of its advocacy of their rights in an adult world. The Bureau has produced a large number of reports on such topics as adoption, foster care, and residential care. Its on-going survey of all children born in one week in 1958 is a major contribution to the study of the needs of all children, whether brought up in their natural families or in some form of substitute care.

Lastly there are various bodies concerned with research and the formulation of policy for the whole of the personal social services, including those for children. In view of the tremendous range of interest, it was considered essential that there should be an independent forum with the duty of advising the responsible minister and of developing resources and training for the promotion of an effective service. To meet this need, the Personal Social Services Council was established on the recommendation of the Seebohm Committee; one of its priorities is the bringing about of greater consumer participation in policy making. The first report of this Council, containing a wealth of comment and information, was published in August1975.[3] In addition to factual data about the financing of the social services, the report contains a number of statements made to members of the Council while they were visiting different parts of the country seeking opinion. These statements were made by Directors of Social Services, councillors, social workers and others in local government and in the voluntary social services. They provide views, not necessarily shared by the Personal Social Services Council itself, on the general position after several years' experience of the working of the Local Authority Social Services Act 1970.

NOTES

1. Report of Committee on the Care of Children, 1946 Cmnd. 6922.
2. Local Authority Social Services Act 1970, s. 1, amended by Local Government Act 1972, s. 195.
3. First Report of the Personal Social Services Council 1975.

Chapter 2

LOCAL AUTHORITIES

SUMMARY

THE SOCIAL SERVICES COMMITTEE

Every local authority which has the duty of implementing the Local Authority Social Services Act 1970 must establish a committee with direct responsibility for the service to be provided, but two or more local authorities may establish a joint committee for this purpose if they wish. This is unlikely in view of the disappearance of small authorities in the re-organisation of 1974. The features of the committee may be listed as follows.

a The Committee must have referred to it by the local authority all matters relating to the exercise by the authority of its functions under the legislation concerned.

b Having referred these matters to the Committee, the local authority may delegate the functions themselves to the Committee.

c Before itself exercising functions under the legislation, the local authority must, unless the matter is urgent, consider a report of the Committee.

d Except with the consent of the Secretary of State, the local authority may not require the Committee to deal with any matters other than those which stand referred to it. Consent has been given for the Committee to play its part in the corporate management of the whole authority.

e Any matter which stands referred to the Committee, but which also relates to a general service of the authority, may be referred to another Committee of the authority, but only after a report by the responsible Committee has been considered.

f The Committee may appoint sub-committees, and may delegate to them any of the functions of the Committee itself.

g The Committees of two or more local authorities may establish
joint sub-committees and may delegate to them any of the
functions of either or any of the Committees themselves.

h The Committee may co-opt persons who are not members of
the authority provided that a majority of members of the
Committee are also members of the local authority.

i Sub-Committees and joint sub-committees may include persons who are not members of the authority, or authorities,
concerned, provided that at least one member of each of the
authorities is a member of the sub-committee.[1]

ROLE OF COUNCILLORS

The Act itself is based on the Seebohm Report (Cmnd. 3703)
which recommended that the local authority welfare and children's
services and certain of the health services should be unified within
each authority into one personal social service. This Report made a
number of other far-reaching recommendations for the improvement
of the existing services, but as the Act confines itself to organisational
changes only, the translation of the Seebohm ideals into reality rests
primarily in the hands of the councillors who serve on the statutory
Committee.[2]

Since councillors are elected to represent the community as a
whole, they are well placed to be aware of social needs, not only of
the elderly, the handicapped and the lonely, but also of the homeless,
the mentally ill, the "problem family" and children in difficulties. It
is the councillors who are best in a position to shape the authority's
social policy and to forge close links between all the committees and
other agencies which contribute towards the care of the community.
It is they who can ensure that services are not only provided, but that
they readily reach those who need them, and it is they who are called
upon to evaluate the effectiveness of services and to make difficult
choices of priority within the local authority's corporate management structure.[3]

Whether or not committees decide to use their power to co-opt,
they have many opportunities of obtaining the views of "consumer
groups" or social workers by means of working parties on particular
subjects or through specially constituted local consultative groups.

CHIEF OFFICER

In addition to establishing a Committee to administer the Act,
the local authority must appoint a Director of Social Services. The
Secretary of State may prescribe the qualifications required for
appointment, but until such time as he does so, he must be given
particulars of the persons who are being considered for appointment,

as he has the power of veto. Once appointed, the Director may not be employed by the authority in any other capacity unless the Secretary of State consents. Consent has been given for the Director to take part in the general management process of the local authority. The Act requires the authority to ensure that the Director, as the statutory chief officer, has adequate staff to assist him in his duties.[4]

FUNCTIONS

The Social Service functions of the local authority were, before 1971, carried out by various committees, the following being a typical distribution; in some authorities, however, the Health Committee dealt with both health and welfare matters.

Former Health Committee

National Health Service Act 1946	Care of mothers and young children. Domestic help for certain households.
Nurseries and Child-Minders Regulation Act 1948.	Regulation of nurseries and child-minders.
Mental Health Act 1959.	Welfare of mentally disordered persons in hospital or otherwise. Accommodation for children suffering from mental disorder. Regulation of residential homes for the mentally disordered.
Health Visiting and Social Work (Training) Act 1962.	Research into matters relating to local authority welfare services.
Health Services and Public Health Act 1968.	Prevention of illness, care and after-care of the sick. Provision of home help and laundry facilities for certain households.

Former Welfare Committee

National Assistance Act 1948	Accommodation for the aged, infirm or needy. Welfare of handicapped persons. Provision of meals and recreation for old people. Registration of homes or charities for aged and disabled.
Disabled Persons (Employment) Act 1958.	Facilities for the employment of the disabled.
Health Service and Public Health Act 1968.	Promotion of welfare of old people.
Chronically Sick and Disabled Persons Act 1970	Promotion of welfare of chronically sick and disabled people.

Former Children's Committee

Children and Young Persons Acts 1933–69.	Protection of the young in legal proceedings, children appearing before courts and committed to care. Promotion of welfare of children. Research, accommodation for children in care, supervision of children under court orders.
Children Act 1948	Provision for orphans and children in care. Registration of voluntary children's homes.
Children Act 1958.	Protection of children living away from their parents.
Adoption Act 1958.	Supervision of children placed for adoption. Regulation of Adoption Societies, placing children for adoption.
Matrimonial Proceedings (Magistrates' Court) Act 1960. Matrimonial Causes Act Family Law Reform Act 1969. Guardianship Act 1973 (added since 1971)	Supervision or care of children subject to Court Order in matrimonial wardship and guardianship proceedings.

None of these committees now exists. The Welfare and Children's Committees gave way to the Social Services Committee, the Health Committee was abolished in 1974 when all health functions were transferred to the Area Health Authority, leaving all social work functions with the Social Services Committee, including social work in hospitals. Each committee and its staff tended to deal with individuals or families according to the problems which became apparent. As a result of this specialist system-based approach, social workers from two or more departments were often involved with members of the same family; in many instances other social agents such as the Probation Service or the N.S.P.C.C. may also have been involved. Though all the services endeavoured by various means to co-ordinate their activities in respect of members of a family, it was not possible to attain full co-ordination of effort because each department or agency saw itself as having a duty in relation to the individual problems of members of the family rather than to the family as a whole.

It is now the duty of the Social Services Committee and its Director to administer all the listed legislation within a unified family social service, the only guidance being that put forward in the Seebohm Report of 1968. The separated child care service of the authority from 1948 onwards has thus come to an end. Its various duties, powers and resources are now absorbed into what may be called the Community Care Service. The child care functions continue and still call for specialist skill, but this should be exercised within the framework of the local authority social service which should be designed to strengthen family life and to preserve it whenever possible.

This is rather a generalised aim however; it needs to be set out in terms appropriate to the corporate approach mentioned in the last chapter. For this purpose it must be stated as a programme area which consists of an overall objective served by first-level objectives, which are in turn served by second-level objectives. All the many and varied activities of the service in its day-to-day operation must then be set out in such a way as to show which second-level objective they serve. Activities should not be carried out without a realisation of their true purpose; this applies whether they are "statutory" in the sense of being precisely controlled by statute or regulation, or "permissive" in that they are carried out under enabling legislation but only to the extent determined by the local authority. Whatever the type of activity, it must be possible for its true cost to be measured against its effectiveness in bringing about the stated objective. It should then be possible to decide that one activity is preferable to another in given circumstances. In times of economic pressure (which, for the social services, is always), such decisions can be used to alter the investment of staff and resources as between one activity or one part of the programme area and another. It is obviously difficult to conceive of a social service in these terms, because its effectiveness must ultimately be measured in terms of human happiness, but social care is now one of the most costly of an authority's total services, and cannot escape the challenge of effective management at every level.

There are various ways of describing objectives, but the outline programme shown on p. 14 may serve as an illustration.

This particular example suggests that any local authority using it would have a high regard for personal freedom and choice and would look upon long-term care or treatment in hospitals, prisons or residential establishments as a last resort. While it would be prepared to provide good long-term care when it was needed, and wanted, it would use its resources in such a way as to enable people to retain their independence for as long as possible, and it would provide different kinds of long-term care, not all residential.

If the authority had accepted that as a deliberate policy, it would follow that each separate activity and service would be seen to be serving one of the sub-objectives and thus ultimately the overall objective itself.

The activities and services need not be limited to those of a particular service. The first-level objective A, for instance, would obviously be mainly carried out by planners, though social services should be

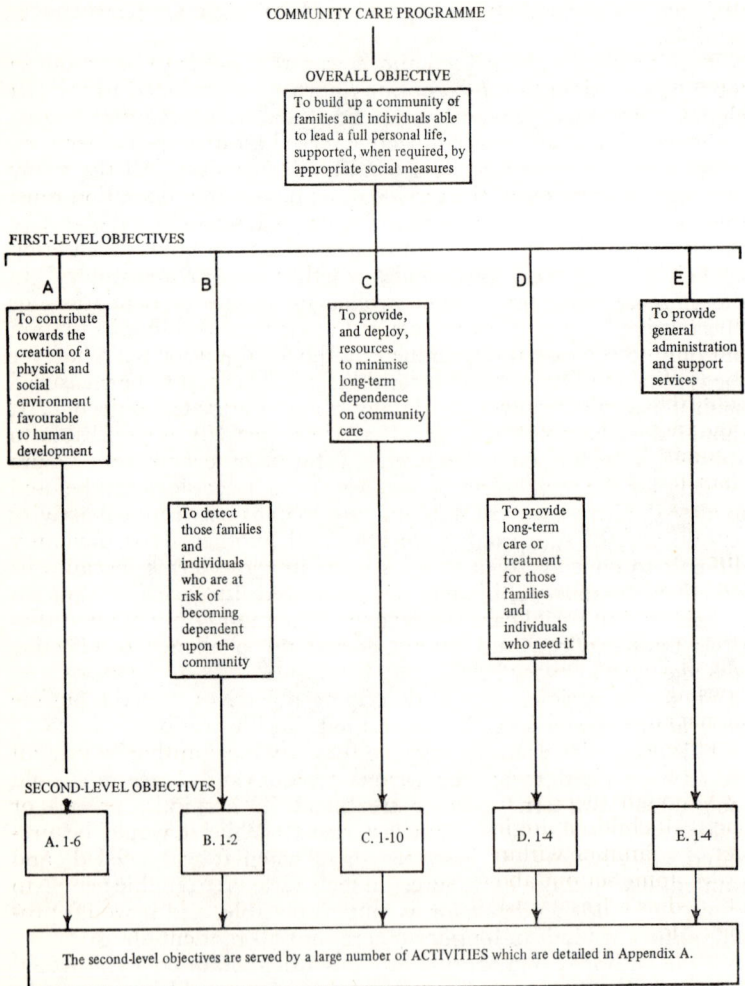

involved in it. The same objective would also be served by a number of the activities of the education service, playgroups, for example, or adventure playgrounds or community centres.

This is because under the corporate approach to local authority management, all objectives are those of the authority as a whole, and they need not therefore correspond exactly with the contents of service provision. In community care, for instance, the bulk of the activities are provided by the Social Services Committee, but other committees also provide services which to some extent serve the stated objective.

So far as children are concerned, this concept was envisaged as long ago as 1963 when the Children and Young Persons Act of that year laid on the local authority the duty to "make available such advice, guidance and assistance as may promote the welfare of children by diminishing the need to receive them into care or keep them in care, or bring them before a juvenile court". The Act also, for the first time, gave the authority power to use resources of staff and material or financial aid for this purpose.

It will be seen that although the duty was laid upon the authority as a whole, and was to stand referred to the children's committee of those days, there was no restriction as to the ways in which the advice, guidance and assistance could be provided, but because the existing committees and departments were directed towards services rather than towards children and their families, the opportunity was not grasped. Efforts were made to achieve progress by various forms of "co-ordination" but these rested on attempts to deploy together different separated services which all had their own diverse and specialist objectives.

The integration of some services under the Local Authority Social Services Act goes some way towards making co-ordination a reality, but of course there are still other local authority services such as housing and education which have a strong social element. Corporate management offers the best prospect of ensuring that they are used to serve an authority's community care objectives as well as to meet the needs of their own committees.

Although there is no longer a separate "child care" service as such, all children are individuals in the community, and their families are families within the community. The whole of the outline programme set out above can therefore be applied to them and can be used as a framework into which all the authority's social services for children, as for adults, can be fitted with meaning and purpose.

RESOURCES

The resources available to the Committee consist basically of voluntary workers, buildings, staff and finance.

VOLUNTARY WORKERS

Chapter XVI of the Seebohm Report[2] examines the concept of "welfare through community" and makes a number of recommendations about the participation of the public in the planning, organisation and provision of the personal social services. It then goes on to state clearly that the increased demands on the local authority services will be so great that it will be unable to meet them without enlisting "large numbers of volunteers" to supplement the statutory services. Though the Report refrains from suggesting exactly how this should be done, it recommends that the members of Social Service Committees, who are themselves volunteers in a way, should, with their Chief Officer, find ways of including both voluntary organisations and individual volunteers in their plans for the administration of the service.

In 1969, a report *The Voluntary Worker and the Social Services* (the Aves Report)[5] examined the subject in great detail, and made a number of specific recommendations relating to the recruitment and training of volunteers, their relationship to full-time social workers, the organisation of their work and such administrative matters as the payment of expenses, insurance cover and authorisation by an appropriate form of certificate.

The conclusions of the Aves Report follow that of Seebohm, that voluntary workers have an *essential* part to play in the provision of personal social services, and that this should be fully recognised. They should not, however, be expected to undertake duties which require professional training. (Presumably this means work which involves the use of particular skills, or perhaps, in some instances, the wisdom of experience. It is doubtful whether it can only mean professional training as such, since only about 40% of full-time social workers are so qualified, but are carrying full social work responsibities every day.)[6]

In 1974, the Government gave explicit recognition to voluntary service by making a grant of £300,000 to the Volunteer Centre, the money to be used in part for the improvement of training of what might be called Voluntary Family Counsellors. People who have a sense of community and feel a responsibility for their neighbours and friends, or for the district in which they live, are capable of doing more than digging old people's gardens, washing their windows, driving them from home to a day centre, or taking part in fundraising activities. Their qualities of compassion, understanding, and concern can all be used in a much more liberal way, and, given some basic training in essentials, can go some way to easing the burden on full-time social workers, while at the same time giving practical expression to community concern.

The Seebohm Report envisaged a "large untapped supply" of such people willing to give their time to voluntary social work, provided that they are treated as responsible, that they are given worthwhile tasks, and that they feel that their help is relevant and is needed. If there is such a reservoir of help available, it could be seen as potentially a most important resource to any Social Services Committee which really wishes to develop the involvement of the community in its work, but it is still an uncertain quantity because it has been neglected.

Traditionally, voluntary effort so far has been provided by a large number of "specialist" voluntary societies, and by more general bodies such as W.R.V.S., Citizen's Advice Bureaux, Councils of Social Service, the Samaritans and church organisations. The most apparent individual volunteers are those who actually deliver meals to the homes of elderly and handicapped people, foster parents, prison and hospital visitors, members of "good neighbour" schemes or "Fish" schemes which have developed in small localities.

There must be many more ways in which people of commitment could help in the provision of services, but if community involvement is to become a reality, it should be borne in mind that to any citizen, his real community is quite small: a hamlet, or part of a village, or, in a town, perhaps two or three streets, or a block of flats.

The voluntary organisations can provide support over a wide area, but the individual volunteer is more likely to be effective near his or her own home. In Chapter 7 and Chapter 9 we shall be discussing the private foster parent, the playgroup leader and the child-minder and considering whether they are "volunteers" too.

BUILDINGS

Some of the Committee's functions require buildings as a base for advice or services. Such buildings house:

Administrative services;
area social work offices, or sub-offices, administering the Home Help Service, the Meals Service and general social work;
day nurseries for younger children;
workshops for handicapped people;
playgroups;
community services;
day centres and clubs for the elderly or handicapped;
day centres and clubs for the mentally or physically handicapped under 65;
adult training centres, or clubs, for the mentally handicapped over 16.

Some of these services may be provided in one and the same building (multipurpose day centres are being developed in some areas). Some of the buildings may be directly provided by the local authority, others by voluntary or community groups or private individuals, or by the Area Health Authority.

Other functions can only be carried out in buildings where people can live either temporarily or on a more permanent basis. These consist of residential accommodation for:

Elderly persons (over 65) and/or younger physically handicapped persons;
mentally handicapped adults;
mentally handicapped children;
mentally ill persons;
mothers and babies;
special groups such as alcoholics, single homeless people, families needing temporary accommodation, young people of working age,
young children;
children of school age, who are in care;
children and young persons placed for assessment and observation;
children and young persons in care who require education training and care.

Here again, the authority may either provide such accommodation itself, or may use homes which have been provided by private persons or by voluntary organisations. So far as children and young persons are concerned, all the types of accommodation bracketed together, consisting of both local authority and voluntary provision, are provided under what is known as a Regional Plan, which, as it applies to a group of local authorities, and not to one only, requires some brief explanation.

REGIONAL PLANNING

Every local authority has been designated by the Secretary of State for inclusion in a large geographical region of up to five or six million population; the authorities within each of these regions are required jointly to establish a Regional Planning Committee, to obtain information about all the various establishments within the region and assess the total needs of the constituent authorities for the accommodation of children and young persons in their care.

Each Regional Planning Committee was required to prepare and submit a regional plan for the provision and maintenance of homes to be known generally as "community homes". These include homes formerly provided by the constituent authorities and any voluntary homes *which have elected to be included in the plan* on the understanding that a local authority will take part in its management. In this context, the phrase "voluntary homes" includes those former approved schools which were not provided and maintained by local authorities, together with probation homes and hostels for young persons under the age of 17. Such a voluntary home must be designated as a *controlled* community home, in which case it will be managed, equipped and maintained by a specified local authority, or an *assisted* community home, in which event it will be managed, equipped and maintained by a voluntary organisation, though a specified local authority will appoint one-third of the members of the managing body.

The Regional Plan proposes the nature and purpose of each community home and in particular sets out proposals for the provision of observation and assessment facilities for children in the care of the constituent authorities. The detailed provisions relating to the Regional Planning Committees are to be found under ss. 35 to 48 of the Children and Young Persons Act 1969. When the plan is completed it will be subject to review and modification from time to time.

It is important to note that the Regional Planning Committee is concerned solely with planning for the region. It does not manage, maintain or provide any establishment nor directly employ any staff for such establishments. The staff is provided by the local authority or the voluntary organisation as the case may be. Since the plan came into operation there have been no establishments known as approved schools, remand homes, reception centres or junior probation homes or hostels, as the term "community homes" is applied to them all; they may, of course, retain their previous names. Those which were formerly approved schools are usually referred to as "community homes with education on the premises" or, by the staff as "community schools". Others are known as observation and assessment units, as that is their primary function. The extent to which each authority has access to each establishment for its children will be determined by the plan which requires the approval of the Secretary of State.

The Secretary of State himself has power to provide other homes for specially disturbed children who cannot reasonably be accommodated within the community home system.[7] This is a resource in the sense that places in the homes may be provided, but only on application to the Secretary of State. (Such homes are not yet available to the expected extent.)

Another function of the Regional Planning Committee is to plan facilities which can be used in conjunction with supervision orders made by the Courts. It is intended that these facilities will eventually replace attendance centres and detention centres as a means of providing activity and control for those children and young persons who are the subject of supervision orders. The facilities are usually referred to as "intermediate treatment" which will be discussed in detail in the context of supervision orders in Chapter 14. The existence of regional planning opens up a number of possibilities; some staff recruiting is being done regionally, and there is scope for innovation in the planning and sharing of accommodation, for instance for mentally or physically handicapped adults or children.

OTHER LOCAL AUTHORITY RESOURCES

In addition to centralised services, such as those of the Solicitor, Treasurer and Architect, a local authority provides other resources which may be available to its Social Services Committee, especially in the context of overall corporate management. Such resources, while under the administration of another committee and not therefore a resource of the Social Services Committee as such, play a vital part in forwarding the community care objective of the whole authority.

There are many such resources, two of the most important being:

a the social service element of the education service, including such matters as provision of free school meals, clothing and maintenance grants and the services of educational welfare officers, who are now recognised as providing a social work service to the schools administered by the authority;

b the provision of housing, accompanied by housing advice and a social work service for tenants. (In non-metropolitan counties, this is a resource not of the county, but of the district councils within its area; elsewhere housing and social services are both the function of one and the same authority.)

Both the police and the probation and after-care services may also be regarded as providing important resources in the promotion of community care, but are not mentioned here because both have a special relationship with the local authority and are not local authority services in the usual sense of the word.

NON-LOCAL AUTHORITY RESOURCES

Two of the most important resources available to the population as a whole have special relevance for the Social Services Committee. One is the health service, now separated from local government, which is now organised in such a way as to recognise the special needs of patients; the other is the Department of Health and Social Security's system of welfare rights and benefits, with its recognition of the special needs of particular groups of people, such as the handicapped.

STAFF

The Committee's staff is the most essential resource, since without it none of the other resources, not even volunteers, can operate. For this reason, staffing costs account for about 60% of all the expenditure of a Social Services Committee; hence the concern for the effective management of man-power referred to in the previous chapter.

It will be clear from the range of its functions and resources that the Committee must provide its Chief Officer with a great variety of staff in accordance with s. 6 of the Act.

These will include:

1. Senior management staff for the conduct of what is a very large enterprise.
2. Administrative and clerical staff for the servicing of the Committee, dealing with finance, supplies, personnel, research, forward-planning, training, records, assessments, and general support work.
3. Liaison staff for effective contact with other committees, Area Health Authority, D.H.S.S., district councils, public bodies, voluntary organisations, and the community, including voluntary social workers.
4. Advisory and supervisory social work staff, team leaders, advisers, inspectors.
5. Social work staff in contact with the community, carrying out a number of statutory and non-statutory duties, social workers in hospitals and clinics, specialist social workers for the blind, the deaf and other groups, such as child-minded children, foster parents and prospective adopters.
6. Administrative and clerical support for social work staff.
7. Managers of workshops, training centres, day centres, day nurseries and other non-residential services such as the meals and home help services.
8. Administrative and clerical support for domiciliary services.
9. Care and domestic staff for the whole range of residential establishments, and teachers in some of the community homes.
10. Administrative and clerical support for the residential services.
11. Home helps (numerically the largest group of all staff).
12. Ancillary staff who are indispensable in the provision of services.

FINANCE

The budget of the Social Services Committee of any local authority will be of the order of several million pounds and one of the highest after that of the Education Committee. The amount available for the provision of services is subject to the constraints mentioned in Chapter 1 and cannot be readily expanded to meet new or unforeseen needs. The budget therefore plays a key part in the monitoring of expenditure and income; finance, though an essential resource, is also a limiting factor in the development of the Committee's services.

GENERAL

In 1972, the Government asked local authorities to provide information for the preparation of a ten-year-plan of investment in the local social services. Suggested guidelines were set out for each group of people considered to require services; the estimated numbers of staff were shown in terms of those needed for a stated population; similar estimates were given for the number of "places" in both day and residential establishments, and authorities were asked to use those in an imaginative way in preparing plans.

So for the first time Social Services Committees were able to form a realistic and detailed assessment of the goals they should be striving to approach by the end of the ten-year period, that is, by 1982. This exercise was very valuable in exposing those areas of need in which there was either no service at all or one far below the suggested level. It also provided a means of comparing existing services with the norms set out for consideration. In general the resources of buildings and staff were found to be well below the suggested criteria, and the finance which would have been required to bridge the gap has not yet been made available, nor is there any prospect of it.

While local authorities may use their ten-year plans as a general guide to their decision on priorities, when planning such limited development as is possible, they have small hope of implementing the entire plans in the foreseeable future, and there is little likelihood that resources will be available for any progress beyond the recommended standards, or for the innovation of new services, specially those involving capital expenditure. In this situation, it is for the members of the Council to decide, with the advice of chief officers, the priorities to be followed as between one programme area and another, (for instance community care and transportation), and also as between one part of the community care programme and another. The chart on p. 14 and the specimen programme in Appendix A set out what the choices really are.

NOTES

1. Local Authority Social Services Act, ss 1–5.
2. Report of the Committee on Local Authority and Allied Personal Social Services, Cmnd. 3703.
3. *Social Services: the councillor's task* B.A.S.W., 1973.
4. Local Authority Social Services Act, s. 6.
5. G. Aves, *The Voluntary Worker and the Social Services*, London, Bedford Square Press, 1969.
6. D.H.S.S. Staffing Returns as at 30 September 1974.
7. Children and Young Persons Act 1969, s. 64.

Chapter 3

THE SOCIAL SERVICES DEPARTMENT: PART I

SUMMARY

TASK

GENERAL

The Social Services Department consists of the Director and his staff, and exists primarily to carry out the policy of the Social Services Committee in implementing the legislation for which it is responsible. The Seebohm Report's recommendations went far beyond a purely organisational approach and showed particular concern for the ways in which the service should be developed. It may be helpful to set out a few of the ideas in the Report as a reminder of the intentions.

1. The new local authority department should provide a community-based and family orientated service which would be available to all. The department should be able to reach out far beyond the discovery and rescue of social casualties; it should enable the greatest possible number of individuals to act reciprocally, giving and receiving service for the well-being of the whole community (Para. 2).[1]

2. Social problems are of tremendous magnitude compared with the resources available. Much more needs to be done, but especially for the under fives, the elderly, the physically and mentally handicapped, and the "neglected flotsam and jetsam of society". Services should be better deployed, and there should be a far greater effort to involve the community in preventing social breakdowns (Para. 139).[1]

3. People must be treated as people, rather than as separate groups divided by age and type (Para. 142).[1]

4. People should no longer be deterred, by the fear of stigma, from seeking help when they need it; on the contrary a positive effort should be made to encourage everyone to learn about the personal social services, and to use them (Para. 145).[1]

5. It is to be expected that a service which is community-based will be subject to criticism because of the non-provision or under provision of services; it will also reduce the gap between "givers" and "takers" of services because it will be increasingly realised that all members of a community are "consumers" either directly or indirectly, and pay for services through taxes and rates (Paras. 491–492).[1]

6. Already in some small ways citizens are taking part in providing services either personally, or in planning, or in the formation of special interest groups of many kinds. This is to be encouraged, though there are difficulties to be faced, one of them being the association between popular pressures and traditional democratic processes, and the possibly conflicting loyalties of social work staff (Paras. 493–494).[1]

The Seebohm Committee realised that its far-reaching proposals for a really effective family social service would need not only the help of the community but also greater resources, especially of manpower. This would depend upon money, training, recognition of needs, and better deployment of staff already available. But the explanatory and financial memorandum of the Local Authority Social Services Bill, which led to the Act, stated that "the Bill is not expected to result in any significant increase in expenditure out of public funds", and "the Bill is not expected to have any appreciable overall effect on public service manpower requirements". Resources have, in fact, been increased, but not yet to the point of enabling Social Service Departments to see the Seebohm Report as much more than an ideal to be attained at some far future date. The Act, as we have seen, was confined to creating a new administrative committee and structure: a skeleton which has yet to be clothed with the flesh of fulfilment.

Since its inception in 1971, the Social Services Department has been fully occupied in re-organisation, and in the very practical demands made upon it. It was committed from the outset to the implementation of the better services for the physically handicapped, which were required by the Chronically Sick and Disabled Persons Act of 1970; and to the development of entirely new services for children and young persons arising from the Act of 1969. Within a few months it was faced with the prospect of carrying into effect the White Paper *Better Services for the Mentally Handicapped.*[2] The large and increasing number of elderly people in the population was already a cause for concern, as was the growth of homelessness of both families and single persons.

A HYPOTHETICAL LOCAL AUTHORITY

Since 1971, all these challenges to the Department have continued, together with many more; they are insistent and cannot be avoided. To take a few examples of the potential pressures, the figures which follow are shown for England as a whole and applied to a hypothetical medium-sized local authority X with a population of 464,350 (one-hundredth part of the estimated national population for 1974).

	England	*Authority X*
Population	46,435,000	464,350
Aged under 5 years	3,384,400	33,840
Aged under 18 years	12,877,500	128,775
Of all under 18, number in care	91,316[3]	913
Aged over 65	6,467,500	64,675
Of these, aged over 75	2,300,100	23,001
Severely mentally handicapped—estimated at 3 per 1,000 total population. (Mildly handicapped not known.)	38,632	386
	—	—
Estimated physically handicapped		
Very severe	127,000	1,270
Severe	305,000	3,050
Appreciable	533,000	5,330
Blind	98,141	981

(The number of the mentally ill at any one time is not known, but is considerable.)

Authority X will be closely involved with the 913 children actually in care, and with their families and the people providing substitute care; it will also be working directly with a considerable number of the mentally and physically handicapped and the blind. Of the 23,000 elderly persons over 75 (ignoring those aged 65–74), there will be many who live alone, or with no younger person; every year the number of those aged 85 and over is increasing, especially amongst elderly women without the support of a family in the household. Of all those described as physically handicapped, about 65% are elderly as well.

Existing resources are fully occupied in the many activities required to serve this authority's population of 464,350 and they are in no real sense meeting the needs that are known to exist. The activities include direct social work support, personal services, including the provision of practical help, the day-care services and, for a small proportion, residential services. But alongside this personal work, there is the continuing complex of the planning of services in association with other local authority departments, housing authorities or departments, the Area Health Authority (which serves the same area as authority X), and voluntary organisations. There is a continual effort to attain the higher standards which are set out in official circulars, or in Acts or White Papers.

This is something like the reality of the position in any authority, though naturally there are variations from one to another. In one place there may be an overwhelming proportion of elderly in the population, in another a high incidence of delinquency, or homelessness. But in any authority the people known and receiving services will form only a small percentage of those who are in need of help of some kind.

THE CHILD-CARE TASK

The child-care figure can serve as an example of this. The figure of 913 means merely that on 31 March 1974, there were 913 children in the care of authority X and that this represented just over seven children in every thousand of the population under 18 (a figure which is rising each succeeding year). Many of these children would be in care for a few weeks or even days, while some would be at some stage in a period of care which may already have lasted for years. But the bare figures give no idea of the potential need for services to families with children; the position may be gleaned from the National Children's Bureau's survey, *Born to Fail?*[4] This is based on the Bureau's long-term study of all children born in one week in March 1958. Of the 10,504 children concerned, only 64% could be described as having an "ordinary" family background. The other 36% were members of families in which one or more of the following factors were present:

Only one parent
Family of five or more children
Poor housing accommodation
Low income.

In 30% of the cases, one or more of these factors was present, but in 6% all four were found.

Assuming authority X to be average, with a child population of 128,775, the expected numbers would be about:

One or more factors: 38,000 children
All four factors: 7,600 children.

But there were in fact variations in the incidence of the factors, ranging from 2% in southern England to 10% in Scotland (for all four factors), so that at the least authority X might well have 2,530 children in this category, and at the most 12,877.

When it is remembered that these figures relate only to the poverty of the physical environment, and leave out all children who may be disadvantaged physically, educationally or emotionally, the total potential problem for any authority is seen to be of daunting proportions. The national scale of disadvantage is set out in detail in Appendix Q of the Seebohm Report.[1]

Similarly the White Paper *Better Services for the Mentally Handicapped* draws attention to the basic needs of mentally handicapped adults and children and urges the development of services which will enable many of them to live in the community and with their own families. This Paper stresses that the people to be helped are not only the handicapped themselves, but the families who care for them often under great difficulties and who need all kinds of support to help them. This kind of support is also needed for an unknown number of families who are caring for less severely mentally handicapped persons who are not included in the figures set out in the previous paragraph.

There are thus very large potential demands for services from those members of the population of whom something is known either because they are registered in a certain category, or because the department has actually been involved with them or their families in some connection. To this potential must be added the pressure from self-help groups, voluntary bodies concerned with specific needs, public authorities, other local authority services, the courts, the health service, schools and a host of other agencies who are all quite rightly bringing families or individuals to the notice of the department so that appropriate help can be supplied.

It is likely that authority X will receive about 10,000 referred cases in the course of a year, some for simple advice, some for fuller investigation and some for long-term help which may continue over a period of years.

ORGANISATION

In a department with so many varied functions and such considerable resources, even though they are always likely to be inadequate, first-class management is essential. The Seebohm Report recognised this very clearly, but in making recommendations about the qualities required in a Director it laid equal emphasis on management ability and social work qualification or experience (Para. 620).[1] Partly as a result of this, social work and administration seem to have become entangled in a structure which apparently values social work less than management. This has already led many experienced social workers to leave the work they were doing to take up advisory, supervisory and managerial posts for which they might not be so well equipped. But because of the knowledge and experience which they took with them they became involved in a mixture of administrative and social work functions which tended to take away responsibility and accountability from the social workers who succeeded them. This subject is fully discussed in the report of the B.A.S.W. Working Party on Career Grades for social workers which broadly suggests, among other things, that the two elements should be entirely separated as in the health service, with administration providing the resources and the social workers using them.

STRUCTURE

The Act of 1970 gave no guidance as to ways in which the Director should organise his staff, and it was to be expected that in local government a traditional hierarchy would develop. In its most simple form, this could have been done by allowing the three former services to continue functioning as they were at both central and area level, with the Director acting as unquestioned co-ordinator, with the control of integrated records, statistics and other management resources, as illustrated below:

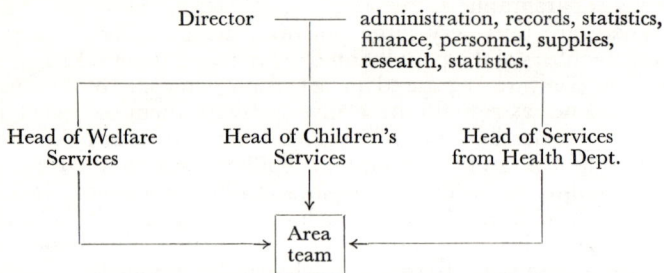

Director ——— administration, records, statistics, finance, personnel, supplies, research, statistics.

Head of Welfare Services   Head of Children's Services   Head of Services from Health Dept.

Area team

A similar structure would have been imposed for each of the area staff and services in the community, so that social workers and existing domiciliary services, and day and residential services would have operated as before, even in separate offices, except that there would be overall co-ordination by someone appointed as Area Officer. There might then have been time for adjustments to be made in the size and shape of areas, and for the area staff to find out whether the traditional services were wanted, whether they were used, and whether there might be real alternatives which would be more acceptable.

However, this was not generally done. In an effort to bring about some form of integration of services the pattern usually became:

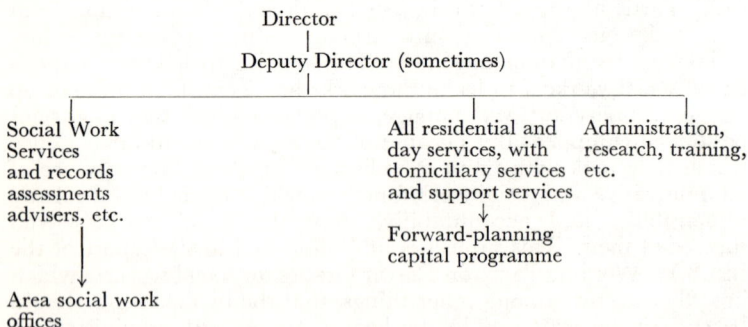

Director

Deputy Director (sometimes)

Social Work Services and records assessments advisers, etc.

All residential and day services, with domiciliary services and support services

Administration, research, training, etc.

Forward-planning capital programme

Area social work offices

There were various permutations of this, but essentially the general principle was to have several assistant directors each dealing with a specific aspect of the work, and with or without a deputy Director.

The separated existing area offices were amalgamated under an Area Officer, who had usually no control whatever over the support and residential services in his area. These were still controlled from the centre, so that area staff could only recommend that people should receive a service; they could not supply it themselves.

By the nature of its setting in local government a Social Services Department tends to be bureaucratic. One of its purposes is to "deliver" services to some of its customers, while telling others that the service they want is "not in stock", but may be available at some time in the future; another purpose is to provide some people with services which they may need, but do not want, such as supervision under a court order, or being placed for residential care or treatment which they would rather do without.

SURVEY OF SOCIAL SERVICES DEPARTMENTS, 1973

These functions alone take up a great deal of the attention of the department which is simultaneously involved in servicing the Social Services Committee, trying to assess the potential demand for existing services, dealing with the day-to-day problems of personnel, buildings, allocation of finance, statistics, controlling the service through managers and advisers at various levels, and developing systems of communication between the fragmented areas of responsibility. The difficulties of Social Services Departments as they were in 1973 are well described in a D.H.S.S. publication covering thirty-four different representative authorities.[5] Some of these departments had made progress in delegating from the centre, but rather less in making communication and monitoring effective. In others, specialists of the former separate departments, such as home help organisers and occupational therapists were still working more or less in isolation from social workers, while in yet others there was a marked dearth of special staff for dealing with the needs of handicapped people and with difficult adolescents. In a number of authorities, separate registers of groups of people were still being maintained because integrated record systems had not been established. In these authorities the area staff were having to rely on a "living memory bank" due to the lack of continuous inclusive written case papers.

The D.H.S.S. Report was prepared before local government re-organisation in 1974, and expresses hope that some of these matters will be put right by the new authorities. It draws special attention to the need for better overall management, with particular reference to:

1. Improved management of work loads. This entails an adequate record of work being undertaken, together with a realistic approach of what must be done, what can be done, and what cannot be done at all. This is largely the responsibility of the leaders of social work teams.

2. Better ways of providing resources to teams without lengthy and complicated lines of decision-making.

3. Efficient administrative record-keeping systems. (In what

aims to be a family orientated service, records should be kept on a family basis, rather than on a basis of individuals known to the department because of different services, so that the whole family picture can be seen immediately. Separated records do not easily reveal that an elderly blind person is otherwise physically or mentally handicapped, or that a mentally ill mother has children in a private foster home, or that she has her own mother living with her. This kind of total information can be incorporated into a suitable case paper, and some kind of integration of the kind is urgently needed. Whether or not record systems are eventually computerised, which is open to doubt, there should be a manual system which can be related to the families and members of families who are the concern of the department.)

Similarly the assessment of charges for the variety of services should be integrated, rather than being dealt with on a piecemeal basis according to the services provided, even if the assessment is "nil", as it often is. If efforts are being made to support a family for instance by providing a home help and placing one child in a day nursery, there is no point in making two separate assessments, or, as is possible, making yet a third because another child may be in care already, or because the mother has been given a recuperative holiday. There is also a constructive side to the question of assessment. If all the necessary financial facts are collated, it is then possible to advise the family about its rights to a wide range of benefits available from both the D.H.S.S. and the local authority (rent and rate rebates, school meals and clothing).

A Steering Group appointed by the Government and the Local Authority Associations is at present experimenting in the use of a form which has been designed for this purpose; after test it may be introduced on a national scale, but this will probably take some time. There would not seem to be any reason why a Social Services Department should not put the principle into effect at once.

4.   The quality of service. This may imply that within a department there is a need for a group of staff acting as inspectors, each with specialist knowledge in some sphere of social work, and all having the authority to investigate and report upon the standard of practice throughout the whole of the departmental activities. Such a group of staff would link with inspection a helpful response to requests from social workers for advice in specific cases, which would probably be more acceptable than the more usual method of pushing cases up through the system for a decision.

All these points, however, are internal to the organisation; they do not really touch upon the Seebohm ideal of a Social Services Department "working effectively through area teams, drawing strength from the community they serve, and with a substantial measure of delegated authority . . ." (Para. 594).[1] Progress has been made in this direction. Some departments have established local advisory or consultative groups or panels which represent the community, being composed of members of district councils, members of the Social Services Committee living locally, members of voluntary organisations, and some individual citizens chosen for personal interest and qualities, and not representing any particular section of the community.

Such a panel certainly gives a community some opportunity of stating its views and criticisms, but it is still some way from real involvement, and does not do very much to provide "strength" to the department. If the community is to be involved it must have rather more understanding of the social services than it has at present. A study in South Wales and Southampton in 1969–72 disclosed a marked lack of knowledge of the functions of the various groups of social workers, with the exception of the Probation Service, the N.S.P.C.C. and the Citizens' Advice Bureaux. The study also describes public attitudes towards the people who receive services, current ideas about the extent to which stated needs were unmet, and an indication of the kinds of social situation in which "self help" is seen as the answer, and those in which the people being questioned would *themselves* be prepared to help.[6] If the level of understanding is to be improved, and if there is to be any prospect of taking up the offers of "community help" it would seem essential that social workers should be based in the community, as was indeed the Seebohm concept.

For towns, the Report envisaged teams of social workers in an area office serving a population of 50–100,000 (Para. 590)[1] but pointed out in Para. 593 that this population would also need to be served by teams in specific sub-areas, neighbourhoods and communities. These paragraphs indicate that the *team* is the basic unit, and that its size and composition will need to vary according to a number of factors.

THE SOCIAL WORK TEAM

The word "area" seems sometimes to have been taken as applying to the former areas of the Children's and Welfare Departments which, in counties, often had a population far bigger than 50–100,000. In the first instance, therefore, some departments set up area offices for very large populations and it was only later on that they began to establish teams in smaller neighbourhoods and districts. On the other hand, Islington prepared a scheme for siting team offices in the borough on the basis of maximum accessibility. Their approach to the task is set out in "Social Priority Areas and Seebohm".[7]

Where area offices for a large area were set up first, and team areas were later evolved, the area teams tended to be regarded as still forming part of the area office, which with its Area Director and administrative and supervisory staff, could easily become a miniature central headquarters, though even this was without the authority to provide directly resources for the teams. Even the files and record of referrals might still be retained by the area office so that the teams themselves were without their own administrative and clerical support.

By contrast, in the Seebohm Report, the team is seen as comprising social workers, occupational therapist and home help organiser (who might also generally promote voluntary service). Such a team would presumably have its own clerical staff and records, would operate independently within its own small community, and would make its own decisions apart from those involving the use of resources controlled from headquarters, or divisional or area offices. In this way, the lines of communication would be shortened, the accountability of the team and of the social workers would be easily apparent, the team leader would perforce act as an effective manager, and the social workers themselves would increasingly identify themselves with the community.

The introduction of the inspecting staff mentioned earlier would help the team to avoid any feeling of isolation, but in any event the individual members of the team would probably be able to undertake part-time attachment to other community bases, such as schools, health centres, courts, and hospitals, and in this way widen their horizons and at the same time develop a special interest in some aspect of social work, while remaining firmly based within the team.

To some extent events have overtaken the attachment idea as schools are now to have their own social service provided by educational welfare officers, and the social workers within the hospitals are now members of the Social Services Department staff. But there is still scope for the attachment of a social worker to the courts in the team areas and for a similar attachment to a primary health care team in the health service; the other members of such a team are the doctors and nurses caring for patients outside hospital.

It is not necessary for a team social worker to be attached to a hospital if a colleague is already working within it, but arrangements have to be worked out for liaison between the team in the community and the team or single social worker in the hospital. There are problems about the different catchment areas for instance, but it is essential that these should be solved on the general lines of the Working Party on the Health Service (March 1974).

Discussions are currently being held about the position of the fairly small number of social workers in Child Guidance Clinics, who are now employed by the education authority. They may also enter the Social Services Department, either retaining their own special position or helping to broaden the guidance "clinic" into a guidance "service" designed to investigate in some depth a number of children who are present do not receive this help because of administrative boundaries.

It will be obvious that Social Services Departments have still a great deal to do in the realm of organisation, and that they are still in the throes of dramatic change. They cannot help but be large organisations, needing on the one hand order and effectiveness, on the other, enough disorderliness to encourage creative activity. The first characteristic is embodied in centralisation, the second in decentralisation. Between the two is conflict and tension, which cannot be resolved by compromise; ways must be found for both to exist together. To quote E. F. Schumacher, "The fundamental task is to achieve smallness, *within* large organisations".[8]

NOTES

1. Report of the Committee on Local Authority and Allied Personal Social Services (the Seebohm Report), Cmnd. 3703.
2. Better Services for the Mentally Handicapped, Cmnd. 4683.
3. Children in Care 31 March 1974, Cmnd. 6147.
4. National Children's Bureau.
5. *Social Work Service*, No. 6.
6. "Community perceptions of Social Work," *Policy and Politics*, March 1973; Journals Ltd. and Reactions to Integration, *Social Work Today*, 1 November 1973.
7. *Social Work Today*, September 1970.
8. *Small is Beautiful*, E. F. Schumacher, London, Bliss and Blight, 1973.

Chapter 4

THE SOCIAL SERVICES DEPARTMENT: PART II

SUMMARY

    The identity of the social worker; Specialisms; Methods of work; Framework of activities.

THE PUBLIC AS "CONSUMERS"

As we have seen, the ideal contained in the Seebohm Report is that the Social Services Department should provide services which are available to "everybody" (Para. 32).[1] This is implicit in the emphasis on the whole community, but in fact only a minority of the population so far actually either receives or gives services. Those who do receive them first became known as "clients", because social work aspired to being a profession; but more recently they are becoming known as "consumers", and as such have opinions which are important to those who supply the services. So far, little attention has been paid to finding out what these opinions are, though there have been several books and a number of articles, together with a fair amount of local research.[2] *Social Work Today* has published several down to earth reports on what it feels like to be a consumer, and it is cheering to find that not all the comments are unfavourable; some show a great appreciation both of departments and of social workers.[3] When the comments are unfavourable they point the need for departments to be aware that in the eyes of the consumer they barely exist; or, rather, they exist only in the person who represents them, whether this is a social worker in the community, or in an establishment, or any other member of staff who for the moment *is* the department.

As opposed to individuals, a group of "consumers" is in a very different position. There are many such groups comprising well-known organisations such as the Claimants' Union, the Child Poverty Action Group, and Gingerbread, which operate on a national or local scale, with the aim of influencing policy.

The general run of social service consumers, however, is usually less articulate than a group and has not yet formed, or been formed, into an association, though the day may not be far distant. But whatever may be done by such groups, or by the Personal Social Services Council and other influential bodies, a department should ensure that there are ways in which views can be openly expressed, as a means of challenging existing organisation or patterns of work. Possibly this can be done through the local consultative groups, if they are representative enough, or through group meetings or joint working parties. There is a growing trend towards the full and proper consideration of the views of "consumers"—expressed, for instance, in the new children's legislation—and this has important implications for all members of the staff of a Social Services Department, in whatever capacity they may be employed.

THE SOCIAL WORK STAFF

The staff of a Social Services Department is its fundamental resource. In the specimen Community Care Programme in Appendix A, the sub-programmes A, B and E are relevant to administrative provision and staff, while sub-programme C puts *counselling* as an integral part of the use and deployment of all services. In sub-programme D there are many activities either in the community or in residential establishments which clearly contain a counselling element. So that, in this example, all social services depend upon social work, but social work itself has particular functions in relation to some of the activities which may be applied, whether other services are needed or not.

But if social work is defined as what a social worker does, there are many people who may claim that in the course of their other duties they are at times social workers. Police, for example, clergy, local councillors or Members of Parliament, marriage guidance counsellors, health visitors, prison visitors and the many other volunteers in agencies may consider that at times they are "doing social work". Perhaps they are.

Further attempts to define a social worker as a "professional" or as "qualified" or "unqualified", so that they can be distinguished from other people, have all so far run into difficulties, partly because more than half the social workers in local authorities are not eligible for membership of the professional body, the British Association of Social Workers, while many who are eligible are not members. Taking the question of "qualification" it can be seen from the annual staffing return of the D.H.S.S. that there is a higher proportion of qualified social workers among the management and supervisory staff than there is among the basic social workers, so that in fact much of what is called social work is being done by people who are not "qualified" though some have considerable experience.[4]

For many years, and especially since 1971, there has been an overwhelming outpouring of books, periodicals, journals, magazines and articles concerned with social work; if anyone had the time to read them all, it is certain that he would not have time to attend the many courses, conferences, seminars and discussion groups he would learn about during his reading. The ordinary person who wants to follow events and even to sense what is going on in social work therefore usually has to confine himself to one or at most two periodicals, perhaps with the addition of one publication relating to some sphere in which he is particularly interested.

The amount of literature may be some measure of the uncertainty which both social workers and administrators feel. It gives the impression that very often some vaunted development of last year was totally mistaken, that there is little agreement on the very nature of social work, and that though there are theories to account for what social workers do, there is still no definition of what they are. Some of the confusions were examined at some length in a preliminary report by the Professional Development and Practice Committee of B.A.S.W. called *The Social Work Task*.[5] Within a few weeks, this preliminary report was criticised by a group of social workers as being "pretentious, verbose, confusing and dehumanising" which seems to suggest that they did not entirely agree with it. Though *Social Work Today* deserves credit for opening its columns to all shades of opinion, on this and many other issues, it seems that at present not even B.A.S.W. can speak with unchallenged authority on issues which are fundamental both to its own members and to the many others who are "doing social work" in either a paid or voluntary capacity.

This is not surprising in view of the many strands which went to make up the Association, and of the many other strands which were left out of it; but the present lack of certainty is confusing to those already in Social Services Departments, and to those who seek to enter them.

The uncertainty centres around several salient questions which can be stated briefly, but cannot be answered satisfactorily.

THE IDENTITY OF THE SOCIAL WORKER

Local government now has a near monopoly of social workers, the only alternative openings being in child guidance clinics, government and voluntary societies. There is little prospect of earning a living in private practice or in industry. The great majority of social workers are therefore employed by local authorities; they receive the benefits of local government staff and are subject to the conditions of service, and to the terms of their contract of employment, which usually requires them to carry out certain statutory responsibilities, and to perform tasks assigned to them by the Chief Officer. Many of them will also have a written authorisation enabling them to take action on behalf of the employing authority, such as appearance in court in some court proceedings, or visiting specified premises.

So the social worker in a local authority draws his right to practise from the authority, which itself draws its powers from statute and from the law itself. It is difficult to escape the conclusion that he is primarily a local government officer, and within the community he will generally be seen as being part of "the welfare". In many situations he is also exercising his right to practise on the basis of the permission of the person being helped, since there is no power to impose help except when it is done with statutory authority.

The social worker may think that his first loyalty lies towards the people he helps rather than to his employing authority, and this may lead him into conflict if he feels that the authority is not serving the best interests of the community, or a part of it. He may find it necessary to take part in social action intended to change the departmental structure or policy, or to bring about the allocation of resources to a specific group of people. This is one illustration of the ways in which conflict between "order" and "freedom" becomes real, unless the department and the social worker have identical goals. For a fuller discussion of this issue, see *Social Action and Social Work*, the report of a B.A.S.W. Working Party on the subject,[6] and *A Code of Ethics for Social Work*.[7]

SPECIALISMS

As in the realm of organisation, there seems to have been some misunderstanding of the Seebohm Report, resulting in an idea that social workers were in future to be "generic" as opposed to being specialists in adoption, mental health or work with homeless families, for instance. The Report refers in para. 555[1] to *already existing* generic training, but this was confined to the principles and methods common to all types of social casework, and did not refer to the application of this central core to all individuals and families, whatever their problems. Chapter XVII of the Report[1] dealt with the question of specialisation in social work, and concluded that it needed to be radically altered. It also suggested that as far as possible a family or individual should be served by one social worker, who should alone decide whether other social workers should be involved to deal with specific needs. But the Report recognised that each social worker will be more effective in some fields of work than in others, because of temperament or inclination, and that this should be taken into account (para. 522).[1] The whole principle of the suggested attachment of social workers to various social institutions gives further recognition to the fact of specialisation by reason of interest. It is true that the Report saw the end of the rigid specialism of the former separate departments, but it pointed out that new specialisms would arise, and this has been borne out by the formation of special teams for intake work, home finding, advocacy of welfare rights, and other innovations for specialist work "across the board", regardless of age or other categories.

There was in the early days a tendency to regard all social workers as "generic", but it is more and more realised that though the service and the teams are generic, the individual social worker himself is not. This point is clearly made both in the report of the Working Party on Social Work Support for the Health Service, and in the D.H.S.S. publication *Social Work Service*, No. 6; on page 10 of the latter this passage appears:

> "It therefore needs stressing that it is a misunderstanding of the Seebohm Report to suppose that the creation of an integrated social service department entailed the integration of social work skills to such a degree that specialisms must disappear."[8]

To sum up, there *is* a central core of principles and method which is common to all casework practice, but the ways of applying it are many and diverse; they often depend upon knowledge which lies outside the central core; and such knowledge is one of the factors which give rise to specialism, old or new.

METHODS OF WORK

Traditionally social workers have worked with individuals and families on the well-known one-to-one basis, but in recent years more attention has been paid to the importance of working with groups of, for instance, foster parents, young people under court supervision orders, mothers of young families, the elderly, and many more. Such groups need not be "in the community", since there is also much scope for this method in residential or day establishments as a part of the process of enabling people who are receiving help to participate in providing it. This form of social work may be derived from social casework, or from statutory duties, but it is a different concept which has its own literature.

In the same way, various methods of working within a whole community have been developed over the past few years. In some places a team of social workers may have operated in a particular district without letting themselves be publicly identified with their department. In others, the team may have been publicly identified but acting as an interpreter of local needs to the local authority. Here again there is a considerable literature.[9]

All that needs to be said here is that there are different methods of social work. The question often at issue is whether each of the methods comprises a separate specialism, or whether all social workers can, or should, be using them all at different times in the course of their daily work.

FRAMEWORK OF ACTIVITIES

If the three questions discussed above do nothing else, they give some idea of the complexity of the social work task, bounded as it is by law and by society in the shape of the local authority, the community, and the people in search of services. All social workers whether in the community or in establishments or administration need to be as well informed as they can be on basic principles. The Central Council for Training and Education in Social Work is drawing attention to training requirements in some of the more important aspects, one of which is law, since it is felt that this subject has not always and everywhere been accepted as essential for social workers. In its paper *Legal Studies in Social Work Education*,[10] the Council points out that legal studies form a necessary part of training for all social workers, and adds that they can be very interesting if seen in the context of day-to-day work. The Report outlines four areas in which law affects the social worker:

Professional law (which is related to practice in special fields);
General law (which affects the lives of all citizens);
Administration of law (the legal profession, legal aid, the courts and tribunals);
Law and society (the need for a legal system and its positive qualities).

The last three aspects have been covered in *Social Workers, their Clients and the Law*.[11] This gives a simple outline of the legal system, and deals with the many points of law which arise for most people at some stage in their lives. Professional law is naturally more specialised and covers the legislation which affects the Social Services Department and which is listed in Chapter 1. Those statutes which relate to Children and Young Persons give precise and detailed guidance for what is probably the widest range of work in the whole department.

The standard work is Clark Hall and Morrison's *Law Relating to Children and Young Persons*[12] which is revised from time to time, but the essentials are to be found in J. K. Bevan's *Law Relating to Children*[13] which is a much smaller volume.

The present work is not therefore so much a book on law as an attempt to relate the law to practice in a Social Services Department's wide range of work with children and young persons and their families. There are some situations which arise only rarely and which may need specialist legal advice; this book is concerned more with points which often have to be dealt with, and tries to show that a proper understanding and use of legislation and regulations can help to ensure a high standard of practice in the sensitive area still known as "child care".

Not everyone may accept the suggestion, made above, that the social work task is carried out within a framework of the law and of society in its various forms. The concept may not be very exciting, but it can perhaps offer some kind of base at a time of great unrest and uncertainty as described in "The Cross-Roads for Social Work".[14]

NOTES

1. The Seebohm Report, Cmnd. 3703.
2. For example *The Client Speaks*, Mayer and Timms, London, Routledge, 1970; and *Social Work Today*, 6 March 1975.
3. "Community Perceptions in Social Work", *Policy and Politics*, March 1973.
4. D.H.S.S. Staffing Returns as at September 1974, S/F/75/1.
5. *Social Work Today*, 6 March 1975.
6. B.A.S.W. Publication, No. 6.
7. B.A.S.W. Discussion Paper, No. 2 (later revised).
8. *Social Work Service*, No. 6.
9. For example *Community Work, Theory and Practice*, edited Philip Evens, Alistair Shornach Ltd., P.O. Box 70, Headington, Oxon., and C.C.E.T.S.W. Paper No. 8, *Teaching of Community Work*.
10. C.C.E.T.S.W. Paper, No. 4.
11. Michael Zander, London, Sweet and Maxwell, 1974.
12. London, Butterworths, Eighth edn. 1972.
13. London, Butterworths, 1973.
14. Professor Martin Rein, *Social Work*, October 1970.

Chapter 5

CHILDREN AND YOUNG PERSONS

SUMMARY

DEFINITION OF "CHILD" AND "YOUNG PERSON"

Among the people who are dealt with by Social Services Departments are many children and young persons, who are usually members of a natural family. Within the overall objectives of the department they are no more important than other people, but they are more vulnerable, and because of their immaturity need protection from many surrounding pressures which do not affect older people so strongly.

There is no definition of "child" in social service terms, but the word usually means a minor (*i.e.* under the age of 18). This is the meaning in the Children Acts of 1948 and 1958, but in the other major Acts (the Children and Young Persons Acts from 1933 to 1969), it normally means a person aged under 14. But in looking at the Act of 1969, special care must be taken because the Secretary of State has power to define from time to time the upper age of childhood. Similarly a person aged 14 to 17th birthday is normally in these Acts a "young person", but owing to the Secretary of State's power under s. 34, the age limit is below 14.[1] There are special reasons for this, which will be dealt with later, but it is important to realise that "child" or "young person" when they appear in the Act of 1969 do not always refer to those under 14 and those over 14 respectively.

Of all the Social Services Departments' responsibilities, that towards these two groups attracts by far the greatest public attention and concern. If young children are ill-treated by adults there is quite rightly an immediate outcry; if social workers are in any way involved, or it is thought that they should have been involved, there is public indignation. Several tragic cases have recently been the subject of official enquiries whose reports, when published, urge the need for improvement of services, better communication between social agencies, a higher degree of skill in detecting children at risk of injury or neglect, and more emphasis on the protection of helpless children.

Quite apart from these well-known cases, much attention has been paid for some years to the problem of child abuse, or the battered baby syndrome; all social agencies are well aware of the danger signals, and have established various ways of forestalling injury, or of taking appropriate action when non-accidental injury by parents or others is suspected. The ill-treatment of children is nothing new and is not confined to physical injury, but certainly much more attention is now given to it and it has assumed larger proportions altogether.

Young persons, those between, say, 12 and 17, attract almost equal attention but for very different reasons. Some of them commit extremely serious crimes against property and against the person, they arouse condemnation by attacking and robbing houses or people, who may be elderly and handicapped, and they often forfeit any public sympathy they might once have had because of their "unfortunate backgrounds", whether these exist or not; others commit less serious offences but commit them frequently and are often defiant and aggressive towards authority and society.

This again is no new phenomenon, as we learn from *A Winter's Tale* written by Shakespeare in 1610:

> "I would there were no age between sixteen and three and twenty or that youth would sleep out the rest; for there is nothing in the between but getting wenches with child, wronging the ancientry, stealing, fighting."

Nothing has changed much except the age group.

But although both these problems of childhood and youth are of very long standing, and are still with us, this does not mean that they have been ignored. Over the years there has been a steady stream of legislation designed to provide help for both the groups usually called "the deprived" and "the depraved", with the result that Social Services Departments now have heavy responsibilities towards both, even if they are not in local authority care. Those who actually enter care create another dimension of responsibility, which again comes under the searchlight of public opinion if anything goes wrong.

CHILDREN AND YOUNG PERSONS ACT 1969

Before the Children Act 1975, the last piece of legislation was the Children and Young Persons Act of 1969, which has been in partial operation since 1971, and which has caused so much concern that it has been considered by the Expenditure Committee of the House of Commons. This Act rests upon the philosophy that, broadly speaking, the young child at risk of injury or neglect, the child in care and the young offender have basically the same social needs and may be suitably provided for in similar ways. There are however some situations in which the protection of the public must be taken into account, as well as the interests of the child or young person concerned. This Act will be considered in more detail later, but it may be helpful at this stage to set out the philosophy, then the various sections of the Act in which the philosophy can be seen, and finally the effect the Act has had so far. Following this are some generalised summaries of comments which have been made by police, magistrates and the British Association of Social Workers during recent discussions. These show that while there may be broad acceptance of the principles of the Act, there is some conflict between those who wish to see it amended in some way, and those who wish to see it implemented more fully.

PHILOSOPHY

The Act does not stand by itself, but is the last step in a progressive modification of the criminal law in its application to children and young people. Starting with the Departmental Committee of Young Offenders (1927), this theme has run through the Children and Young Persons Acts of 1933–63, the Ingleby Committee Report on Children and Young Persons (1960), the White Paper, *The child, the Family and the Young Offender* (1965), and the further White Paper *Children in Trouble* (1968).[2] The Act itself stems largely from this last mentioned White Paper.

What is the philosophy?

For many years there had been debate about juvenile delinquency as though it were something which in itself could be "prevented". During the 1960s the figures were always increasing, and in particular there were marked failures in the methods then in operation. Of all children discharged from approved schools 80% committed further offences within three years of discharge, 68% of all those released from borstal and 61% of all released from detention centres were known to have committed offences. It seemed that, whatever their merits, these measures were not outstandingly successful.

The present philosophy attaches much less importance to the distinction between "good" and "bad" children, and much more to the kind of treatment which is necessary, irrespective of the cause of the "trouble", which may or may not manifest itself in delinquency. Very few people have grown up without committing acts which could be called offences, and allowance must be made for the differing rates at which young people grow up into personal responsibility. Moreover, and this may be lost sight of, the upbringing of a child is the prime responsiblity of his parents and if they need help in this obligation, it must be provided by society as a whole. The intention, therefore, is that in taking action to deal with a child who comes to notice, full regard must be paid to his family and wider social background with a view to drawing out whatever strengths are to be found there.

Formal procedure, such as appearance in court, should be reserved for those situations where intervention is necessary in the interests of the child, or of society. Firm and consistent discipline is a part of upbringing; if parents cannot provide it, society must do so.

The methods of providing for all children in trouble must be flexible, and not geared solely, as in the past, to their particular problems, e.g. delinquency, non school attendance etc.

In general, this philosophy has not been seriously challenged, but there are differing views on the age at which young people arrive at personal responsibility; there is also doubt in some quarters about the principle of relying on the support of family and community when either or both of these influences may in fact be tolerant or even encouraging towards deviance from acceptable behaviour.

THE PHILOSOPHY AS EXPRESSED IN THE 1969 ACT[3]

		Effect
1. Recognition of varying rates of personal development.	s.4 No child under 14 to be charged with an offence, except homicide. s.5 No young person to be charged with an offence (except homicide and other serious offences to be specified by the Secretary of State), unless it is considered that the case cannot be dealt with in some other way, after consultation with the local authority.	Neither s. 4. nor s. 5 is in operation yet. There is however a good deal of co-operation between police and Social Service Departments, by which the latter are notified of children and young persons who have come to police notice, and have the opportunity of making their own enquiries into personal and social background, so that full information can be exchanged with the police. Because of the large numbers of such cases they receive far too little attention.
2. Recognition of the desirability of dealing with young people without taking	s. 1 (2)(f) A child or young person who has committed an offence (except homicide)	As a result of the joint discussions children may be offered services by the social workers, or may be cautioned by the police, or

Effect

criminal proceedings.	may be brought before the court as being in need of care or control, instead of being charged with the offence.	may be summoned to appear before the juvenile court. The use of police cautions varies widely from one part of the country to another, so that court appearances are misleading.
3. Recognition of the need to involve the family and other influences on a basis of voluntary co-operation.	It is not enough in such cases for the offence to be proved or admitted. It must also be proved that an order of the court is required if the necessary care or control is to be provided. (In other words full enquiry and possible voluntary help must reveal that compulsion is needed.)	This procedure seems to be very little used. Only a handful of young offenders are dealt with in this way, most, if they appear in court at all, being charged with an offence.
4. Recognition of the need to replace punitive measures	s. 7(1) Minimum age for committal to Borstal to be raised from 15 progressively to 17.	This section is not operative. Borstal committals doubled from 1969 to 1973 (859 grew to 1,767).
	s. 7(3) Detention centres and attendance centres to be phased out.	Detention centres are still in use, and a greatly increased number of young persons go there. Custodial sentences in all have increased, contrary to the intention of the Act, and will be encouraged by the extension of Eastwood Park.
5. Recognition of the need for a flexible variety of provision, not related to the reason for appearance in the court.	s. 7 Probation orders, approved school orders, and orders of committal to a remand home abolished, to be replaced by care orders, supervision orders, and remand to the care of the local authority.	In operation.
6. Recognition that the social needs	ss 11/12 Supervision under	Supervision orders are being made in considerably fewer

Effect

of delinquents are similar to those of other children in trouble, and may be met in similar ways.

order of the court removed from the probation concept in criminal proceedings. Unlike probation orders, supervision orders are not dependent on consent. They may not contain any condition about residing at a particular place. They may however contain general conditions to assist the supervisor, some about maintaining contact, others about various activities usually referred to as intermediate treatment, *i.e.* intermediate between supervision without any conditions, and removal from home. The supervisor however chooses whether or not to apply the conditions. There are no statutory rules for the exercise of supervision by local authority social workers.[4]

cases than were formerly dealt with under probation orders. There was a decline of 3,025 between 1969 and 1973; it seems significant that committal to borstal, detention centres and attendance centres increased during the same period by 2,903.

The ninety-day residence under an intermediate treatment order was intended to replace a period at a detention centre; other provisions were intended to replace attendance centre orders. The facilities were to be planned by the Regional Planning Comittee, but not until after the residential provision had been planned. Facilities so far made available are disappointing and unimaginative—there is little scope for any form of community service, for example. The development of these facilities depend upon the appointment of a specialist member of staff, but not enough authorities have taken this step.

s. 20
Courts may commit a child or young person to care of a local authority, which then has certain powers and duties. It must decide upon and provide suitable accommodation (which may be the child's own home), must exercise its powers in the best interests of the child, but must also take into account the

Though the use of supervision has declined, care orders have continued at roughly the same level.

The Act contains provision for dealing with the persistent offender who may in fact be in custodial care for longer (if he is under 15) than was the case under an approved school order. There are however other factors besides the decision of the care authority. notably the lack of facilities protection of the public (ss. 24, 27).

It must review each case every six months to ensure that the care order is still necessary. There is no time limit regarding a placement at a particular place, except that of age for the expiry of the care order.

for highly disturbed young people, and the powers of heads of establishments to decide which cases they will and will not accept.

7. Recognition of the need for residential provision.

ss. 35–48
All approved schools, observation centres, nurseries, local authority homes and hostels and some voluntary homes, to be merged into a community homes system, administered in regions. Regional Planning Committees set up, but not to provide facilities, only to advise authorities as to regional needs, *e.g.* on the extent of required secure accommodation.

In operation.
Pressure is being exerted to obtain sanction for more secure accommodation—representing another movement away from the concept of treatment in the community. It has been estimated that one-third of the children in long-term residential care could be better provided for by facilities developed under the intermediate treatment concept of partial care with supervision.

8. Recognition of the need for special provision for children outside the community homes system.

s. 64
The Secretary of State has power to provide homes for children needing special facilities and services which are unlikely to be available within the community homes, however varied and specialised they may be.

In operation.

Only one such home is open, others are planned, but the total provision will be small, as it is intended that the great majority of children however disturbed will be contained in community homes.

The one home which has been opened (at Brentwood) since 1973 has never been fully operational due to staffing difficulties. No further provision will be made before 1977/78.

GENERAL COMMENTS ON THE WORKING OF THE ACT[3]

Police	*Magistrates*	*British Association of Social Workers*

It is important that early preventive action is taken and co-operation with Social Services Departments has been developed. But there are difficulties when these measures have not been effective, and young people continue to commit offences. What positive action can be taken after a care order has been made and a further offence is committed?[2]

When neither care orders, attendance centre orders, or detention centre orders are made, as in some assault cases, fines are useless, as they are virtually unenforceable until age of 17. Attachment of Earnings Orders only useful if there are any earnings.

Regret losing powers to order remand to a special place and now use remand centres, for those young people too refractory for Local Authorities care

Regret loss of power to select cases for long-term residential treatment. Are often dealing with young people who have already been under supervision orders, and care orders, and feel unable to make any other order which will be effective.

Supervision by local authorities less effective than supervision by probation officers, who are directly responsible to the court.

Suggest that the Act was brought into operation before facilities and staff were available.

This Act by itself will not and cannot bring about a reduction in juvenile crime. If this is to be done, it will be by better policy in health, housing, education and poverty relief agencies, *e.g.* the recognition of needs as shown by the Finer Report.

Important parts of the Act have not been brought into operation.

Community care by preventive measures has still not been provided as proposed under the Act of 1963, but the Act of 1969 is based on the assumption that these are to be available.

Plans for intermediate treatment have low priority in local authority departments. They should be developed before plans for residential care and should contain provision for short-term placements with a constructive purpose.

Though there is an increase in crimes committed by juveniles, this must be seen in the context of an increase in crimes committed by persons of all ages.

Of all indictable offences in 1970, 23·7% were committed by persons under 17. By 1973 the percentage had increased to 24·6%. In the last quarter of 1974, adult crime showed an increase of 18%, but juvenile crime by 15%.

While all these increases are to be deplored, it can hardly be said that they are directly due to the operation of the Act.

Because of lack of resources children are not receiving the help they need. Community homes are not in the right locations, many being quite separate from the surrounding com-

Police	*Magistrates*	*British Association of Social Workers*
		munity. There are not enough qualified or skilled residential staff; there is a need for much more provision for observation and assessment of children coming to notice. Plans for fifty-five centres were submitted, but so far only fourteen have been approved, these all having been brought forward from previous programmes.
		While secure accommodation is not seen as desirable in itself, there is a need for more, so that it can be used constructively to deal with the more highly disturbed young people who are committed to care.

The Social Work Service itself carried out a survey of the working of the Act towards the end of 1971, when the new provisions had been in effect for rather less than one year. The results are contained in a memorandum issued with D.H.S.S. Circular 29/72 of 26 July 1972.[5]

The Children Act 1975, referred to earlier, deals with entirely different aspects of child care and will be referred to in Chapter 17. Its provisions will have little immediate effect on the Act of 1969, or on the treatment of young offenders.

Clearly, children and young persons must make very large demands on Social Services Departments and their staffs, not only because of the potential numbers involved, but also because of the wide range of needs and services. In considering these, and the legislation which governs them, it may be helpful to relate comment to the specimen community care programme at Appendix A, which of course applies to all "consumers" irrespective of age, social difficulties or kind of service provided. In this way it may be easier to study details while at the same time keeping in mind the ultimate goal, which is the well-being of all individuals and families in the community.

NOTES

1. *Guide to Part I of the 1969 Act*, paras 249–251, London, H.M.S.O., 1975.
2. Cmnd. 3601, 1968.
3. "B.A.S.W. states the case", *Social Work Today*, 20 February 1975.
4. The Children Act 1975 contains powers for such Rules to be made.
5. For a fuller examination of the Act and its working, see the Eleventh Report of the Expenditure Committee of the House of Commons, July 1975, H.M.S.O.

Chapter 6

PREVENTIVE WORK

SUMMARY

PAGE

STAGES 51
Discovery and Referral; Recording; Investigation; Assessment; Treatment

Bearing in mind the overall objective, the duties and resources of the Director of Social Services in relation to children and young persons, we should now consider what is really meant by preventive work. It is certainly much more than the mere prevention of the admission of children to care, as this can be done in an entirely negative way.

By "prevention" is meant a positive promotion of the welfare of children and young persons by meeting their social needs whatever they may appear to be, so that only when there is no alternative will long-term care or treatment be provided.

This concept has been mentioned in many reports during this century, culminating in the White Paper "Children in Trouble" of 1968; the fundamental basis is that the prime responsibility for the welfare and upbringing of children belongs to their parents. Social services exist to help parents to carry out this duty and to enrich the lives of their children. When help of this kind has not been forthcoming in the past some families have disintegrated, the individual children have suffered, some have become delinquents and of those a number have joined the well-trodden road from supervision through various forms of care to enforced and repeated detention in borstal or prison, or, sometimes mental hospital.

The aim of the Director of Social Services and his staff must, therefore, be to prevent the unnecessary separation of children from their families by taking every possible action to help parents and to look upon this as the first priority. But it is only the unnecessary separation which is to be discouraged. The purpose of s. 1 of the Act of 1963 is not "to diminish the need for children to be admitted to care, or to appear before a juvenile court . . .". It is to "promote the welfare of children". This may be done by preventing admission or committal to care, but equally in some cases it may be done by actively ensuring that admission to care takes place.

STAGES

As suggested by the Ingleby Report[1] (which preceded the Children and Young Persons Act, 1963) preventive work should be thought of in terms of the four following separate stages which should not be confused with each other:

1. DISCOVERY AND REFERRAL

The former Children's Departments were providing advice, guidance and assistance in 1963 or even earlier; in consequence, the machinery for discovery and referral was well established, though capable of improvement and development.

Almost all families containing children are known to the health service or to the schools and education welfare service; both these services are well placed to learn of families and children who are in difficulties and to refer them to the Director of Social Services when specialist social work help is needed. Other "general" referring agencies include clergy and ministers, family doctors, members of the public and parents or children themselves.

There are, in addition, a number of agencies of various kinds which may become aware of difficulties of a specialist nature, such as:

Housing Departments	Arrears of rent, unsatisfactory care of children, threat of eviction.
County Courts	Debts, threat of eviction from tied houses or houses being purchased on mortgage.
Police N.S.P.C.C. }	Children and young persons receiving unsatisfactory care or control or in physical or moral danger, or being ill-treated.
Department of Health and Social Security	Families in financial difficulties.
Citizens' Advice Bureaux	Family problems.
Probation Officers	Problems affecting families or individual children.

It is unlikely that any family or child in need of social help can long escape discovery by one or other of these agencies, and the Director of Social Services will need to ensure that when a situation is discovered, it is referred as soon as it becomes clear that social work help, which cannot perhaps be given by the referring agency, is needed (see specimen Community Care Programme C 1 in Appendix A).

2. RECORDING

The efficient recording of all referrals is a task which is vital to the Department as a whole. There must first be a policy as to what does and what does not constitute a referral: is it a case not dealt with before? Is there any previous record? Is it merely a request for advice? Does it need investigation? If so, to what extent? It is also important to record the source of the referral (to check on the effectiveness of the "discovery" procedures) and on the presenting problem, even though this may later prove to be less important than some other factor. Referrals are likely to provide useful material for the Department's research staff, so that there is a lot to be said for noting in each case the home area, within a defined small area, such as village, hamlet, or, in towns, enumeration district (which can be allocated from the appropriate map). Information about each individual or family must also be recorded, whether there are children concerned, family structure and other agencies known to be involved. This information may be either very simple or, if it is to be used for compiling a case history, more detailed, but this will depend upon the administrative pattern adopted. Lastly there should be some easy means of recording each referral in such a way that it will be easy to see what degree of work it entailed, how long it took to deal with it, and whether it is completed, as a referral, or whether it is still outstanding.

This aspect of a department's work is obviously most important, and takes up so much time, effort and skill that the concept of "intake work" has developed in many departments, as one of the new specialisms, at least in larger urban districts. Social Services Departments have developed more positive methods of encouraging referral, rather than waiting for a crisis situation to arise. This is an administrative task as explained[2] in sub-programme B which involves two functions:

a Encouraging the possibility for people to refer themselves, either to the Department itself or to other referral points, such as probation officers, hospitals (where some social work teams are based), Citizens' Advice Bureaux or Councils of Social Service. There must be enough centres of this kind, they must be publicised, and the needs of remote areas must not be forgotten. In this context, the Department has to make decisions about the number and location of its team offices and calling offices, the use of its other establishments which are not social work offices, the possibility of mobile office units, and the provision of an "on-call" service, and its method of operation.

b The setting-up of a series of early warning systems, by which other agencies may know how and when to refer people to the Department.

The extent to which referrals are encouraged in both these ways will of course depend on the relative value placed on this activity as against others, such as the provision of services. If there are far more referrals than can be dealt with effectively, accessibility may have to be reduced, but there is some choice between functions **a** and **b**.

The idea of specialist intake teams[3] is very attractive, as one of its purposes is to relieve part of the social work staff from the continual "bombardment" of new work of all kinds; another purpose of course is to improve the quality of this first contact with people who may be in a state of stress. But the method is not a panacea for all ills, and gives rise to particular problems. It needs very careful planning, a clear delineation of the area of referrals to be dwelt with, and a precise understanding as to when a referral is to be passed over for long-term work. It is also essential that staff carrying out this task should be committed to it, should perceive its relevance to the rest of the work of the team, and should not be allowed to become depressed by the constant pressure of demand and the lack of adequate resources. It is generally felt that social workers should only specialise in intake work for a limited time, during which they will gain invaluable experience. The control of intake teams is a management problem as the way in which the team works has a profound effect on the whole team, or groups of teams in the area. There is now good reason to think that quite a high proportion of new referrals need only a short period of intensive work, and it is necessary to know enough about the facts to be able to decide how many staff should be allocated to long-term work, and how many to "intake". There might well be a case for intake staff to outnumber long-term staff, possibly by two to one, in some districts.

Many social work teams, specially those operating on a small patch will probably not be able to develop this specialism, however, and may have to rely on the conventional method of making good reception arrangements, either by using an experienced reception clerk, or social worker, or by operating a system of duty roster. Whatever method is preferred, there is likely to be a constant stream of referrals coming in by telephone, letter, form, or personal call and dealing with these is an important social work task. Referrals are likely to fall into the three classical groups contained in the phrase "advice, guidance and assistance" or into some combination of these.[4]

"Advice" may be taken to include the many requests which are made for information, for instance, about whether some service such as child-minding is available. It will also include requests for advice about departmental or external services, and may be dealt with simply by referring the enquiry to the appropriate agency. But the aims of the department will be far better met if, in addition to this, accurate advice can be given immediately. The range of requests will be extremely wide and advice can only be given if the team has available up-to-date literature on the many questions which arise. A number will call for basic knowledge of legal aid, simple law on a number of family situations such as rent, eviction, matrimonial disputes, child care, and welfare rights or benefits. Many of these can be dealt with directly and simply if the appropriate books and booklets are available.[5] A rural team, especially, ought to be equipped to play the part of the local Citizens' Advice Bureau which may in fact be in a distant town, though it will no doubt answer questions by telephone if necessary when there is a good contact with the team.

"Guidance" can take the form of either one interview or a series of interviews about more personal problems which may exist quite apart from the need for factual advice. There may often be a need for the factual advice as well, but guidance is something rather separate, and should only be offered when it is requested as a rule.

"Assistance" is the most complex of the three factors, because it may well contain the other two. The aim should be to help the enquirer to deal with his own problems as far as this is feasible: he can be helped to fill in a form of claim for some right to which he is entitled, or be offered personal support before a tribunal, or in dealing with a housing authority. There is a wide area of help of this kind which is certainly assistance, but which does not necessarily involve social casework, or any form of on-going support. In some instances, however, it will be apparent that there is a need for something more than practical advice, guidance and assistance; this should lead to the offer of referral for social work support. From this has grown the idea of the "contract", by which a mutual agreement is made for the offer and acceptance of some form of social work help, individually or by group, or community, for an agreed time, during which it is intended to achieve some stated goal. Whether this contract is to be carried out by the intake team, or duty officer, or whether this is the stage at which the case is passed on for longer-term work, will depend on the pattern adopted by the team or department concerned.[3]

3. INVESTIGATION

As a first stage, it will be necessary to enquire whether the family is willing to accept assistance; this cannot be imposed, but it is unlikely from previous experience that it will be refused. Investigation should normally be carried out by one social worker and may be the beginning of "a casework relationship" unless, of course, this relationship already exists by reason of a previous referral. The immediate reason for the referral will be taken into account but will need to be considered in the whole context of the case. A request for reception of a child into care for instance, may stem from some other underlying problem within the family, which may become apparent during the enquiry and which needs to be identified as a basic social need. Investigation calls for great skill on the part of the social worker and should be given the highest priority on account of the effects which flow from it. In some cases investigation will be sufficient; in others there may be a need for assessment.

4. ASSESSMENT

Assessment has a long history and literature, especially in relation to children and young persons. As long ago as 1948, local authorities were obliged to provide accommodation for the observation and assessment of children who were admitted to care. Remand homes existed partly to assess children who had appeared before the courts, so that they could make recommendations for treatment. At the same time there were separate child guidance clinics for the assessment of children with emotional difficulties, diagnostic units for physically handicapped children, and the school psychological service for assessing children with educational or mental handicaps. Recent discussion about the future of the child guidance service have once again highlighted the present vast network of assessment agencies concerned with children and young persons. There are many sources of referral which usually take a pre-determined course, for instance, police to social services, school to school psychologist, doctor to child guidance clinic and so on. Assessment by the chosen agency is carried out without reference to the others, which might have relevant knowledge, and recommendations often only take into account one part of the total available resources. In this way, children who come to the notice of the Social Services Department because they are to appear in court may have had no formal assessment, or some form of special assessment, but no overall assessment of their needs. All too often this is finally supplied when they have been before a court and have spent some time at a special assessment unit; by then it may be too late to be of help. Comprehensive assessment for children was being urged as long ago as 1968,[6] but has not yet been brought about. However, the corporate approach of local authorities, which are providing the various forms of assessment in their own departments, may now lead to the introduction of a central *referral unit*, or units, which will be for all children, whatever their apparent difficulties. There are practical problems to be overcome, but thought is being given to the possibility, and at the very least there should be more effective exchange of information about children, wherever they are referred.

In the former Children's Departments "assessment" was thought of too much in terms of residential assessment. This was perhaps due to the fact that there were establishments which carried out most of the task; and though remand homes as such no longer exist, there is still a kind of hierarchy of establishments from the small reception home to the sophisticated assessment units with highly skilled staff, which receive children and young persons for observation, and report upon them to the Social Services Department which placed them. Even now, however, there is a tendency for children who have been before the court for offences, especially boys, to be sent to the sophisticated units; other children who come to the notice of the department rarely receive that kind of comprehensive assessment and probably only few need it.

But there are other forms of assessment which ought to be used more than they are. A number of ideas were contained in a booklet[7] issued by the Ministry in connection with the Children and Young Persons Act 1969. Here assessment facilities were seen as absolutely vital to the working of the Act, and to the whole range of children who were expected to come to notice. As will be seen in Chapter 9, for instance, no child should come into care in any way without *investigation*. This booklet stresses the fact that in some cases this will not be enough; it should be followed by assessment.

However, we need no longer think of assessment as being carried out solely in a residential setting. The following methods are available and the most suitable should be used in each case:

1. Assessment of a child in his own home by a social worker aided where necessary by others, such as educational psychologists, etc.
2. Daily attendance at an assessment centre near the child's home, foster home or other children's home where he usually lives.
3. Placement in an assessment centre providing a specialist consultation as in present reception centres and remand homes.
4. Assessment of a child wherever he may be by visiting specialists from an available assessment centre.
5. Placement in a highly specialised assessment centre with full facilities, corresponding to the present classifiying unit including the provision of secure accommodation.

There should therefore be a graduation of assessment procedures to be chosen solely in relation to the child's need and with the exception of (5) above all these procedures should be directly within the Authority's control. The purpose and content of the assessment should however in all cases be the same. Moreover, assessment will not always be a once and for all requirement and must be available at all times during a child's period in care.

Assessment in its simplest form is used almost daily by a social worker. The other forms of assessment involve other services which should be used only when necessary, otherwise they will be placed under too much strain and will not be readily available. The type of referral unit mentioned earlier on should bring about a greater comprehensive use of whatever facilities are available.

Something of this kind has already emerged in the detailed schemes of consultation which have been worked out for dealing with referrals of battered children as regards whoever receives the first intimation. The mounting concern about these cases has been strong enough to overcome most of the problems in co-operative consultation. But these children, important though they are, form only a small proportion of those who would benefit from the same kind of careful, ordered assessment. It is to be hoped that this will be developed in the near future.

5. TREATMENT

It is only after proper investigation, that treatment can begin.

Treatment is the bringing together of the identified social problem and the resources which are available to meet it. An essential part is the acceptance by the family of the social worker and his acceptance of the family; whatever else may be provided or done it is usually necessary that some one person shall be seen by the members of a family as being concerned for them and being the means of bringing the right resources to bear on their difficulties.

The first and most important resource is the continuing support and interest and concern of the social worker himself.

Over and above this, there is no limit to the amount of help which can be given, except any limit imposed by the local authority as regards finance and staff. The resources available to the Director are set out in Chapter 1 and need to be applied in such a way as to promote the welfare of all children referred, by providing constructive help when it appears that in the short term or long term there is a likelihood that a child or children of a family may need to be admitted to care or committed to care for one of many reasons. These reasons are indicated in the annual statistics; those for the year 1973–74 being as follows:

Admitted to Care

a	No parent or guardian	394
b	Abandoned or lost	988
c	Death of Mother; Father unable to care	670
d	Deserted by Mother; Father unable to care	4,354
e	Confinement	2,725
f	Short-term illness (up to six months)	13,374
g	Long-term illness or incapacity	958
h	Child illegitimate (Mother unable to provide)	1,770
i	Parent or guardian in prison or remanded in custody	855
j	Family homeless because of eviction	673
k	Family homeless through cause other than eviction	1,531
l	Unsatisfactory home conditions	4,503
m	Other reasons	7,533

Committed by juvenile courts:

n	Offenders	3,389
o	Non-offenders	5,553
p	Others	636
q	Committed by Matrimonial and other Courts	446

Total 50,352[8]

Incidentally, these figures show some change from those for the year 1969–70. Without quoting them all, there has been quite a marked fall in the numbers admitted for reasons **d**–**g**, and **j**, but a marked increase in those admitted for reasons **l**–**p**. The total admissions have fallen from 51,171 to 50,352 (about the same per 1,000 under 18). The age groups of children coming into care are interesting. Of these 8,862 (18%) were under 2, 10,010 (20%) aged 2–4, 28,942 (57%) were of school age, and 2,508 (5%) were over school age.

The reasons stated above are taken from the returns made by each local authority at the end of the financial year. The returns are based on the information supplied by social workers or teams responsible for the admissions, and are not anything like as clear cut as they appear. Frequently more than one reason applies, but one has to be selected for the return. In 7,533 cases, "in other reasons" in category **m** it seems to have been impossible to assign any of the more precise reasons. There is most probably a misuse of "unsatisfactory home conditions" which was originally intended to relate to physical conditions, condemned dwellings for example, and from the numbers quoted, it is possible that a number of emotionally unsatisfactory home conditions have been included.

As admission, or committal, to care was the form of treatment which was in fact applied in these thousands of cases, it must be assumed that it was preceded by investigation, or even assessment. Leaving aside those committed by courts, the local authorities made a conscious decision to admit to care 40,328 children and young people, about a third of them under 5, for a variety of reasons amounting to family misfortunes, many of which might affect anyone.

Many people have short-term illnesses, many parents desert their partners, or have unsatisfactory home conditions. Why do some cope with their own problems, while others come to the Social Services Department for help? This question becomes even more pertinent in view of the fact that a great many voluntary admissions to care are for a short period only. Not very many last *more* than six weeks (42% in a study in one authority), and only 22% for *more* than six months.

This subject was studied some years ago by a method involving a comparison of 100 child-care families with a control group of 100 other families who made their own arrangements for children during a mother's confinement.[9] One of the conclusions was that the application for care was rarely the result of practical difficulties. It often arose because of a basic weakness in the family life, with poor family relationships and a disregard of the effects that separation would have on the lives of the children. Even short-term admission to care, then, is probably only an indication of the need for prolonged support, and continuous assessment. Other aspects of this report will be discussed in Chapter 9.

But there is every reason why the local authority should develop new resources and new preventive services designed to support social workers in their dealings with families and children. It is in this area of social work that the many voluntary organisations and services may be able and willing to pioneer schemes to meet particular situations, in co-operation with the local authority. But the time has come for less reliance on the casework method—the "one to one" approach which makes enormous demands on limited resources of time and skill. More stress should be laid on stimulating and encouraging group work, neighbourhood work, and community development. Using these methods, it may be found that the people of any given neighbourhood can themselves make a great contribution to the solution of their own problems and difficulties, especially those which spring from isolation and a sense of inadequacy. The greatly needed corporate approach by the whole local authority to the promotion of the welfare of children by the use of existing services has so far not been much in evidence. Even social workers often think in terms which do not go beyond using money provided under s 1 of the 1963 Act to pay overdue electricity or gas bills, rent arrears, debts or other embarrassing liabilities, on the grounds that payment will "keep children out of care, and be much cheaper". The power to use money *in exceptional circumstances* which was given by this Act was to enable social workers to assist a family with counselling, knowing that finance would be available if it was needed in that context. It was never intended to provide money without the counselling that went with it. In the event, payments under the 1963 Act have gone far beyond the intention of the Circular 204/1963 and are being used largely to subvent or replace supplementary benefits.[10, 11] This raises once again the question of a social worker's awareness of the field of welfare rights, mentioned earlier in this chapter.

It must be remembered that among the cases of families and children referred from many official and unofficial sources, there will be some which demand primarily the *protection* of a child or young person. There will be others to which preventive measures and voluntary support have been applied without success. It is essential that the social worker should recognise these situations and should be able to take appropriate steps to provide either the *protection* or the *care* which is seen in any particular case to be necessary for the child. This is a hard decision, and the failure to make it lies at the heart of much controversy and conflict about the rights of a child as against those of his parents, or other adults. All through the process of discovery, referral, investigation, assessment and treatment the rights of the child in his own right are at issue and at no stage can they be ignored.

NOTES

1. Report of the Committee on Children and Young Persons 1960, Cmnd. 1191.
2. Specimen Community Care Programme, Appendix A.
3. "Work in a Social Services Department—intake", *Social Work Service*, No. 5, December 1974.

4.   "Family Advice Service," Leissner—B.H.J. 17 January 1969.
5.   For instance, *Social Workers their Clients and the Law*, Zander; *Family Benefits and Pensions*, D.H.S.S., *Exceptional Needs Payments*, London, H.M.S.O., 1973; *National Welfare Benefits Handbook*, Child Poverty Action Group; *Legal Aid*, B.A.S.W.; *The Rent Act 1974*, Shelter, 86 The Strand, London, WC2R OEQ; *Small Claims in the County Court*, free from Lord Chancellor's Department.
6.   *Caring for Children*, National Children's Bureau and Longmans.
7.   *Community Homes Project: assessment* (1969).
8.   Children in Care, 31 March 1974, Cmnd. 6147.
9.   *Child Care and the Family*, Schaffer, London, Bell 1968.
10. "Section One Money: a survey of use", *Social Work Today*, 3 April 1975.
11. "The Problem of Disconnected Electricity supplies", *Social Work Today*, 15 May 1975.

Chapter 7

PROTECTION

SUMMARY

IMMEDIATE PROTECTION

One of the important functions of a Social Services Department
is that of acting as a sentinel, especially as regards children and young
persons under seventeen. The word implies constant vigilance and
readiness to take action when danger threatens. Among the referrals
coming to a department, either in or out of office hours, there will be
some which primarily call for immediate steps to safeguard a child
who needs either care or control, which must now be defined.

DEFINITION OF CARE OR CONTROL

At one time the Children and Young Persons Act 1933 provided
ways of dealing with those who were found to be in need of *care or
protection*. That Act also allowed parents to bring their children before
the court as being *beyond parental control*. The Act of 1963 took away
this right from parents and provided means of dealing with children
who were in need of *care, protection or control*. The Act of 1969 refers
only to children in need of *care or control* but states that care includes
protection, and control includes discipline.[1] The circumstances in
which a child or young person may need either care (including protection) or control (including discipline) are set out in the primary
conditions described in s. 1 (2), as follows:

a his proper development is being avoidably prevented or neglected or his health is being avoidably impaired or neglected or
he is being ill-treated; or

b it is probable that the condition set out in the preceding paragraph will be satisfied in his case, having regard to the fact that
the court or another court has found that that condition is or
was satisfied in the case of another child or young person who
is or was a member of the household to which he belongs; or

bb having regard to the fact that a person convicted of a First
Schedule offence is, or may become, a member of the same
household as the child; or (Children Act 1975, Schedule 3)

c he is exposed to moral danger; or

d he is beyond the control of his parent or guardian; or

e he is of compulsory school age within the meaning of the
Education Act 1944, and is not receiving efficient full-time
education suitable to his age, ability and aptitude; or

f (he is guilty of an offence, excluding homicide) will be dealt
with separately.

Under condition **a**, there is a general power for *anyone* acting in
the interests of a child to act in a case of emergency affecting a child
or young person.

CHILDREN AND YOUNG PERSONS ACT 1933, s. 40

Anyone acting in the interests of a child or young person and
suspecting that:

a the child or young person has been or is being assaulted, ill-
treated, or neglected in any place within the jurisdiction of the
justice, in a manner likely to cause him unnecessary suffering,
or injury to health; or

b that any offence mentioned in the First Schedule to the Act of
1933 (cruelty, ill-treatment, assault, etc.) has been or is being
committed in respect of the child or young person,

may lay *information on oath* to that effect before a justice of the
peace who may issue a warrant authorising a constable to search for
the child or young person, who need not be named, and to take him
to a place of safety if the information is found to be correct.

For this purpose the constable may enter a house or building, by
force if necessary, and may remove the child or young person from
it. Although the warrant may only be addressed to and executed by
a constable, the justice may direct that the constable shall be accompanied by a medical practitioner; the person laying the information
may also go with the constable unless prohibited by the justice.

This section sets out the lawful way of gaining entry to a house by
force if need be: This mainly concerns the police, acting under the
authority of a J.P. and may also involve a doctor, and the complainant. The power may be used when there is an unreasonable refusal
to allow the visiting of a child in a private foster home or a pros-

pective adoptive home. (See under General Protective Functions, *post.*)

In the generality of cases however this dramatic action will not be necessary so that when conditions **a** to **e** are thought to exist, they can normally be dealt with by the social worker, armed with a place of safety order, or by the police without an order.

BATTERED BABIES AND OTHERS IN NEED OF PROTECTION

This is the situation which arises in the cases of what are sometimes known as battered babies, though of course they are often not babies and may be of any age up to 17. Basically, these are children (or young persons) who are thought to come within condition **a** above, but where additionally there is a likelihood that injury has been caused by an assault which is a criminal offence under Schedule 1 of the Act of 1933.[2] As suggested in the previous chapter, concern about such cases has led to the setting up of highly structured arrangements to deal with the sometimes conflicting elements of physical and mental health, social considerations and the law. Such arrangements are made under the guidance of the D.H.S.S., and are associated with continuing research into causes, and measures for prevention of tragedy.

The very complex factors to be taken into account are set out in the report of Tunbridge Wells Study Group of 1973.[3] Different authorities have evolved various methods of providing instant advice to parents on the lines of experiments mounted by the N.S.P.C.C. The report estimates that there may be about 4,600 cases of battering each year, some 700 resulting in death. This is therefore a most serious problem,[4] but it should not be overlooked that there are far more cases in which one of the conditions **a** to **e** applies, and especially perhaps where apparent injury may be emotional rather than physical.

The local authority has the duty of investigating any case in which it receives information suggesting that any of these conditions apply to any child or young person residing or found in its area, unless it is satisfied that such enquiries are unnecessary.[5] A parent may still ask the local authority to bring his child before the court, subject however to s. 3 the Children and Young Persons Act 1963. Furthermore, the authority has the duty of bringing care proceedings in such a case unless satisfied that it is not in the child's interests or the public interest to do so, or that some other person is about to bring proceedings.[6] (The "other person" would be a police officer or an officer of an authorised society, the National Society for the Prevention of Cruelty to Children; or in cases described in **e** above, the local Education Authority.[7]) Information received by a local authority may refer to a number of situations some of which may require urgent action to bring about the removal of the child or young person from the persons who have his care or control for the time being, whether parents or not. Such an emergency situation could arise, for instance, if there is imminent danger to an unwanted stepchild or adopted child, a child who is rejected by one or both parents, anyone under 17 found to be suffering from unexplained injuries, a child or young person who has been punished excessively by a physical attack or by being locked in a room, or a child or young person who is "beyond control" to the extent that he may have been turned out from his own home. It does not follow of course, that care proceedings *will* be taken in all such cases and indeed it is intended that they will not; but there are some instances in which it might be thought essential that the child or young person should be removed for the time being to a place of safety.

Social workers sometimes try to deal with this situation by using voluntary admission to care, and then placing the child in a foster home or children's home. This is of doubtful validity, and is often futile. If the first need of a child is for protection, even for a short time, this will not be achieved by admission to care since the parent can at present remove the child at will, leaving the position much as it was before the admission.

DETENTION IN PLACE OF SAFETY

The proper course is removal to a place of safety where the child can be *detained* under proper authority. Being detained is not the same as being in care and is more akin to a form of arrest, though for purely protective reasons, and may be arranged in one of two ways.

1. Any *constable* may detain a child or young person if he has reasonable cause to believe that any of the above conditions **a** to **d** is satisfied or that condition **b** would be found to be satisfied by an appropriate court or that a juvenile is being taken from place to place by a vagrant. (A constable has no power to detain a child or young person in respect of condition **e** as failure to attend school does not itself warrant immediate removal. He would, therefore, have to consider in such cases whether any of the conditions **a** to **d** is satisfied.) In detaining the child or young person or arresting him without warrant, the constable must take such steps as are possible to inform the parent or guardian of the detention and the reason for it.[8] The constable must then ensure that the case is enquired into by a police officer not below the rank of inspector; that officer shall, after completing the enquiry, release the child or young person, or if he thinks fit, arrange for his *detention in a place of safety*, informing him and his parent or guardian of his right to apply to a justice for his release. The child or young person may lawfully be detained in the place of safety for a period of only eight days from the beginning of the detention. If, during that period, the child or young person or his parent or guardian, applied to a justice for release, the justice must direct that he be released unless he considers that further detention is necessary in the interests of the child or young person.[9] In this event, further detention would be authorised under an interim order.

2. *Any other person*, for example, an officer of a local authority or Inspector of the N.S.P.C.C., wishing to *detain* a child or young person and take him to a place of safety, must apply to a justice, who may grant the application if he is satisfied that the applicant has reasonable cause to believe that:

a any of the conditions set out in **a** to **e** above is satisfied; or
b an appropriate court would find condition **b** satisfied; or
c the child or young person is about to leave the United Kingdom in contravention of s. 25 of the Children and Young Persons Act 1933, which relates to persons under 18 going abroad for the purpose of performing for profit.

On the authority of the justice, a child or young person may then be detained in a place of safety for a period not exceeding twenty-eight days. Here again, the child or young person and the parent or guardian must be informed of the detention and the reason for it.[10] Whichever method of detention is intended, it is only necessary for there to be "reasonable cause" for belief that a child's circumstances fall within the conditions set out in s. 1 of the Act. Proof is not required at this stage, but may be sought later.

The main differences between the two methods are:

a the constable may detain on the authority of a police inspector, without obtaining a justice's order, but any one else must obtain an order.
b the constable can only detain for a maximum of eight days, whereas a justice's order authorises detention for up to twenty-eight days.

A place of safety is defined as "a community home provided by a local authority or a controlled community home, any police station or any hospital, surgery or any other suitable place, the occupier of which is willing temporarily to receive a child or young person".[11] The place of safety need not therefore be a place within the control of the local authority and can, for instance, be a private house.

The Tunbridge Wells report, referred to earlier, recommends that the first essential step in dealing with a child suspected of being damaged by non-accidental injury is immediate admission to hospital. A hospital may of course be used as a place of safety, and is defined as such, but mere admission to it does not necessarily provide protection. The parents may, as the report suggests, attempt a panic withdrawal of the child while investigations are going on. It is therefore advisable for the admission to be made on the authority of a place of safety order obtained in the usual way. A note on the content and use of the order will be found in Appendix B. No one but the local authority or the N.S.P.C.C., however much concerned in a case, has the power to apply for a place of safety order. The police do not need one. Another point about detention in a place of safety is that it need not continue for the full period of eight or twenty-eight days as the case may be. The detention can be brought to an end by an application procedure or by reception into care.

INTERIM ORDERS

While a child or young person is detained whether by a constable for a period of eight days or under the authority of a justice's order for a period of up to twenty-eight days, an application may be made to either a magistrates' court or to a justice of the peace for an interim order to be made. On such an application the interim order must either be made or refused; the application cannot be adjourned. If the order is refused, the court or justice may direct that the child or young person be released forthwith. An interim order may only be made if the person is present, unless he is under the age of 5 or cannot be present because of illness or accident. An interim order commits the child or young person for a period of not more than twenty-eight days to the care of the local authority in whose area the person resides or where the circumstances arose, the decision as to which being at the discretion of the court or the justice.[12] It may be necessary to obtain further interim orders in some cases, but those can only be made by a juvenile court and not by a single Justice of the Peace.

The order lays upon the local authority a duty to bring the child or young person before the court on the expiration of the order or such earlier time as the court may require; but if the child is under 5 or unable to appear by reason of illness or accident, the court need not require his attendance; it may make a further interim order for a period of twenty-eight days.[13] In the case of a young person over the age of 14, if the court or justice certifies that he is too unruly to be safely committed to the care of the local authority under an interim order and if there is a remand centre available to the court, the court or justice may commit him by warrant to the remand centre for twenty-eight days or for a less period. If an interim order is already in force, such a warrant may only be issued on the application of the local authority, and may not in any case run beyond the date fixed for the expiry of the interim order. On the issue of such a warrant an interim order will cease to have effect.[14]

A person in respect of whom an interim order has been made may apply to the High Court for the order to be discharged and the High Court may discharge the order on such conditions as it thinks fit. If, however, the High Court refuses to discharge the order, the local authority to whose care the child or young person is committed may not allow the parent or any other person to be in charge of him without the consent of the High Court and in accordance with any directions which the court may give.[15]

There are, therefore, provisions for removing children and young persons from actual or suspected perils with the authority of the law and there are safeguards for their appearance before a court within a specified time unless it is more in their interests for them to be released.

GENERAL PROTECTIVE FUNCTIONS

These apply in a number of cases where there may not be any element of crisis or danger but none the less protection (by supervision) is available for children and young persons who, for various reasons, are living either entirely or partly with people who are not of their own family. The two principal Acts concerned are the Children Act 1958 (Part I) as regards "foster" children, and the Adoption Act 1958 (Part IV) as regards "protected" children. There is no provision in either of these two Acts for regulations to be made by the Minister, as for example in the Children Act, concerning the boarding out of children. The two Acts have many similarities and for this reason the following notes have been set out in two columns for convenience of comparison. *The numbers in the margins refer to the sections of the appropriate Act.* This method makes the functions appear to be extremely dull, and probably legalistic, but the details are important even if they are uninteresting. Very briefly, there are certain ways in which people who are looking after other people's children have to notify various events to the Social Services Department. (There are a number of exceptions which are all set out.) The Department has duties towards these children because they all need protection, though not all to the same degree. It also has powers which it can exercise over the people who are providing the care for the children. It has powers to prohibit placing in stated circumstances, and can take steps to remove children by stated procedures, when this is in their interests. Other comments follow after the summary of the two Acts.

SUMMARY:

CHILDREN ACT 1958— (AS AMENDED) FOSTER CHILDREN	ADOPTION ACT 1958— PROTECTED CHILDREN
Introduction	
1. The work undertaken by local authorities under this Act is referred to generally as "Child Protection" and was previously known as "Child Life Protection". The Infant Life Protection Act 1897, laid down a maximum age of 5 years for children with whom the Act was concerned and this age was raised to 7 years by the Children Act	**1.** Local authorities have various duties in connection with children who are to be legally adopted but in this chapter we are dealing with the supervision of children being cared for by persons who are proposing to adopt them. The whole question was discussed by the Curtis Committee who recommended in 1946 that these children

1908; to 9 years by the Children and Young Persons Act 1932, and to the upper limit of compulsory school age by the Children Act 1948.

should fall under supervision in the same way as foster children fostered for reward.

Legislation

2. The principal Act is the Children Act 1958, as extensively amended with effect from 1 January 1970 by the Children and Young Persons Act 1969 see Schedule 7.

2. The necessary legislation was effected in the Adoption Act 1950, and was re-enacted in Part IV of the Adoption Act 1958. Part IV of the Adoption Act 1958, bears a strong resemblance to Part I of the Children Act 1958, and details will not be repeated in the case of provisions which are identical in both Acts.

Definition

3. *Meaning of "foster child"—* A foster child is defined as a child below the upper limit 2 of compulsory school age whose care and maintenance are undertaken by a person who is not a relative or guardian of the child; the child becomes a foster child as soon as the person who has given the undertaking receives him. There is no definition in the Act of the term "guardian". But see list of exemptions at **4** below.

3. *Meaning of "protected child"—*

a The powers and duties of local authorities in this part of the Adoption Act relate only to "protected children" so that it is important to establish precisely the meaning of the term.

b There are two main categories of protected children. In the first category are those children below school-leaving age who are placed in the actual custody of persons who 37 are not parents, guardians or relatives of the child (but who propose to adopt him), under arrangements made *by* another person not being the parent or guardian of the child. There is sometimes doubt as to whether or not a person has in fact taken part in arrangements for the placing of a child with another person and in this connection it is helpful to refer to s. 57(2) of the Act which sets out quite clearly that taking part in the arrangements includes entering into, or making any agreement or arrangement for, or for facilitating, the adoption of the child by any other person whether the adoption is effected, or is intended to be effected, in pursuance of an adoption order or otherwise. It also includes agreements or arrangements for, or for facilitating, the placing of the child in the care and possession of another person. The section goes on to say that if the third party initiates or takes part in any negotiations of which the purpose or effect is the conclusion of an agreement or the making of any arrangement for the purpose of adoption or if he causes another to do so, then he has taken part in the arrangements for the placing of the child within the meaning of s. 37 and the child will be a protected child.

c In the second category are children in respect of whom notification of intention to apply for an adoption order has been

37

given to the local authority under s. 3(2) of the Act. An adoption order cannot be made unless such a notification has been given in respect of the child, except where the applicants or one of the applicants is a parent of the infant, or where the child is over compulsory school age at the time.

d It follows, therefore, that all the children in the first category will also fall within the second category if and when notification of intention to adopt is given; but there will also be children falling in the second category who have never been in the first, as will be the case where adoption is arranged by a registered adoption society, a local authority or by direct arrangement between the parent or guardian of the child and the proposed adopter.

e The child will only be a protected child while he is actually in the care and possession of the person referred to in the first category, or of the person giving the notice in the second category.

Exemptions

4. Children are not regarded as foster children within the meaning of the Act in the following circumstances:

a While in the care of a local authority;

2

4. The provisions with regard to exemptions are very similar to those contained in the Children Act 1958, in respect of foster children:

a Children in the care of local authorities are not

37

exempted from becoming protected children and the obvious case will be where a child who is boarded-out becomes the subject of an application for an adoption order and the notice of intention is given under s. 3(2) of the Adoption Act.

b While in the care of a voluntary organisation;

b The provisions with re-
to gard to exemption for
d protected children are the same as in para. **4b** to **d** opposite;

c While boarded-out by a Health Authority;

d While boarded-out by a local Education Authority;

e While in premises in which any parent, adult relative or guardian of his is for the time being residing;

e A child is not exempt from becoming a protected child by virtue of the fact that he is in the care of any person in premises in which a parent or adult relative or guardian of his is for the time being residing.

f While in a voluntary home;

f The provisions with re-
to gard to exemption for
k protected children are the same as in para. **4f** to **k** opposite;
"Guardian" now includes a father who has custody of an illegitimate child (Children Act 1975, Schedule 3.)

g While in any school within the meaning of the Education Acts 1944–53 in which he is receiving full-time education;

h While in a hospital or nursing home registered or exempted from registration under the appropriate legislation;

i While in any home or institution not specified above but maintained by a public or local authority;

j While in the care of any person by virtue of a supervision, or care order;

k While liable to be detained or subject to

guardianship under the Mental Health Act 1959, or resident in a residential home for mentally disordered persons within the meaning of Part III of that Act.

1 While in the care of a person who does not intend to, and does not in fact, undertake his care and maintenance for a continuous period of more than six days, or, if that person is not a "regular foster parent", for a continuous period of more than twenty-seven days. The period may be continuous (even though broken within the period). See *Surrey County Council* v. *Battersby*, [1965] 1 All E.R. 273. A person is a "regular foster parent" for this purpose if she has during the preceding twelve months had the care of one or more children for a period of three months, or for periods totalling three months, or for at least three continuous periods each of more than six days. Children who are cared for for periods of not more than six days are subject to supervision under the Nurseries and Child Minders Regulation Act 1948. The above provisions regarding persons who are not "regular foster parents" give exemption from supervision in the case of children placed for short holidays or in an emergency.

1 There is no time limit for protected children.

n While placed with a person who proposes to adopt him under arrangements made by a local authority or registered adoption society, or while he is a protected child. (A child placed by a parent or guardian or a third party, not for adoption, is not exempted.)

Reward

5. It is no longer necessary to establish "reward" in order to bring a child within the definition of a "foster child". (But see **12** below—Insurance.)

5. There is no reference to "reward" in connection with protected children. On the contrary there is a general prohibition of payments in respect of children who are to be adopted, in Part V of the Adoption Act. 50

Duty of Local Authority

6. Local authorities for the purpose of this Act are non-metropolitan councils and metropolitan district councils and their duties are allocated to the Social Services Committee. The local authority has the duty to ensure the well-being of foster children in their area by causing officers of the authority to visit the children from time to time, at the discretion of the authority and give such advice as to the care and maintenance of the children as appears to be needed. It is for the local authority to decide in each case whether continuous visiting is necessary. 2nd Sch. 1

6. Here again, local authorities for the purpose of the Adoption Act are the councils of non-metropolitan counties and metropolitan districts and their duties with regard to the visitation of protected children are similar to those in respect of foster children, the difference being that there is no discretion allowed as to visitation; the requirement is that all protected children must be visited from time to time by officers of the authority, who must satisfy themselves as to the well-being of the children and give such advice as to their care and maintenance as may appear to be needed. 28 38

Notices to Local Authority

7a. A person who proposes to maintain a foster child not already in his care must give *written* notice to the local **3** authority of his intention to do so not less than two weeks and not more than four weeks before he receives the child unless he receives the child in an emergency (undefined). In the case of a child received in an emergency, the person must give *written* notice to the local authority not later than forty-eight hours after he receives the child, and the same provision applies to the case where the person had in his care a child who was not a foster child but who became a foster child while in his care. The notice is to be given to the local authority for the area in which the premises concerned are situated. The notice must give the date of reception, as to other information, see para. **7f** below. The reception of subsequent foster children need not be notified to the local authority provided one or more foster children have been maintained continuously since the first notification was given (but see **8b** below).

b A person maintaining a foster child must notify the local authority, in writing, if he changes his address, at least two weeks and not more than four weeks before the change. If the change is made in an emergency then the notification may be made not later than forty-eight

7a. The provisions of the **40** Adoption Act with regard to notifications to local authorities are very similar to those required for foster parents under the Children Act 1958. Where, however, arrangements are made for placing children who would come within the first category referred to above, the responsibility for giving the notice to the local authority falls on the third party or agent and not on the person in whose care and possession the child is to be placed, nor by the parent or guardian of the child.

See also **7f** below.

b The requirement for giving written notice of change of address is similar to that required for foster children under the Children Act 1958.

hours after the change. If the new address it situated in the area of another local authority, the first mentioned authority must notify the authority concerned and send particulars in respect of the child.

c If a foster child dies, the person having the care of the child must inform the local authority and the person from whom the child was received within 48 hours of the death. Where the child is removed or removes himself the local authority may require notice to be given to them of the name and address of the person into whose care the child has been removed. Such notices must be in writing.

d Although there is no requirement to notify the local authority of the removal of individual foster children, a person who ceases to maintain any foster children at particular premises must notify the local authority thereof in writing within forty-eight hours, unless notice is already required by **c** above, or unless the person intends to maintain any of the children again within twenty-seven days. If this intention is abandoned, however, or if the child is not received again within the twenty-seven-day period, notice must be given.

e Local authorities no longer have the power to grant exemption from the giving of notices of intention to act as foster parents.

3

c If a protected child dies, the person having the care of the child must notify the local authority in writing within forty-eight hours of the death. There is no provision in the Adoption Act for notification of children being removed or removing themselves as under the Children Act 1958.

d There is no equivalent in the Adoption Act to that contained in the Children Act 1958, in respect of notification of children ceasing to be foster children.

e Local authorities do not have the power to grant exemption from the giving of notices in respect of protected children.

f The local authority *may* require a person maintaining or proposing to maintain a foster child to give the following particulars, *i.e.* the name, sex, date and place of birth of the child and the name and address of every person who is a parent or guardian or acts as a guardian of the child or from whom the child has been or is to be received.

8. *Power to Inspect Premises, Impose Conditions or Prohibit the Keeping of Foster Children.*

a Any local authority officer who is authorised to visit foster children may inspect any part of premises in the area of the authority in which foster children are to be or are being kept, but before doing so the officer must, if so requested, produce a duly authenticated document saying that he is entitled to visit foster children. If admission to the premises is refused, or refusal is expected, or the occupier is temporarily absent, a justice of the peace may on production of sworn information in writing issue a warrant authorising entry to the premises, by force if need be, within forty-eight hours, for the purpose of inspecting the premises. The warrant may only be issued if there is reasonable cause to believe that there is a foster child in the premises. The power to inspect premises

3

4

f The requirements of the Adoption Act in respect of protected children are identical with those of the Children Act 1958, in respect of foster children, as regards the information to be supplied to the local authority on request.

8. *Power to Inspect Premises, Impose Conditions or Prohibit the Keeping of Protected Children.*

a Officers of a local authority have the same authority to inspect premises as is contained in the Children Act 1958, in respect of foster children. In the event of refusal, note **11** applies.

39

must be distinguished from the duty to visit foster children referred to in paragraph **6** above.

b A local authority *may* impose requirements on a person who is keeping or proposes to keep foster children in premises used wholly or partly for that purpose. The requirements may relate to the following:

i The number, age and sex of the foster children who may be kept at any one time in the premises or any part thereof.

ii The accommodation and equipment to be provided for the children.

iii The medical arrangements made for protecting the health of the children.

iv The giving of particulars of the person for the time being in charge of the children.

v The number, qualifications or experience of the persons employed in looking after the children.

vi The keeping of records.

vii The fire precautions to be taken in the premises.

viii The giving of particulars of any foster child received in the premises and of any change in the number or identity of the foster children kept therein.

4

b There is no power for a local authority to impose requirements in respect of protected children in the same way as is referred to in the paragraph opposite.

This requirement is important as it enables local authorities to keep themselves informed of all admissions and discharges of foster children, if they so desire, notwithstanding the last sentence of **7a** above.

If the authority so desire, the requirements may only apply when the number of foster children in the premises exceeds a specified number, or may relate to a particular class of foster children only.

c Local authorities may prohibit persons from keeping foster children as follows:

    i If the premises are unsuitable, from keeping any foster children in those premises.

    ii If the person is unsuitable, from keeping any foster children in any premises in their area.

    iii If the premises or the person are unsuitable for a particular child only, from keeping that child in particular premises.

Any such prohibition may be cancelled by the local authority. The requirements and prohibitions referred to must be imposed by notice in writing addressed to the person concerned. Any person aggrieved by any requirement or prohibition imposed in the preceding paragraph may appeal to

4 **c** The local authority under the Adoption Act has no *general* power to prohibit a child being received in 41 any premises but the local authority may prohibit a person from taking over the care of *a child* if the authority consider that it would be detrimental to the child to be kept by that person in those particular premises. This power may not, however, be exercised if a Registered Adoption Society or another local authority was the agent. There is a similar provision for persons aggrieved by any prohibition imposed by the local authority to 42 appeal to a juvenile court.

a juvenile court within fourteen days from the date of notification of the requirement. Although the prohibition takes effect at once, a requirement does not take effect while an appeal is pending. Local authorities imposing requirements or prohibitions are required to include in the notice a statement notifying the person concerned of his right to appeal and of the time within which he may do so.

9. *Disqualification for keeping Foster Children.*—A person may not maintain a foster child if:

a An order has been made against him under this 6 Act removing a child from his care.

b A child has been removed from his care after having been found to be in need of care or control under the Children and Young Persons Acts 1933–1969.

c He has been convicted of any offence specified in the First Schedule of the 1933 Act or has been placed on probation or discharged absolutely or conditionally for any such offence.

d His rights and powers with respect to a child have been vested in a local authority under s. 2 of the Children Act 1948.

e A local authority have made an order under sub-s. 4 of s. 1 of the

9. *Disqualification for keeping Protected Children.*—There is no provision comparable to that under section 6 of the Children Act 1958, disqualifying certain persons from 34 keeping foster children. Local authorities will, however, no doubt make the same enquiries about the foster parents of protected children as they make about other foster parents.

Nurseries and Child Minders Regulation Act 1948, refusing his registration under that Act, or have made an Order under s. 5 of that Act cancelling his registration or the registration of any premises which he occupies.

f An order has been made under s. 43 of the Adoption Act 1958, for the removal of a protected child who was being kept or was about to be received by him:

unless he has disclosed that fact to the local authority and obtained their written consent.

These disqualifications apply also to persons who live or are employed in premises in which it is proposed to keep foster children.   6
(2)

10. *Removal of Foster Children kept in Unsuitable Surroundings*

a A local authority may complain to a juvenile court that a foster child   7 is being kept or is about to be received by any person unfit to have his care, or by a person disqualified under the preceding paragraphs for keeping foster children, or in any premises or any environment detrimental or likely to be detrimental to him, and if the court, on hearing the complaint, is satisfied of the truth of the allegations they may make an order for his removal to a place of safety until he can be

10. *Removal of Protected Children kept in Unsuitable Surroundings*

a and **b** The provisions of the Adoption Act with regard to the removal of protected children kept in unsuitable   43 surroundings are identical with those for foster children.

restored to a parent, relative or guardian or until other arrangements can be made for him. In cases where there is imminent danger to the health or well-being of the child the application may be made by a person authorised to visit foster children and the order made by a justice of the peace.

b The order referred to in the previous paragraph may be executed by an officer of a local authority or by a constable.

c The order may require the removal of all the foster children in the premises if the ground of the complaint is that a prohibition by a local authority made under s. 4 of the Act has been contravened.

d Any children removed from premises under this paragraph may be received into care by a local authority under s. 1 of the Children Act 1948, whether or not the circumstances fall within s. 1 of the Children Act and the child may appear to be over the age of 17.

e The parent or guardian of any child removed under this paragraph must be notified by the local authority if this is practicable.

c This does not apply to protected children.

d and **e** The provisions of the Adoption Act with regard to the reception of children on removal into care and the 43 notification to the parent or guardian of the child are identical with those in respect of foster children.

Power to Issue Warrants to Search for and Remove a Child

11. This section extends the power under s. 40 of the 8

11. This provision is identical with that contained in 45

Children and Young Persons Act 1933, to search for and remove a child under warrant. Under that section the warrant may be issued if it appears from information on oath that there is reasonable cause to suspect that a child has been or is being ill-treated or neglected or is the victim of certain specified offences. This section provides that a refusal to allow the visiting of a foster child or the inspection of any premises by a person authorised to visit under Part I of the Act shall constitute reasonable cause for such a suspicion and hence for the issue of a warrant to search for and remove the child.

the Children Act 1958, in respect of foster children.

Insurance

12. The Life Assurance Act 1774, provides *inter alia* that no insurance may be made unless the insurer has some interest in the life of the insured and that he may not recover more than the value of the interest. The section provides that a person who maintains a foster child for reward shall be deemed for the purposes of the Life Assurance Act 1774, to have no interest in the life of the child.

9

12. This provision is identical with that contained in the Children Act 1958, in respect of foster children, except that the reference to "reward" is omitted.

46

Sittings of Juvenile Courts

13. This section relieves juvenile courts, while they are dealing with appeals under s. 5 or complaints

10

13. This provision is identical with that contained in the Children Act 1958, in respect of foster children.

47

under s. 7, from the restrictions imposed by s. 47(2) of the Children and Young Persons Act 1933, as to the time and place of sittings and the persons who may be present. The appellant or defendant will be an adult and the respondent or complainant will be a local authority. There is thus no need in such cases for these special provisions that govern the work of juvenile courts when they are dealing with juveniles.

Appeal to the Crown Court

14. There is a right to appeal to the crown court from any order made under Part I of the Act by a juvenile court or any other Magistrates' Court within the meaning of the Magistrates' Courts Act 1952. The expression "Magistrates' Court" is defined as "Any Justice or Justices of the Peace acting under any enactment or by virtue of his or their commission or under the common law". The effect is to provide a right of appeal to the crown court against an order made by a justice of the peace acting in an emergency under the provisions of s. 7(1) as well as from an order made by a juvenile court under that section or s. 5.

11

14. This provision is identical with that contained in the Children Act 1958, in respect of foster children.

48

Extensions to Certain School Children During Holidays

15a. Where a child resides during school holidays in a school for a period exceeding

12

15. This paragraph is inapplicable to protected children.

one month, Part I of the Act shall apply to him, subject to the following modifications, as if children in schools were not excepted from Part I:

b Where the provisions of the Act in relation to such children obtain, the duty to give the local authority on request the particulars specified in para. **7f** above is applied, but instead of the duties previously referred to, to give notice of intention to maintain a foster child, to notify change of address and to notify the death or removal of a child, there is a duty to notify the local authority of the estimated number of children, if any, who will reside in the school for a period of more than two weeks during the school holiday. The local authority retains the duty to inspect the premises, but not the power to impose requirements or a prohibition under s. 4.

c A local authority may exempt any person from the duty of giving notices under this section either for a specified period or indefinitely and the exemption may be revoked at any time by notice in writing.

d The schools concerned in this paragraph are schools within the meaning of the Education Acts 1944–53, which are not schools maintained by local education authorities, *i.e.* in effect independent and direct grant boarding schools and non-maintained special schools.

Extension of Age

16. A foster child on attaining the upper limit of compulsory school age remains a foster child until he reaches the age of 18; or lives elsewhere than with the person with whom he was living when he attained school leaving age; or apart from his age ceases to fall within the definition of a foster child; whichever event occurs first. 13

16. A protected child ceases to be a protected child on the making of an adoption order; or on his attaining the age of 18 years; or on his leaving the care and possession of the persons intending to adopt him; or if he should come within the scope of any of the exemptions referred to in para. **4** above. A child, therefore, may remain a protected child if an adoption order in respect of him is refused or if an interim order is made. 37

Offences

17. The offences under this Act are as follows:

a Failing to give any notices or required information within the time specified or failing to give the information within a reasonable time or knowingly making or causing or procuring any person to make any false or misleading statement in the notice or information. 14

b Refusing to allow an authorised officer to visit a foster child or to inspect premises, or obstructing an officer entitled to inspect premises by virtue of a warrant issued by a justice of the peace under s. 4(1A) of the Act.

c Failing to comply with any requirements imposed by a local authority or keeping any foster children in any premises in contravention of a prohibition.

17. The definition of offences in this part of the Adoption Act and the penalties on conviction follow very closely those contained in the Children Act 1958, in respect of foster children. 44

d Maintaining a foster child in contravention of s. 6 of the Act, but a person is not guilty of an offence in respect of a person referred to in s. 6(2) if he proves that he did not know and had no reasonable grounds for believing, that a person living or employed in the premises was a person to whom the section applies.

e Refusing to comply with an order for the removal of any child or obstructing any person in the execution of such an order.

The Act provides a maximum penalty on a summary conviction of imprisonment for a term of 3 months or a fine of £400 or both. In England and Wales a local authority may institute proceedings for offences under this section.

(Penalties as amended by the Children Act 1975, Schedule 3.)

Service of Notices

18. Any notice of information required to be given, 15 may be given by post.

18. The provision for notices is identical with that contained in the Children Act 55 1958, in respect of foster children.

Authentication of Documents

19. Any notice by a local authority may be signed on behalf of the authority by the 16 Clerk of such authority or by an officer of the authority authorised in writing to sign such a notice.

19. The provisions for authentication of documents is identical with that contained 49 in the Children Act 1958, in respect of foster children.

Advertising

20. Advertisements indicating that a person will 37 undertake or will arrange for the care and maintenance of a child shall not be published unless they truly state the name and address of the person concerned.

b Any person who causes an advertisement to be published in contravention of this paragraph shall be guilty of an offence and will be subject to a fine similar to that referred to in para. 17 above.

c Local authorities may initiate proceedings for offences under this section.

20. The restriction upon advertising in the Adoption 51 Act 1958, is rather different from that in the Children Act 1958. No advertisement may be published indicating that the parent or guardian of a minor desires to cause the minor to be adopted; or that a person desires to adopt a minor; or that any person (other than a Registered Adoption Society or a local authority) is willing to make arrangements for the adoption of a minor. A person who publishes an advertisement in contravention of provisions such an advertisement or causes such an advertisement to be published, shall be liable on summary conviction to a fine not exceeding £50.

Note: Such advertisements must relate to a living child, not to an expected child. See 122 J.P. 289.

Definitions

21. In both Acts "relative" has the same meaning as set out in Chapter 10. In both Acts, "child" means a person under the age of 18. In both Acts "place of safety" means a community home provided by a local authority, a controlled community home, police station, or any hospital, surgery or other suitable place the occupier of which is willing temporarily to receive a child. In both Acts "compulsory school age" has the same meaning as in the Education Acts and is now up to 16 plus.

22. The Adoption Act provisions apply only to children placed with a view to adoption. In all other cases referred to above, the Children Act 1958 applies.

Supervision

Dealing first with the children falling under Part IV of the Adoption Act 1958, supervision in many cases, does not last long because adoption often follows within a few months of notification. But there are cases in which the notification has been given and accepted, when it was not really valid, and there was no prospect of adoption from the start. This leads to so-called "supervision" possibly for many years, and it is not surprising that visiting "from time to time" means hardly ever. Even when visiting is regular and frequent for a few months, it has often been rather purposeless, because it has been looked on as a prelude to the making of a guardian *ad litem* report to the court, and adoption has been thought of as inevitable unless some serious objection to it has arisen

Probably the best use to be made of visiting under s. 38 is to "give advice as to care and maintenance" by thoroughly discussing with the prospective adopters their attitude, and that of their relatives, to the natural parents of the child, and to the child, first as a baby, then on entering school or playgroups, later as an adolescent and finally as an adult. The physical care of the child will usually be satisfactory, but in any event advice on health matters will be available from a health visitor, leaving the social worker free to concentrate on the adoptive relationship. The position with regard to supervision and other adoption matters is, however, altered by the Children Act 1975, and its effect is described in Chapter 17.

The privately placed foster children dealt with under the Children Act 1958 do not generally receive the attention they should, especially as there are so many of them. At 31 March 1974, 29,738 children in local authority care were in foster homes, some of them with relatives.[16] At the same date 9,694 children were known to be in private foster homes, but this is only an unknown fraction of the total, because of ignorance of the duty to notify, or failure to do it. At one time there used to be notices in post offices and other public places drawing attention to the law, in simple language. This publicity now seems to have ceased.

Little is known about this large group of children, but there has been valuable research on a small scale by Robert Holman.[17] Indications in his sample are that:

1. The children's parents are for the most part overseas students, or unmarried mothers, or deserted fathers.
2. Most children are under the age of 5.
3. Placings take place informally as a result of a meeting, or a notice in a shop window.
4. There is no preparation for the placing.
5. Enquiries into notifications are rarely carried out by Social Services Departments, or if they are, they do not prevent unsuitable foster parents from taking children. Thus there are those who have physical illnesses, or criminal records, or whose own children have been committed to care for neglect.
6. Foster care is often provided by the woman alone, her husband taking little part in it.
7. Many of the children themselves suffer from various defects. and difficulties.
8. Private foster parents receive no allowance from the local

authority and depend on amounts payable by natural parents at a low rate, with no certainty of receiving even that.

9. Private foster parents have no rights with regard to the children; they rarely know how long they will stay, or whether they will ever go.

10. Visits by social workers are "from time to time" which often means very rarely. During the visits few children are seen "on their own". (This stems from the use of the discretion mentioned in s. 1 of the Act.)

On the credit side, many foster parents were far more than "baby-farmers" and had loving attitudes to the children, even when there were serious behaviour problems, with which they received little outside help. Sometimes the genuine attachment to the children was so great, that the fear of their removal at any time, without warning, created strong tensions and anxiety; in extreme cases, it could lead to the offer of bribes to parents to let the children stay, or to the foster parents moving from the district to escape the threat of removal.

If these brief comments are compared with the provisions of the 1958 Act, it will be clear that better practice would lead to a great improvement in the lot of these children and the private foster parents. Whatever else may be said about private fostering, it obviously provides a substantial social service as an alternative to local authority care. Ways could be found to turn it into a major resource in the spirit of community care. The Children Act 1975 will greatly change the position of these foster parents in relation to the parents of the foster children; and of the children themselves.

NURSERIES AND CHILD MINDERS REGULATION ACT, 1948
AS AMENDED

In addition to foster children and protected children, there are a number of children requiring the protection of the authority because, although they live at home, they are cared for during the day by people other than their parents. Their supervision is governed by the Nurseries and Child Minders Regulation Act of 1948, as amended by s. 60 of the Health Services and Public Health Act 1968.

a *Introduction*

The need for this Act arose because there were a considerable number of children being cared for in nurseries and in private houses who did not fall under the supervision of the local authority. To come within the scope of the child protection enactments, as previously described, children placed privately by their parents had to be cared for by persons other than relatives who undertook their *care and maintenance for reward*. Owing to the demand for female labour, the practice of placing children with daily minders spread to many parts of the country, and these children did not fall under supervision because they were cared for by the day and were not, therefore, being *maintained* in such a way as to bring them within the scope of child protection. Similarly, children placed by their mothers in nurseries provided by the employers in mills and factories were also outside the definition of foster children for child protection purposes.

b *Registration*

The Act of 1948 introduced a dual system of registration of premises and persons and the distinction between the two is maintained throughout the Act. So far as *premises* are concerned, the obligation to register applies where the premises are used for the reception of children under compulsory school leaving age to be looked after for the day, or for two hours either continuously or in the aggregate each day, or for a period not exceeding six days, whether for reward or not, but does not apply where the premises are used wholly or mainly as private dwellings, or in the case of a home or institution as defined in the Children Act 1958, or a school. The term "wholly or mainly" has no precise meaning and many such children are cared for without the premises being registered. Premises used mainly for the reception of children for a period exceeding six days, to which the child protection provisions apply, are also exempted from registration under this Act. The registration relates to the premises or buildings and not to the person in charge of the children.

A *person* caring *for reward* for one or more children under 5 years of age to whom she is not related, looking after them for the day or for two hours either continuously or in the aggregate each day, or for a period not exceeding six days, *must* apply for registration

In both cases changes in circumstances require fresh registration. Failure to register is an offence for which the penalty on summary conviction is a fine up to £50 and for a second or subsequent offence £100 and/or three months' imprisonment. A local authority must issue a Certificate of Registration and may also impose conditions in respect of both premises and persons concerning the number of children to be kept; the precautions to be taken against exposing the children to infectious disease; the qualifications and number of staff employed; the adequate maintenance and safety of buildings; the diet and feeding arrangements; and the records to be kept. Additional requirements may be laid down for premises only in respect of the qualifications of the person in charge and the medical supervision of the children. These requirements may be varied or revoked by the local authority and must be specified in the Certificate of Registration. Local authorities may refuse registration if they are not satisfied with the fitness of the persons who are to look after the children or with the premises in which they are to be kept. Playgroups may be established either in "premises" (*e.g.* church halls or in private houses and fall to be registered accordingly).

c *Appeal*
Any person aggrieved by the action of the local authority in refusing registration, cancelling registration, or imposing conditions may appeal to a Court of Summary Jurisdiction.

d *Inspection*
Local authority inspectors are empowered to enter *premises* used for child-minding to inspect the children, the records and the premises, also the home of a *person* registered as a child-minder.

e *Avoidance of dual supervision*
Where *premises* are used both for day-minding and for the care and maintenance of foster children within the meaning of the Children Act 1958, there is provision for the avoidance of dual supervision. If the premises are used mainly for the reception of children falling within the 1958 Act, *i.e.* for a period exceeding six days, then the provisions of the 1958 Act with regard to visitation, entry and inspection apply and the requirements regarding registration in the 1948 Act do not apply.

In the same way, a *person* required to register under the 1948 Act is exempted from registration if she receives one or more children falling to be dealt with under the 1958 Act or subject to supervision as boarded out children under any other Act.[18]

f *Entry*
Entry when there is reasonable cause to believe that premises or persons are child minding without registration can be effected by obtaining a warrant issued by a Justice of the Peace.

g *Prosecutions*
Proceedings for offences under the 1948 Act may be taken by the local authority.

h *Definitions*
A "local authority" for the purpose of the Nurseries and Child Minders Regulation Act 1948, is the Social Services Committee.

In this Act a "Child·' is a person who has not attained the upper limit of compulsory school age; that phrase and "relative" have the same meanings as in the Children Act of 1958.[19]

Comment
Though the Regulations covering child-minding are somewhat confusing (as between premises and personal child-minding), the intention is quite clearly to protect children who are placed by the day in the care of people who are not their parents. Most of these

children are placed in the houses of individual child minders who should be registered and may be visited by social work advisers.

Reports from the Child-Minding Research Unit suggest however that about 57,000 children are placed with registered child minders and a further large number, at least 100,000, with people who are not registered, thus committing an offence against the Act.[20] The standards of care provided, however, do not seem to depend on registration, some of the unregistered persons giving a better service than some of the registered.

When the standards are low, young children may spend many hours a day, sometimes from as early as 6 a.m., sitting in an attic or back room and being kept out of sight of callers and passers-by for fear of detection. Often there is no stimulus, no play equipment or experience and in some instances children may even be tied to furniture to keep them out of the way.

Compared with more fortunate children who are taken shopping, play in the park, visit friends, and enjoy both books and toys, many day-care children lead an extremely deprived life which will seriously affect their later development. Like the privately placed foster children mentioned earlier, this is another very large group of children who are protected by legislation, but not by the way in which it is implemented.

As long ago as 1968, when the local authority Health Department administered the Act, the Ministry of Health issued an excellent memorandum of guidance,[21] with Circular 37-68, on the whole question of the various methods of providing day-care for children under 5, including advice on physical standards of accommodation, recommended equipment, and feeding. It advocated the encouragement of good child-minding, especially for priority groups of children who were defined, and who constitute the kinds of children whose parents for a number of reasons use day-care services. The present position falls very far short of the ideals in the memorandum, even when social workers have been appointed specially to deal with applications for registration and to visit and advise the people actually caring for children. (There is no duty to visit the children.)

As in the case of private foster parents, child-minders are providing a social service; in this case it is an alternative to the expensive day nursery and, if conditions are good, it can be far better. (In the connected field of nursery schooling, the National Foundation for Educational Research has issued a report suggesting that the proposed extension of nursery schools as such, is a "gigantic social hoax", and that nursery education would be more effective if carried out with small groups of children in private houses.[22].) This may give impetus to the positive promotion of good child minding services as well. In some areas, attempts are being made to give child-minders training, to persuade the unregistered to register, to use already existing powers to pay them for their service, and to supply free fireguards, toys and play equipment.

In the context of "protection", the Act certainly results in this being given to those children who are placed with registered child minders; the unregistered are liable to prosecution, but this is unlikely to be as effective as a recognition of the value of the service being provided, together with the use of powers to assist below standard child-minders to attain the levels required for registration. They are, after all, providing a spontaneous community service which is usually available in the districts where it is needed most. Under suitable direction and encouragement it could be made into a valuable resource, without capital investment, and in the process those child-minders who should not be caring for children would be more readily identified and prohibited.

It is apparent that so far as "approval" is concerned, adoptive parents, local authority foster parents, private foster parents and child-minders have a good deal in common. A suggested method of combining the process of investigation in all cases is set out in Appendix C.

"PROTECTION" OF THE YOUNG OFFENDER

The Act of 1969 is intended ultimately to ensure that children under the age of 14 are dealt with under the same procedure, generally speaking, whether they are offenders or not. The Act is not however to be fully implemented at once and can only be put into operation gradually by the Secretary of State's use of his powers under the **very important s. 34.** This will be used virtually to determine at any particular date who is a "child" and who a "young person", a point which has to be borne in mind in consulting the Act. Section 5, restricting prosecution of children over a minimum age, will not be brought into operation by the present Government, nor do they intend to raise the minimum age for prosecution to 12 until they are satisfied that the necessary resources are available. The position, therefore, is that all children become of an age to be prosecuted at 10, which is also the age of criminal responsibility.

For this reason there are still parallel procedures relating to "offenders" and "non-offenders" over the age of 10 years.

Earlier in the chapter we have looked at the procedure for protecting a child or young person when it is considered that one of the primary conditions **a** to **e** is satisfied, and that there is need for immediate action. When the condition **f** (the offence condition) is satisfied, there is a different procedure, set out in s. 29. This provides:

(a) That the person may be arrested without warrant; if so he may be brought before a court at once, or taken to a police station where his case will be enquired into. He must then be released unless it is felt that he should be detained in his own interests, *e.g.*, he cannot at once be handed over to his parents, *or* unless his release would defeat the ends of justice. If he is released a recognisance may be taken for him to report to a police station if required.

(b) Alternatively he may be arrested on a warrant, in which case a recognisance for his attendance at court may be taken.

(c) In all cases of arrest, with or without warrant, the police officer concerned must inform the parent or guardian, and if the child is not released must make arrangements with the local authority for him to be received into care and accommodated in the most suitable way. He must then appear before a court within seventy-two hours, unless this is impossible, *e.g.*, because of illness.

(d) On appearance in court, the court must order release unless the arrest was on warrant, or unless detention is in the interests of the arrested person, or the interests of justice. When the court does not order release, it may remand either on bail, with recognisance, or in custody. In the event of a remand in custody, the accused must be informed of his right to apply to the High Court for bail.

(e) Remands may be to the custody of a constable for one day only, but will generally be to the care of the local authority with provision for committal to a remand centre or prison of any person over 14 who is certified to be too unruly of character to be detained in the local authority's care.

There are further measures for what may be called the "protection" of young offenders from criminal proceedings. Although an offender may be arrested and dealt with as above, or may more simply be alleged to have committed an offence, it does not follow that criminal proceedings will be taken against him. As s. 5 is not in operation there is no actual provision in the Act for consultation between police and local authority for the purpose of deciding whether a child or young person should be dealt with by voluntary methods, or by care or criminal proceedings. It is intended, however, that there should be consultation between the two services as there has been since 1964, and that this should be developed and expanded as the resources become available. In each area the police and the Director of Social Services were asked to consider the method and scope of such consultation, as outlined in paras 92–97 of the "Guide". They should take into account the use of the police caution, the juvenile liaison scheme, where it exists, and other informal arrangements such as the referral of all cases involving persons under the age of 17 to a joint police-local authority bureau for a decision as to whether court proceedings are essential, and if so whether they should be care or criminal proceedings. Generally these consultations affect children up to 14 at present, as social workers would find it impossible to deal in this way with all young persons up to 17. As it is, the inter-service discussion is superficial and does not often include the compiling of full social histories, as was the intention.

Although a local authority may itself institute care proceedings on the basis of the offence condition, this does not mean that it should investigate alleged offences as such. This remains a matter for the police, as does the final decision as to whether or not to prosecute for an offence. In coming to this decision regard will be paid to such criteria as the gravity of the offence, the public interest, and the necessity for a court appearance, for instance in certain traffic offences involving a penalty such as disqualification from driving.

A further point about the young offender is that if he is charged with an offence he will be dealt with summarily, generally speaking. This will not be the case if he is charged with homicide or with other grave crimes punishable with a long period of detention which the magistrates consider would be an appropriate sentence but cannot themselves order; or if he is jointly charged with an adult.

PROTECTION GENERALLY

The overall protection of children and young persons in court proceedings is provided by the Children and Young Persons Acts 1933–69. These Acts deal with such matters as juvenile court procedure, evidence of children, limitations on publication of reports, and the general principles to be observed by courts in cases involving young people.

Finally, all proceedings both care and criminal are subject to the right of Appeal to the Crown Court against orders made by the court. When a more immediate decision is needed, there is now the right to apply to the High Court for the discharge of an interim order, in care cases, or for bail in criminal cases. In all cases legal aid is available and may be granted by the court. Parents of persons under the age of 16 may be ordered to make a contribution to the cost. Explanatory leaflets have been issued, and all local authority social workers should ensure that both children and their parents or guardians are aware of the right to apply for legal aid at any stage of proceedings in the juvenile courts.

PROTECTION IN EMPLOYMENT

This account of the protective functions of the local authority would not be complete without mention of the duty to protect children and young persons in employment, by controlling the conditions in which they work, regulating their appearances as public performers, prohibiting their exposure to injury, and ensuring that their education is not neglected.

This general function is, however, the province of the local education authority, not of the Director of Social Services. The powers are as set out in the Children and Young Persons Acts of 1933 and 1963 (Part II) and the Children (Performances) Regulations of 1968.

NOTES

1. C. and Y.P. Act 1969, s. 70(1).
2. C. and Y.P. Act 1933, Sched. 1.
3. *Non-accidental Injury to Children*, Medical Education and Information Unit of the Spastics Society.

4. Which may still be underrated: see *Severely Ill-treated Children*, Oxford Linkage Study, Old Road Headington, Oxon.
5. C. and Y.P. Act 1969, s. 2(1).
6. *Ibid.*, s. 2(2).
7. *Ibid.*, s. 2(8).
8. *Ibid.*, ss. 28(2) and 28(3).
9. *Ibid.*, ss. 22(1) and 28(3)–(5).
10. *Ibid.*, s. 28(3).
11. C. and Y.P. Act 1933, s. 107, as amended.
12. C. and Y.P. Act 1969, s. 20(2).
13. *Ibid.*, s. 22(3).
14. *Ibid.*, s. 22(5).
15. *Ibid.*, s. 22(4).
16. *Children in Care* 31 March 1974, Cmnd. 6147.
17. *Trading in Children*, R. Holman, London, Routledge and Kegan Paul, 1973.
18. Nurseries and Child Minding Regulation Act 1948, as amended, ss 9 and 10.
19. See Paragraph 21 above.
20. Child minding Research Unit "Action Register" 1974.
21. Ministry of Health Circular 36/68 and 37/68, and Memorandum of guidance to local (health) authorities.
22. National Foundation for Educational Research.

GENERAL NOTE

The contents of this chapter will in due course be affected by the implementation of the Children Act 1975. Some of the more important sections of the Act are briefly commented upon in Chapter 17.

Chapter 8

INVOKING THE COURT

SUMMARY

There are a number of situations which may put young people into the jurisdiction of the courts. There are first the children of parties to divorce or matrimonial proceedings, who may be placed under supervision or, exceptionally, committed to the custody or care of the local authority. As will be seen in the Table in Chapter 6 this power has so far been little used, and it must be presumed that in the majority of such cases the courts have been satisfied that responsibility for the children of the family could be given to one or other parent, or to another person, with or without a supervision order.

The Family Law Reform Act of 1969 empowers courts which have jurisdiction in wardship proceedings to make supervision or committal orders in the same way and under the same conditions as the divorce courts. This is an additional power in respect of young persons who are already wards of the court. It should be remembered that the Family Division of the High Court has inherent powers by which it may make minors "wards of court". An application for wardship can be made by taking out a summons which makes the minor a ward for up to twenty-one days, during which time the court will hear the application and give judgment on the merits of the case. There have been many situations in which wardship has been applied for, including those in which there was already in force an order affecting the minor concerned. When a local authority is involved, the court will rarely review its decisions, provided that its powers have been properly exercised under the relevant statute.

Then there are the courts which are concerned with applications under the Guardianship of Minors Act 1971, as expanded by the Guardianship Act 1973, and which have the power to make orders relating to the custody and upbringing of minors. In these domestic situations, proceedings usually start because of disputes between parents or guardians; the children's welfare is therefore endangered and the courts have power to decide the issue. Whatever the original ground of the application may be, the welfare of the child is the first and paramount consideration, and there is now power for the court to make a supervision order or to commit the care of the child to a local authority.

In other words, parents or guardians who make an application to the courts in domestic, matrimonial or custody proceedings automatically invoke the courts on behalf of the children.

There are many other situations in which it may be necessary for children or young persons to be brought before a court either in their own interests or those of society, or both.

Unfortunately, some social workers mistrust the courts and look upon the legal system as a punitive and coercive machine which, once it is started, cannot be stopped and is largely concerned with prohibitions. It does not seem to be sufficiently realised that the law and the courts provide many necessary safeguards, especially for children and young persons, against adverse circumstances in which they are helpless. They also provide a defence against the possible abuse by social workers of their very considerable powers.

Although the juvenile court, like other courts, is a legal institution, it is the firm ally of the social worker when he feels the need for reinforcement of his legitimate aims, or when he has justifiable grounds for thinking that it may be necessary to intervene in some way in the interests of a child or young person. Among recent tragic cases there have been some in which social workers, after taking the best possible professional advice, have been unable to agree on a right course of action and have taken a case before the court for resolution. In other cases, the social workers did not bring their undoubted misgivings before the court, but continued to work on a voluntary basis in circumstances of great risk. In this they were acting without the support of the magistrates as the representatives of society as a whole.

These considerations are specially important in dealing with very young children who have been ill-treated or where there has been ill-treatment of children within the household. The prospect of repetition of assault is high, and unilateral decisions by social workers are fraught with risk as well as being deplored in the Tunbridge Wells study.[1] For discussion and the accepted warning signs, see "Parental abuse on children".[2]

CARE PROCEEDINGS (C. AND Y. P. ACT 1969)

Under s. 1 of the Act, it is necessary for any of the persons authorised to bring care proceedings to have decided that he "reasonably believes that there are grounds for making an order" under the section.

Before he can decide this, he must clearly have considered whether there are alternative ways of ensuring that the child or young person receives care or control. This involves consultation, and specially with the local authority which may in turn involve other agencies (see Chapter 7).

Care Proceedings may not even be considered of course unless one of the primary conditions, set out in Chapter 7, is satisfied. Paraphrased, these conditions refer to a child who is:

neglected or illtreated, or is a member of a household in which a child has been ill-treated or neglected, and a court has found that that condition was satisfied;* (See para. **a**, page 62).

exposed to moral danger;†

beyond the control of parent or guardian;
failing to attend school;
believed to have committed an offence other than homicide (which involves criminal proceedings).

If any one of these conditions exists there is a ground for social intervention, which may or may not include invoking the court. As we have seen in the last chapter, when the offence condition is being considered, the police may decide to institute *criminal proceedings* for one of several reasons; if they do not, the offence stands only as a prima facie justification for social intervention in the same way as the other primary conditions mentioned above.

The next stage consists of the decision whether or not to institute *care proceedings*. This is a question which must be considered in the light of what is called the "care or control" test. The person considering the case must ask himself "Can the needs of this child or young person for care or control be met by any of the resources which could be made available on a voluntary basis by any means at all?", and "If proceedings are not taken is this child or young person likely or unlikely to receive the care (including protection and treatment) or the control (including discipline) which he as an individual appears

---

* Section 1 (2) (a) uses the words "is being" and there has been some concern about this when, for instance, a child has been detained in a hospital or other place of safety. While there, can it be said that he "is being" ill-treated or neglected? There is reason to suppose that in these circumstances "is being" means "was being" at the time when preventative action was taken. If this were not so, a place of safety order would not lead to protection for the child. This does not apply to a child whose parents refuse consent to a life-saving blood transfusion or operation. (See Ministry of Health circular F/P9/1B of 14 April 1967 addressed to Regional Hospital Board, and Home Office Circular 63/1968 of 5 March 1968.)

† A person aged 16 who is or has been married may not be the subject of care proceedings. A girl under the age of 16 may have married lawfully in another country, but is not *for this reason* exposed to moral danger (*Muhamed v. Knott*, 1968). In any event, it may be felt that much of what used to be regarded as moral danger for girls is now condoned by various means, such as free contraceptive advice to young people under 17. But exposure to moral danger may arise in other ways, for instance by coercion of a child for criminal purposes.

to need?". If the answer, after taking into account all that is known about the total situation, is "unlikely" then care proceedings would be justified.

Put another way, it is no longer enough to know or to be able to prove that a child has been neglected or ill-treated, or is the victim of an offence, or at risk of being neglected, or beyond control, or in moral danger, or that he is not receiving efficient full-time education or that, being over 10, he has committed an offence. While these facts may tend to indicate that the child is in need of either care or control or both, they do not prove it. Nor is it enough to say that the child is not receiving adequate care protection and guidance from his parents or guardians; the quality of parental care is only one of the factors to be considered. The child's total circumstances, past, present and future, must be examined with a view to deciding whether care or control is *unlikely* to be available if a court order is not made.

All these considerations are binding on those who are authorised to bring care proceedings, that is a local authority, a constable or the N.S.P.C.C. If the primary condition is non-attendance at school, it is the local education authority which must, after applying all the tests, institute proceedings.

The recent increase in non-attendance at school (and in actual absences from school of adolescents who are officially recorded as being in school) is a cause for great concern.[3] There is a move to make non-attendance (or absence) in itself a ground for care proceedings, without the need for application of the "care or control" test which at present applies. Whether or not this would be justified in the cases of adolescents, for younger children at primary schools the care or control test should remain. This would make it more essential for the widest possible enquiries to be made before care proceedings are used. In the course of these enquiries, education welfare officers and the schools would be brought into contact with the comprehensive assessment process referred to in Chapter 6. In this way the isolation of the E.W.O.s from other social workers and agencies would be diminished, and the needs of at least some of the children should be discovered and met without the need for care proceedings.[4]

If the offence condition is the basis of proceedings, they will be taken by the local authority or, more likely, by the police. Proceedings in respect of other primary conditions may be instituted by a local authority or the police, or by the N.S.P.C.C. following consultations.

Once it has been decided to start either *care* or *criminal* proceedings, the local authority must be informed; so must the probation service, in cases concerning children over the age of 13.

The person bringing the proceedings will be responsible for the whole of the evidence as to (a) the satisfaction of the primary condition, and (b) the care or control test, as the court itself has to be fully assured that an order is essential. When the local authority institutes proceedings, a solicitor may take the case and the social worker give evidence, as opposed to any report which may be made in addition.

The Home Office "Guide" to Part I of the Act[5] deals fully with consultation, provision of information for the courts, the types of orders which the court may make in care and criminal proceedings, and Part I of the Act generally. As the Guide is available to courts and practitioners it does not seem necessary to cover the same ground in detail in this book, except in so far as the general duties of the Social Services Department are concerned, but the general effect and the salient points are set out here for easy reference to the Guide, which in turn refers to the appropriate sections of the Acts as amended by the Criminal Justice Act 1972.

As a result of the 1969 Act, and the wider use of preventive powers, less young people should appear before the juvenile courts, but at the same time the local authority will be much more vitally concerned in the work of the courts than previously, and may well find it essential to be regularly represented at court sittings, if this is not the case already. There is much to be said for the appointment of a specialist social worker in busy courts.[6]

There are a number of changes in procedure, fully described in the Guide to Part I. The general effect of these is to simplify the whole of the proceedings, and to make it clear that although the local authority may have wider powers than before, the rights of children and their parents are to be safeguarded by the courts and by the availability of *legal aid in all proceedings under the Act.*

The method of taking immediate action, by arrest or detention, followed by consultation as appropriate, has already been dealt with. When this stage is followed by a decision to institute either criminal or care proceedings, the following questions may arise for consideration. (Where numbers are quoted they relate to the paragraphs in the Guide.)

COMPARISON WITH CRIMINAL PROCEEDINGS

	Criminal Proceedings	*Care Proceedings*
How will process begin?	By summons or charge (216).	By notice, or summons or warrant if necessary to secure attendance (176).
May parents be required to attend?	Yes. C. and Y.P. Act 1933, s. 34.	Yes (179).
Who will institute proceedings?	Police.	Police or local authority if offence condition alleged,

	Criminal Proceedings	*Care Proceedings*
		education authority if non-attendance alleged; in other primary conditions **a** to **d** either police, local authority or N.S.P.C.C.
In respect of children of what age?	10, and over from 1/1/71. Age may be raised under s. 34, except for charge of homicide (4).	Any age up to 17, unless over the age of 16 and has been married.
In which court?	·Juvenile, or magistrates court for area where offence committed.	A juvenile court anywhere (189–190).
When would the magistrate's court be concerned?	If juvenile jointly charged with person over 17 (C. and Y.P. Act 1933, s. 46). But this means jointly charged with the same offence not with a different offence arising from the same circumstances.	Not at all, unless child is a witness. If the court convicts a person of offences against a child, it may not now direct that the child be brought before a juvenile court, as it cannot apply the care or control test. It may, however, draw the case to the notice of the police or local authority (26). *But* in school attendance cases only, the court may direct that the child be brought before a juvenile court (37).
Has a juvenile the right to elect to go for trial?	No.	
May he be sent for trial?	Yes, in certain circumstances (217 and 218) but written statements must be taken (C.J. Act 1972, s. 44).	

	Criminal Proceedings	*Care Proceedings*
Can a magistrate's court deal with a case in any other way than committal for trial?	Yes, by fine, compensation, binding over of parent, discharge, or traffic offence penalty. Otherwise must remit to the juvenile court for juvenile's home area (228/9).	
What happens if the original court is not that for the juvenile's home area?	If magistrate's court, as above. If a juvenile court, may try the case, and make an order, *or* remit to court for home area (C. and Y.P. Act 1933, s. 56).	Juvenile court must either dismiss case, or direct that juvenile be brought before court for home area. *But* if offence condition alleged may hear evidence before deciding whether to dismiss or remit (191/2).
If a court remits to court for home area, what happens in the meantime?	Release on bail or remand procedure under s. 23, *i.e.*, remand to care of local authority usually (229, 220–227).	May allow child to return home and inform local authority for home area, or make interim care order committing to care of more appropriate authority (193 –195).
Who takes action in the home area court?	Police.	Usually local authority for home area, within 21 days. Could be the Education authority in respect of condition e.
Who produces evidence?	Police.	Person bringing proceedings (50).
What is the burden of proof?	As in criminal proceedings.	As for civil proceedings (42). But if condition f is alleged, offence condition, and is denied, burden of proof must be as in criminal proceedings. If court not satisfied, it must dismiss the case. If satisfied,

	Criminal *Proceedings*	*Care* *Proceedings*
		there will be separate civil proceedings, with evidence in respect of care or control test (45 and 46). For education cases, see paragraph 44.
How will social reports be supplied to the court?	Police will notify local authority and probation service. Social service dept is primarily responsible for supplying all local authority information but if probation service normally deals with home surroundings aspect it may continue to do so (99, 100, 103) until the age for prosecution is raised under s. 34.	Person bringing the proceedings will notify local authority and probation service. Local authority responsible for all reports in respect of children under 13, and normally in respect of any child brought before the court by the local authority itself (104). Education authority similarly responsible in cases it brings itself (102).
	But even if the home surroundings report is prepared by the probation service, local authority has a duty to supply any information it has which will assist the court (103).	Probation service will still supply reports relating to children over 13 who are not brought before the court by the local authority or education authority, and may in any event be asked for a report in a case of any kind (104/5). (The age of 13 may be raised under s. 34.)
After reports, what are the considerations relating to the use of the court's powers?	The welfare of the child and his need for education and training (C. and Y.P. Act 1933, s. 44).	
What orders can the juvenile court make?	These are set out in para. 77, as amended	These are set out in para. 51, but there

Criminal Proceedings	Care Proceedings
	are additional powers in certain cases to order a young person over 14 to enter into a recognisance, and a person aged 13–17 to pay compensation, (both in respect of care proceedings based on the offence condition). Paras. 58–63.

(The paragraphs referred to above direct attention to other paragraphs giving details relating to the various orders which may be made in criminal or care proceedings.)

What orders may be made by higher courts following committal?	Detention (C. and Y.P. Act 1933, s. 53 (1) and (2), and orders set out in para. 77 modified by para. 250.

Care orders are dealt with in Chapter 9, and supervision orders in Chapter 14.

OTHER ORDERS

These are the two orders which most closely concern the social worker, but it should be remembered that there are other orders which the court may make instead.[7]

A. In care proceedings (including those in which the offence condition is the ground of the application to court).

1. *Recognisance by the parent to exercise proper care and control* (C. and Y.P. Act, s. 1 (3)). This seems to be little used, possibly because of a reluctance to follow the philosophy that the primary responsibility for the upbringing of children rests on their parents. Or it may be that parents are unwilling to accept the responsibility

2. *Hospital or guardianship order* (s. 1 (3)(d), (e)). These can only be used when mental health provisions under the Act of 1959 apply.

3. *Recognisance by the* young person *before the court in a sum of up to £25 for his own good behaviour* (s. 3(7)). This order can only be made with consent, and there is therefore no appeal against it.

4. *Order for compensation*, up to £400·00 which *may* be payable by parent or guardian if he has conduced to the commission of the

offence (s. 3(6)), and if he has been informed of the intention to make such an order.

B. In criminal proceedings, where the child or young person is charged with an offence, as such.

    1. *Binding over parents or guardian with their consent* (s. 7(7)) (See A 1 above).

    2. *Binding over the offender himself, with his consent* (Common Law).

    3. *Absolute or conditional discharge* (Criminal Justice Act 1948, as amended).

    4. *Hospital or guardianship order* (see A 2 above).

    5. *Fine, compensation up to £400, restitution of property.* Fines and compensation may be payable by parent or guardian under certain conditions (see A 4 above). In practice parents are rarely ordered to pay fines or compensation. Fines levied on children and young persons are very difficult to enforce, and there is no effective sanction in the case of non-payment, as default action is not possible until after the age of 17 and is then according to means.

    6. *Attendance centre order.* This is very useful, but only possible if the court concerned has an attendance centre within reasonable reach. Such a centre should not be more than ten miles or forty-five minutes' travelling time from the home of the young offender.

    7. *Detention centre order.* Junior detention centres are for young offenders aged 14–17. Ideally they should not be used for first offenders, but in fact are. Nor should they be used for persons who have previously been sent to a detention centre, or have been in a community home under a care order, or have previously been in borstal. As will be seen in the comments on the use of the Children and Young Persons Act 1969 in Chapter 5, the detention centre order is being made increasingly often in recent years. Attendance centre and detention centre orders can only be made where the offence is punishable with imprisonment. Both types of centre are part of the penal system and are not administered by local authorities. There is considerable conflict of opinion as to their purpose, and especially as to whether they are punitive, or reformative; and in consequence the regime varies from one centre to another. Eventually it is intended that both will be phased out and replaced by other provisions under the Act of 1969.

    8. *Borstal detention.* A juvenile court can only order committal to borstal for anyone already in care and placed in a community home (see Chapter 11). It can however commit a young offender to the crown court with a view to a borstal training. The minimum age is still 15, as s. 7(1) is not in force.

It was mentioned in Chapter 5 that the number of young offenders under 17 in borstal is increasing.

    9. *Deferment of sentence.* Under the Criminal Justice Act 1972, s. 22, a juvenile court may defer sentence for a period of up to six months, without making a remand order.

10. *Deprivation of property.* Under s. 23 of the same Act, a juvenile court may deprive an offender of property which has been used, or was intended to be used, for criminal purposes.

General comment. Before a young person is sentenced to a period of borstal training, or to a detention centre (either of which will deprive him of liberty for an appreciable time), the court must ensure that he has legal aid, or that he has had the opportunity of having it. There is no such requirement before the making of a care order, which may also entail loss of liberty. Social workers may well wish to consider whether they ought to ensure that the provision of legal aid is understood by any young person likely to be made the subject of a care order, and by his parents.

NOTES

1. See Chapter 7.
2. Joan Gibson, *Social Work Today*, 18 April 1974.
3. "The Many Problems of R.O.S.L.A.", *Social Services*, 13 July 1974.
4. "The E.W.O., truancy and School Phobia", *Social Work Today*, 30 May 1974.
5. *Part I of the Children and Young Persons Act 1969* (A guide for courts and practitioners), London, H.M.S.O., 1970.
6. "The Social Worker and the Courts", Brian Harris and Geoff Sage, C.C.E.T.S.W. Paper 7.
7. For fuller treatment of this subject, see *The Law Relating to Children*, H. K. Bevan, London, Butterworths, 1973, and *The Legal Context of Social Work*, J. D. McClean, London, Butterworths, 1975.

GENERAL NOTE

The contents of this chapter will in due course be affected by the implementation of the Children Act 1975, as there will be other ways in which a court may be invoked. Some of the more important sections of the Act are briefly commented upon in Chapter 17.

Meantime, attention may be drawn to the D.H.S.S. Local Authority Circular (75)18 of 25 November 1975 urging local authorities to bring care proceedings when they feel that there is a case for protecting a child. The circular arises from the judgment of the Court of Appeal in *Surrey County Council* v. *S* concerning the meaning of s. 1(2)(b) of the Children and Young Persons Act 1969.

Chapter 9

ADMISSION TO CARE

SUMMARY

It was explained in Chapter 6 that the local authority receives information about families or children "in trouble" of many different kinds; it has wide powers to improve these situations by the use of the family support service and must direct its energies to assisting parents to undertake their responsibilities in so far as they are able and willing to accept such help.

It is inevitable, therefore, that local authority social workers are increasingly working with families and children with their consent. If a family accepts this kind of voluntary support for itself or for one of its members, it may be said to be receiving *care*, in the most natural and constructive way within the family setting. Support of this kind may include the use of any kind of service which the authority has or may develop, for instance, the child guidance service, attendance of children at play-groups, adventure weekends, group sessions for mothers, and in fact anything which can be said to enrich and broaden life experience, while encouraging parents to provide adequate care for their children.

Involvement of social workers with families in this way is "care" and the former concept of a child either being *in care* or *not in care* at any particular time must in future become somewhat blurred, except perhaps for statistical purposes. Local authorities may well be considering whether their case records should be adapted to reflect this continuing nature of care, whether it is provided within the family or outside it for the time being, especially in view of the growing use of five-day or other part-time care as a constructive measure.

There are, however, situations in which it is difficult or undesirable for a child to be cared for by his own parent or parents (because of their present circumstances) or by members of the wider family, and the question of admission to specialised local authority care has to be considered. Whether or not to admit to this form of care is one of the most important decisions a social worker will be called upon to make, especially in a case newly referred, in which there may have been no previous contact with the family.

The child-care figures for 1973/4 in Chapter 6 show that the largest group of children admitted under the Act of 1948 (that is, by the agreement of social workers) came into care because of short-term illness, which together with confinement appears to be by far the most frequent cause. There are other apparently short-stay admissions amongst the figures. The turnover of children in care under this Act is very high, many periods of care ending in a few weeks, and many admissions seem to be associated with poverty, either materially or in family relationships, or both.

These short-stay admissions appear to be arranged somewhat casually, despite the various studies which indicate that even a short separation of a child from a caring family can cause him deep distress.[1] Nor is that all. Admission to care will usually be followed by a financial assessment of the parents with a view to an agreement for contributions. There will often be a re-adjustment of family allowance or supplementary benefit payments, and possibly other benefits. This may well cause temporary hardship and inconvenience to the parents, and will not improve relationships with the social worker concerned with the family. There are of course some really sudden emergencies, but in most cases, even of confinement or illness, there ought to be time to consider the alternatives to admission to care.

Admission to care under the 1948 Act is the opening of a door into the unknown, and may lead by a long, unforeseen process to long-term care or treatment, perhaps in a community home. Not only will this be costly, but it may well lead to a loss of identity and a life of unhappiness. There are children who have been in continuous care for many years, having been admitted ostensibly because of a mother's illness, without any thought at the time that care might be protracted almost indefinitely. The Children Act 1975 gives rise to other anxieties about the possible consequences of admission in the future.

In the proposed "Charter of Rights",[2] B.A.S.W. has included Principle 3, which reads: "Before a child is admitted to care an assessment of his family and home environment should be undertaken which will include the preparation of the child and his family for the admission, and their participation in the plans that are made." There is every reason for applying this principle in every case, however transient the need may seem to be; in an emergency, when it occurs, the same principle ought to be followed after the admission.

In the "assessment of his family and home environment", the weaknesses will be apparent, but if the family is important for the child, the strengths must be sought. Already many Social Services Departments will not receive a child into care simply because the family is homeless; they prefer to accept the far greater cost of providing accommodation for the family as a whole, and in this they have the support of social workers.[3]

There should be a similar attitude to reception into care in other circumstances, especially in those where short-term care appears to be required, or perhaps has been specifically requested. This means a greater readiness to spend time and money under the 1963 Act. If the cost to an authority of maintaining one child or young person in a community home is £4,000 for one year (and it may be more), it is worth reflecting that this sum would help ten families to the extent of £400 or one hundred families to the extent of £40 in the same year.

On the following pages is an algorithm setting out the enquiry which ought to be made in every case in order simply to satisfy the requirements of s. 1 of the 1948 Act as to eligibility for admission. This may seem cumbersome, and, if short-term care is unimportant, irrelevant. But if it is followed through, it should prevent any admission which is not essential in the interests of the child.

It may be said that the alternatives to care are unrealistic, or that they are not available. They would be available to a family able to afford to make its own private arrangements, and should be available to any family which has the will and strength to remain intact.[4] Many Social Services Departments would make money available for the kinds of service set out in the algorithm in Chart C,[5] if social workers stated the case more strongly, rather than making such extensive use of short-term care, apparently without much question. The home help service is obviously one of the principal supporting services, but in its traditional form of a few hours per week, largely to help the elderly, it cannot provide anything like the kind of service needed if children are to be able to remain in their own homes instead of being received into care. Perhaps there is a need for seeking this kind of helper in the locality of the family concerned: are there not people willing to help in the home, without being home helps? There are also great possibilities in the recruitment of full-time salaried home helps willing to live temporarily in the family home, or at least to give full-time service at the time when it is needed. A belief in the value of family care, as opposed to short-term local authority care, should enable social workers to make a very convincing case for the diversion of resources in the direction of this kind of support, as set out in Programme C in Appendix A.

CHART A

RECEPTION INTO CARE   CHILDREN ACT 1948, s.1

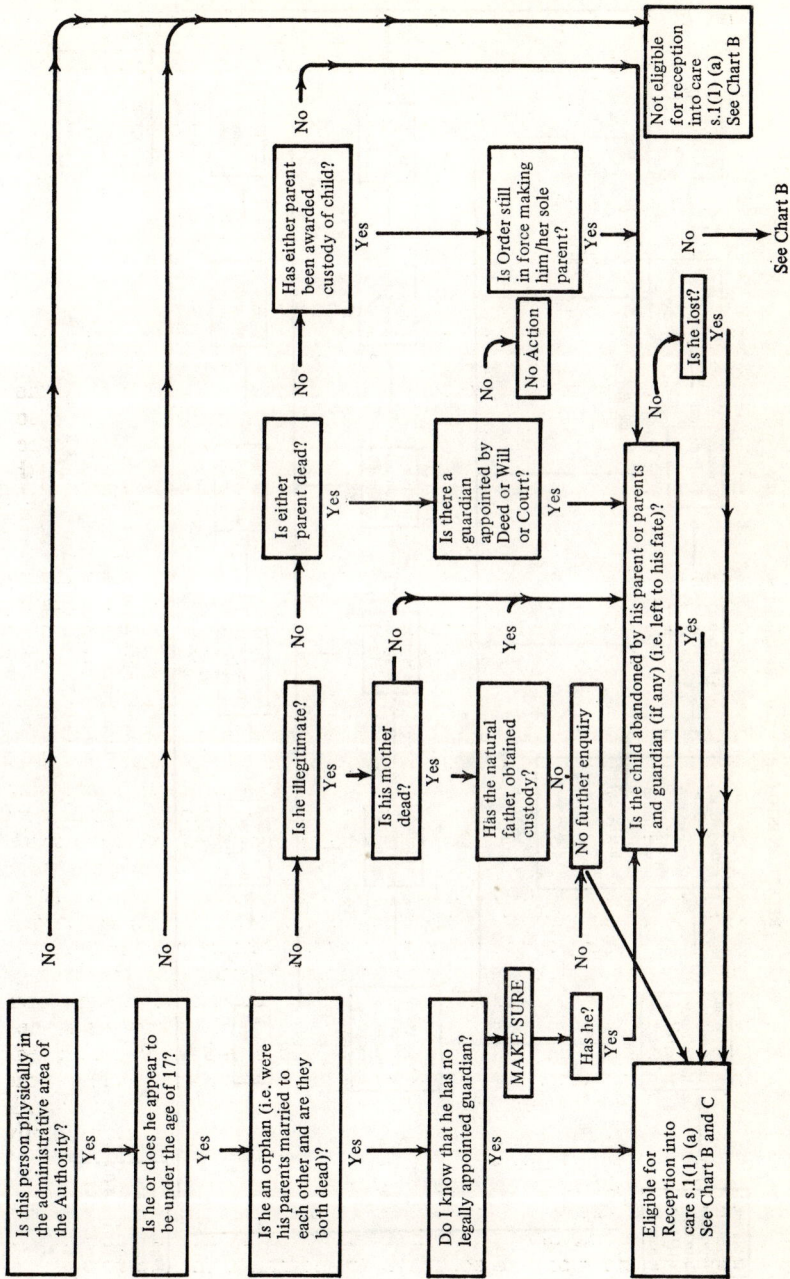

Is this person physically in the administrative area of the Authority? — No →

Yes ↓

Is he or does he appear to be under the age of 17? — No →

Yes ↓

Is he an orphan (i.e. were his parents married to each other and are they both dead)? — No →

Yes ↓

Do I know that he has no legally appointed guardian? — MAKE SURE → Has he? — Yes → / No →

Yes ↓

Eligible for Reception into care s.1(1) (a) See Chart B and C

Is he illegitimate? — No → / Yes ↓

Is his mother dead? — No → / Yes ↓

Has the natural father obtained custody? — Yes → / No → No further enquiry

Is either parent dead? — No → / Yes ↓

Is there a guardian appointed by Deed or Will or Court? — Yes → / No ↓

Has either parent been awarded custody of child? — No → / Yes ↓

Is Order still in force making him/her sole parent? — No → No Action / Yes →

Is the child abandoned by his parent or parents and guardian (if any) (i.e. left to his fate)? — No → / Yes →

Is he lost? — No → / Yes →

Not eligible for reception into care s.1(1) (a) See Chart B

See Chart B

CHART B
RECEPTION INTO CARE CHILDREN ACT 1948, s.1

Is the child eligible for reception into care s.1(1) (a) (Chart A)?

Is the father dead or has he been deprived of custody?

Is the father prevented from providing for his proper accommodation, maintenance and upbringing, by reason of mental disease?

By reason of bodily disease?

By reason of infirmity?

By reason of other incapacity?

By reason of other circumstances? *

Is the mother dead or has she been deprived of custody?

Is mother prevented as above?

Is there a guardian?

Is guardian prevented as above?

Eligible for reception into care s.1(1)(a) and (b) (See Chart C)

Not eligible for reception into care s.1(1)(a) or (b) (See Chart C)

*As this is not a penal statue, the words "other circumstances" in s.1 need not perhaps be construed too strictly, but this algorithm raises the question so that thought will be given to the reality of the circumstances and whether in fact they prevent a parent from providing for the child. Other considerations arise in Chart C which follows.

CHART C
RECEPTION INTO CARE   CHILDREN ACT 1948, s.1

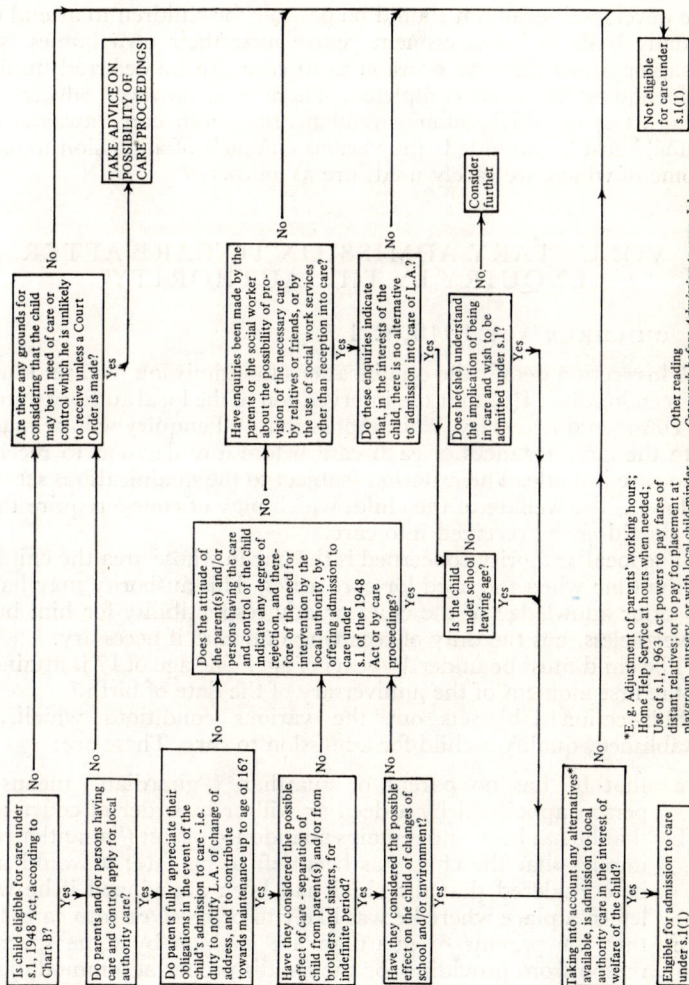

Is child eligible for care under s.1, 1948 Act, according to Chart B? — No / Yes

Do parents and/or persons having care and control apply for local authority care? — No / Yes

Do parents fully appreciate their obligations in the event of the child's admission to care - i.e. duty to notify L.A. of change of address, and to contribute towards maintenance up to age of 16? — No / Yes

Have they considered the possible effect of care - separation of child from parent(s) and/or from brothers and sisters, for indefinite period? — No / Yes

Have they considered the possible effect on the child of changes of school and/or environment? — No / Yes

Taking into account any alternatives* available, is admission to local authority care in the interest of welfare of the child? — No / Yes

Eligible for admission to care under s.1(1)

Does the attitude of the parent(s) and/or persons having the care and control of the child indicate any degree of rejection, and therefore of the need for intervention by the local authority, by offering admission to care under s.1 of the 1948 Act or by care proceedings? — No

Have enquiries been made by the parents or the social worker about the possibility of provision of the necessary care by relatives or friends, or by the use of social work services other than reception into care? — No

Do these enquiries indicate that, in the interest of the child, there is no alternative to admission into care of L.A.? — No / Yes

Does he(she) understand the implication of being in care and wish to be admitted under s.1? — No / Yes

Is the child under school leaving age? — No / Yes

Consider further

Are there any grounds for considering that the child may be in need of care or control which he is unlikely to receive unless a Court Order is made? — No / Yes

TAKE ADVICE ON POSSIBILITY OF CARE PROCEEDINGS

Not eligible for care under s.1(1)

*E.g. Adjustment of parents' working hours; Home Help Service at hours when needed; Use of s.1, 1963 Act powers to pay fares of distant relatives; or to pay for placement at playgroup, nursery, or with local child-minder, or private or L.A. foster parent on payment by parent, without reception into care. Or for placement of child with parent(s), e.g. temporary family accommodation.

Other reading
Casework before Admission to care, Jehu
Casework in the Child Care Service, Timms, Butterworths 1962
"Day Care of Young Children", *Social Work Service*, No. 6

Meantime, full investigation of the circumstances must be made; the social worker should be able to consult a senior colleague on this all important matter and in some cases, it may be possible for the child's need to be assessed during his voluntary attendance at a children's home or other suitable place. When assessment facilities are developed locally, it should be possible for children to attend on a daily basis at an assessment centre near their own homes (see Chapter 6), so that the decision as to care can be deferred until a full enquiry has been completed. There will, however, always be some cases in which, after careful investigation, care (away from home) must be provided; the various channels of admission to care (some of which are rarely used) are as follows:

VOLUNTARY ADMISSION TO CARE AFTER ENQUIRY BY THE AUTHORITY[6]

1.   CHILDREN ACT 1948, s. 1

This section details the qualifications for admission to care; it will be seen in sub-s. 1(c) that the intervention of the local authority must be considered necessary. This implies that full enquiry will be made into the circumstances of each case before any decision to receive into care is made. The criterion (subject to the qualifications set out below) is the welfare of the child, which may of course require that he should *not* be received into care.

The local authority concerned is the one in whose area the child is at the time when the need for care arises. This authority may have no prior knowledge of the child or any responsibility for him but, nevertheless, has the duty of receiving into care if necessary.

The child must be under 17 years of age. The age of 17 is attained at the first moment of the anniversary of the date of birth.[7]

Sub-section 1(b) sets out the various conditions which, if established, qualify a child for admission to care. These are:

a   that he has no parent or guardian ("guardian" means a person appointed by a deed or will or "by order of court"); *or*

b   that he has been and remains abandoned or lost ("abandoned" implies that the child has been left to his fate; it would not be considered that the child had been abandoned if he was left in a place where he was likely to be received into care); *or*

c   that the parents or guardian are *prevented* by some specific reason from providing for the child's proper accommodation, maintenance and upbringing. They may be prevented either "permanently" (*e.g.* under detention in mental hospital) or "for the time being". The reasons stated are mental or bodily disease or infirmity or other incapacity or "any other circumstances"; this last is so wide that it covers many circumstances, including short-term illness of parents, eviction, desertion, unsatisfactory home conditions, and the other reasons for admission to care set out in Chapter 6 (page 57).

Reflecting the spirit of the legislation, the section is flexible enough to meet cases where the parent is in agreement, and the child, if old enough, consents.

Admissions to care must be made within the framework of the Act and there are cases where care may be desirable but cannot legally be provided under this section. A typical case of this kind would be where an uncle and aunt of a child, who have brought him up for some years, apply for financial assistance which could only be given by way of boarding-out allowances, but where the parents of the child are perfectly able and prepared to provide for him themselves.

Mention has been made of "application" from parents for admission to care and although this is usually received it is not essential. A child may be received into care from the home of someone who is not the parent or may be received when the parent is sentenced to imprisonment without making provision for the child, even if she does not apply. It is usual, however, for children to be received at the request of a parent, or both parents, and where the request is made by one parent only, the other one is also seen if this is possible. Under this section the duty of the authority is limited to *receiving* the child—it cannot *take* him. Occasionally a young person may wish to be received into care for some reason. This can be regarded in the same way as the former provision (now repealed) for a child to take refuge in a place of safety, and should be accepted as such.

A further point is that any child may be admitted to care, including one mentally disordered.[8] Such children are the concern of the Social Services Department in any event, whether in care under the Children Act or not, and may be provided with accommodation without being in care at all.

Where an authority has received into its care under s. 1(4) a child who is ordinarily resident in the area of another authority the second authority may agree to take over the care of the child and, even if it does not do so, may agree to accept financial responsibility for the cost of maintenance incurred by the "care" authority. Where there is a dispute between the authorities concerned as to the child's ordinary residence this may be referred to the Secretary of State for determination and many cases have been decided in this way. The general principle appears to be that the child's residence is not necessarily that of his parents, but that if the parents have the intention of taking over the care of a young child at some future time their place of residence may also be his. An older child may, of course, have determined his own place of residence by leaving home voluntarily. Residence, however, is always at the time of admission and not at any time prior to that; but children who are living in a particular place by virtue of some order, or official arrangement, are not regarded as resident there for the purposes of this section. (This provision does not apply to unofficial arrangements, *e.g.* placings by parents or adoption societies.)

2.   CHILDREN ACT 1948, s. 29(6)

Where a voluntary home is to be closed by the Secretary of State (after investigation) he may require the local authority in whose area the home is situated to receive into their care all, or any, of the children concerned. The local authority is obliged to comply with this requirement whether or not the conditions of s.1 apply and notwithstanding the fact that any of the children may appear to be over the age of 17.

3.   CHILDREN ACT 1958, s. 7(4)

When a child is removed from a foster home to a place of safety by order of a juvenile court or magistrate the local authority may receive him into care whether or not the conditions of s. 1 apply and notwithstanding the fact that he may appear to be over the age of 17.

4.   ADOPTION ACT 1958, s. 43(3)

There is a similar requirement under this section with regard to protected children removed from unsuitable surroundings by order of a juvenile court or magistrate.

Note.—see Chapter 7, Protection.

COMMITTAL TO CARE BY ORDER OF A COURT

1.   CHILDREN AND YOUNG PERSONS ACTS 1933–69

The local authority, local education authority, constable or authorised person (N.S.P.C.C.) may institute *care* proceedings in respect of a child or young person if there is a reasonable belief that it is necessary for the authority of a court order to be obtained.[9]

Criminal proceedings may be instituted against a child who is of an age to be prosecuted as in the past. The "qualified informant" provisions of the Act are not in operation.[10]

Neither care nor criminal proceedings will be commenced, as we shall see, without consideration of many factors but if and when it is finally decided that such proceedings will be taken the person responsible for bringing the child or young person before the court must inform the local authority,[11] which is required to make investigations and provide the court with such information relating to the home surroundings, school record, health and character of the person in respect of whom the proceedings are brought as appear likely to assist the court.

Although the making of such investigations and reports have always primarily been the responsibility of the local authority, it has been the general practice for home surroundings reports to be made by the Probation Service under s. 35 of the Children and Young Persons Act 1933, where this was the wish of the court. Now, under s. 9(1) of the 1969 Act, the duty is to be laid entirely upon the local authority but s. 34(3) enables the Secretary of State to apply s. 9 in stages; the practice from 1973 is for the local authority to be responsible for all reports in respect of children under 13, while reports on children and young persons over that age may be made by either the local authority or by the probation service where this is at present the local arrangement. Gradually the age of 13 will be raised so that eventually investigations and reports will be made as a rule by the local authority. The court may in any case, however, require reports from other sources, in particular from a probation officer under para. 3 (5) of Sched. 5 of the 1948 Criminal Justice Act.[12]

In the light of the reports it receives, the court has to decide which course of action to adopt, subject to the general rule that when dealing with a child or young person brought before them, juvenile courts must have regard to the welfare of the child which is not paramount in such cases, and must where necessary take steps to remove him from undesirable surroundings and make proper provision for his education and training.[13]

One of the orders which may be made by the court is a care order.[14] Such an order may only be made when a court finds that

(a) one of the six primary conditions is met (see Chapter 7); and
(b) the child is in need of care or control which he is unlikely to receive unless the court makes an order, *or*

A child or young person has been found guilty of an offence punishable in the case of an adult with imprisonment.[15]

A care order may be made either initially or in substitution for a supervision order; in the latter event a court must still consider whether the care order is necessary to ensure care or control.

The following are the main provisions of a care order, which differs in some respect from the previous fit person order:

a A person may be committed only to the care of a local authority; it is the duty of that authority to receive him into care and to keep him in care notwithstanding any claim by his parent or guardian. The consent of the local authority to the order is not required (Fit Person orders made before 1 January 1971 are now deemed to be care orders—Schedule 4).

b The care order gives to the local authority the same powers and duties in respect of the person committed as his parent or guardian would have, had the order not been made. In addition the local authority may restrict the liberty of the committed person as it considers appropriate, subject to regulations to be made under s. 43. The local authority may not, however, bring up a committed person in any religious creed other than that in which he would have been brought up had an order not been made.

c The authority to be named in a care order is that for the area in which the committed person resides or if that is not known the local authority in whose area the circumstances arise.

d The care order ceases to have effect where the committed person attains the age of 18 unless he was 16 when the order was made, in which case it remains in force until the age of 19. An order expiring at the age of 18 may, however, be extended to the age of 19 in the case of a person accommodated in a community home or home provided by the Secretary of State if this is in the interest of either the person concerned or the public.[16]

e The care order may be discharged by a court on the application of the local authority or the committed person (a parent or guardian may only apply on behalf of the child or young person). If the order is discharged, a supervision order may be made up to the age of 18.

f A person in respect of whom a care order is made will be treated in the same way as a person in care under a voluntary arrangement and, as s. 13 of the Children Act 1948 (as amended) applies, may be allowed to be under the charge and control of a parent guardian, relative or friend though the care order remains in force.

2. INTERIM CARE ORDER

An Interim Care Order is a care order and has the same effect but only for twenty-eight days, after which it lapses and a further Interim order must be made if the circumstances justify it. Interim care orders may be made for the purpose of initial protection as described in Chapter 7 or at any time during care proceedings. There is a right of appeal to the High Court as described in Chapter 7.

3. REMAND ORDER

At any time during criminal proceedings the court may make an order remanding a child or young person on bail *or* may commit him to the care of the local authority for the period of remand.[17]

4. DETENTION IN CARE

Where a person aged 10–17 is arrested with or without a warrant and cannot be brought before a magistrates' court to be charged with an offence; the case must be enquired into by a senior police officer who may release him in certain circumstances or make arrangements for him to be taken into care by a local authority.[18]

5. DETENTION IN A PLACE OF SAFETY

This is detention under an order for the purpose of protection as defined in Chapter 7. All community homes are places of safety which may be used for the purpose of protection, but detention in them is not, strictly speaking, a form of care.

6. MATRIMONIAL CAUSES ACT 1973, s. 43

The law requires divorce courts, when hearing applications for orders, to consider the welfare of any children of the family under the age of 16 or still receiving education or training. This includes children who have been *treated* as members of the family by both parties to the marriage, for instance, stepchildren and adopted children. Where it appears that the custody of a child under 17 should not be given to either of the parties or to any other individual an order may be made committing his care to the local authority within whose area he resides, under s. 43 of the Matrimonial Causes Act 1973. Sometimes if a child is already in care, the court will order that he should not be discharged from care without the consent of the local authority, or alternatively, without an order of the court.

7. MATRIMONIAL PROCEEDINGS (MAGISTRATES' COURTS) ACT, ss. 2 AND 4(2)

This Act contains a similar power in respect of applications for matrimonial orders, except that *no child who is already in the care of a local authority* may be committed, nor may any child who has attained the age of *16 years.*
Note.—In both Acts, "child of the family" includes one who has been accepted and treated as one of the family though not being the child of both husband and wife. This is a complicated issue calling for legal advice. Committal to the care of the local authority under paras 6 and 7, is only open to the courts in *exceptional circumstances* and does not confer parental rights—it only confers care and control. The information on which the court acts in such cases will normally be a report which the court may require from either a probation officer or a local authority social worker. See Chapter 14.

The consent of the authority to committal is not required, but it must be given notice of the proposal to commit and any representations by the authority must be heard with regard to the making of the order itself and with regard to maintenance of the child.

In divorce court cases fourteen days' notice to the authority is required; in magistrates' court cases ten days.[19]

8. FAMILY LAW REFORM ACT 1969, s. 7(2) AND (3)

Under this Act, a court which has jurisdiction in wardship proceedings may, in exceptional circumstances, commit a child who is the subject of proceedings to the care of a local authority.

9. GUARDIANSHIP ACT 1973, s. 2

This Act amends the Guardianship of Minors Act 1971 so that when a court is dealing with an application for custody under s. 9, it may now, in exceptional circumstances, commit the care of a minor to a local authority. This power may be exercised in respect of a minor who is either legitimate or illegitimate, and by the High Court, a county court or a magistrates' (domestic) court, whichever is dealing with the application under the Act of 1971.

GENERAL

As a result of this Act, a court dealing with guardianship, matrimonial, or wardship proceedings, in which minors are involved, has power to commit the care of a minor to a local authority in much the same way, subject to the limitations of the magistrates with regard to age, and other matters. Such orders are not, however, care orders. The differences between children in care under the 1948 Act Care Orders and others whose care is committed by the courts are set out in Chapter 11.

NOTES

1. *Child Care and the Family*, Schaffer, London, Bell, 1968.
2. "Children in Care—a Charter of Rights", B.A.S.W.
3. "Reception into Care because of Homelessness", *Social Work Today*, 5 September 1974.
4. "In defence of Parents", Holman, *New Society*, 1 May 1975.
5. For further reading on the subject of reception into care, see *Casework before Admission into care*, Jehu, and *Casework in the Child Care Service*, Noel Timms, London, Butterworths, 1962.
6. See Algorithm, Reception into Care, s. 1. *ante.*
7. Family Law Reform Act 1969, s. 9.
8. Mental Health Act 1959, s. 9(3).
9. Children and Young Persons Act, s. 1.
10. *Ibid.*, s. 5(9) and para. 75 of Guide to Part I.
11. *Ibid.*, s. 2(3) and s. 5(8).
12. *Ibid.*, s. 9(2).
13. C. and Y.P. Act 1933, s. 44.
14. Children and Young Persons Act 1969, s. 1(3).
15. *Ibid.*, s. 7(7).
16. *Ibid.*, s. 21.
17. *Ibid.*, s. 23(1) and (2).
18. *Ibid.*, s. 29(3).
19. Matrimonial Causes Rules and Matrimonial Proceedings (Magistrates' Courts) Act 1960. See also *Maintenance and Custody Orders in the Magistrates' Courts*, second edition, Brian Harris, Chichester, Barry Rose, 1974.

GENERAL NOTE

The contents of this chapter will in due course be affected by the implementation of the Children Act 1975. Some of the more important sections of the Act are briefly commented upon in Chapter 17, but it should be noted here that there will be more children who will be eligible for committal by a court to the care of a local authority.

Chapter 10

THE POSITION OF PARENTS, GUARDIANS AND RELATIVES

SUMMARY

COMMENT

There are certain inherent powers in the Family Division of the High Court independent of statutes but the lower courts are confined to making decisions in accordance with Acts of Parliament. Parents now have equal rights with regard to their children and may both, for instance, appoint guardians by will, or apply to a court for custody, access or order on matters affecting a child's welfare. The powers of the High Court as regards guardianship are not affected by the Children Act 1975 (s. 104).

DEFINITIONS

As the phrases "parent", "guardian" and "relative" appear fairly often in children's legislation, it would be as well to have these defined.

PARENT

Married couples who have children by their marriage are parents. The Children Act 1948 defines the mother of an illegitimate child as the parent, to the exclusion of the father. Definitions of "parent" as including adoptive parent, as in the Children Acts 1948 and 1958 are repealed by the Children Act 1975 as being unnecessary in view of the status of the adopted child set out in Schedule 1. ("Parent" is not defined in the Children and Young Persons Acts 1933–69 but is capable of a similar interpretation.)

The position with regard to the natural father of an illegitimate child is not, however, quite as simple as it appears because of the fact that a child may be legitimated by the subsequent marriage of his natural parents, even if they were not free to marry at the time of the child's birth. Similarly, a child of a void marriage (*e.g.* bigamy) may in certain circumstances be regarded as legitimate, the natural father becoming the lawful father.[1] Moreover, a natural father may apply under the Guardianship of Minors Act 1971 for the custody of his illegitimate child or for access. If he is given custody he acquires some of the powers of a lawful father for the purposes of the Guardianship Acts, and for other purposes becomes the guardian of the child.[2] The Family Law Reform Act of 1969 makes changes in the relationship between an illegitimate child and his father, specially with regard to inheritance and registration of the child's birth.

GUARDIAN AND LEGAL GUARDIAN

A "guardian" is defined in the Children and Young Persons Act of 1933 as including any person who, in the opinion of the court, has for the time being the charge of, or control over, the child or young person.[3] The Department of Health and Social Security will regard as "guardian" anyone looking after an orphan child, or a child one of whose parents is dead and the other cannot be found.

There is a further definition of *legal* guardian in the Act of 1933, which means a person appointed according to law to be the child's guardian by deed or will or by order of a court. This latter definition is similar to the one included in the Children Act 1948, and in the Adoption Act 1958 as amended by the Children Act 1975, Schedule 1.[4]

RELATIVE

A "relative" means a grandparent, brother, sister, uncle or aunt, whether full-blood or half-blood or by affinity. All references in these Statutes to relatives by adoption are repealed by the Children Act 1975, under the provisions of Schedule 1.

As regards illegitimate children, the father of the infant is regarded as a "relative" as also are his relatives within the foregoing definition.[5]

Relatives have few rights but may be consulted in certain adoption cases.[6]

In legislation affecting the supervision of children there are certain commonsense exemptions where relatives are concerned.[7]

PARENTAL RIGHTS

Generally speaking, both lawful parents of a child, or any legal guardian of a child, are presumed to have the custody of the child, and a father does not lose custody simply by deserting the family or living separately from it.[8]

With regard to a child in the care of a local authority, therefore, the authority only has "actual possession or control" and this does not diminish the parents' rights *except* in the circumstances set out below. The rights of a parent may be affected in one or more of the following ways:

1 CUSTODY ORDERS

These may be made by the Family Division of the High Court or, under the Guardianship of Minors Act, by the Family Division of the High Court, county court or court of summary jurisdiction. They may also be made by the High Court under the Matrimonial Proceedings and Property Act 1970 in divorce cases or by the magistrates court in hearing matrimonial proceedings under the Matrimonial Proceedings (Magistrates' Courts) Act 1960.

In any of the foregoing cases custody may be given to one parent as against the other *or* may be given to a third party. (As mentioned above, a natural father may be granted custody in preference to the mother.)

A court hearing an application for an adoption order but deciding to make an interim order may give the *custody* of the child to the prospective adopters for a period of not more than two years.[9]

The existence of any custody order as described above has an effect on the reception of children into care under the Children Act. Whether the word "parent" or "guardian" appears in ss. 1–5. of the Act it is to be interpreted as referring to the person who has the custody.[10] It is, therefore, quite lawful for the child to be received into care from a parent or other person having custody without the consent of the parent or parents deprived of custody, but an important consideration in such cases is that the parent or parents deprived of custody may nevertheless have the right of access to the child and probably, therefore, a right to be informed of the action which is being taken. He, or she, cannot however claim the child from the local authority as of right. This has a particular bearing on discharges from care and will be considered later. Similarly, in juvenile court proceedings any parent or guardian may be required to attend, and this *may* be held to include a person who has been deprived of custody by order of court.[11] When a custody order is made under the Guardianship of Minors Act 1971, the consent of both parents may be required for marriage and for adoption.[12]

2. CARE ORDERS (CHILDREN AND YOUNG PERSONS ACT 1969)

These may be either full care orders, interim orders or warrants remanding to the care of the local authority. Such orders commit the child or young person to the care of the local authority which then has the duty of receiving him into care and keeping him in care for the duration of the warrant or order notwithstanding any claim by his parent or guardian. The authority then has the same powers and duties as the parent or guardian would have, but for the order.

No care order permits the authority to bring the committed person up in any religious creed other than that in which he would have been brought up apart from the order. Nor does it empower the authority to consent to adoption or arrange emigration for the child without parental consent. The power to consent to marriage is uncertain, so that these custodial powers remain with the parents, while the care order conveys the care and control of the child and possibly such powers as applying for a grant of administration, or changing the name of the child by deed poll. There is one additional power for the local authority. It may, subject to Regulations, restrict the liberty of the committed person to such an extent as it thinks appropriate. (This is referred to in Chapter 11.)

There are provisions for application for the discharge of interim orders and care orders.[13] There are also provisions for appeals against orders in criminal and care proceedings and for legal aid to be granted by the court.[14] Applications for legal aid may be made to the clerk of the justices or the court Administrator, as the case may be, in advance of the hearing.

3. RESOLUTION

When a child is already in the care of a local authority under s. 1 of the Children Act 1948, the Council may pass a resolution assuming parental rights in the following circumstances.[15]

a   that both parents are dead and the child has no guardian;
b   that *either* parent or guardian has abandoned the child;
c   that he, or she, suffers from some permanent disability rendering him, or her, incapable of caring for the child;
d   that he, or she, is of such habits or mode of life as to be unfit to have the care of the child;
e   that the parent has allowed his, or her, whereabouts to be

unknown to the local authority for a period of not less than twel' e months (this is to be deemed to be abandonment);[16]

f that he, or she, has so persistently failed without reasonable cause to discharge the obligations of a parent or guardian as to be unfit to have the care of the child;[17]

g that he, or she, suffers from a mental disorder (whether permanent or not) which renders him, or her, unfit to have the care of the child.[18]

In the case of **a**, a resolution would be in respect of both parents (if married) on the same ground, but otherwise it will be noted that a resolution may be passed in respect of *one* living parent or guardian and while it is in force that parent or guardian loses his or her rights in respect of the child except those mentioned above under care orders.

It is possible for a parent to agree to a resolution being passed, but failing that, notice of it has to be served upon him and he is entitled to serve a notice in writing objecting to the resolution within a period of one month. In such cases the resolution will lapse unless the authority lays a complaint before a juvenile court within fourteen days. The court may order that the resolution shall not lapse by virtue of the notice served by the parent. Moreover, at any time while the resolution is in force the parent may apply to the authority for it to be rescinded or to a juvenile court for the resolution to be set aside.[19] This procedure is discussed further in Chapter 11.

4. ADOPTION AND OTHER ORDERS

An adoption order confers a new status on the child who is to be treated in law as if he were not the child of any person other than the adopter(s).[20]

5. MATRIMONIAL PROCEEDINGS ACTS

In either divorce or separation proceedings the court may in certain circumstances commit the care of the child, or children, to the local authority. It will be noted that it is the *care* and not the child which is committed and such orders do not confer parental rights on the local authority. The child must, however, continue in the care of the local authority notwithstanding any claim by a parent or other person. The court will not include any order as to access in such orders as this is a matter left to the discretion of the local authority concerned. A divorce court may declare a parent unfit to have custody of a child.[21]

6. WARDSHIP AND GUARDIANSHIP PROCEEDINGS

In such proceedings, as in matrimonial proceedings, the court may in certain circumstances commit the care of a child to a local authority.[22]

7. GENERAL

It will be seen, therefore, that in dealing with children who have come into the care of the Council in any way it is most important that full information should be available as to the *method* of admission and the position with regard to parental rights and/or custody, especially as regards the natural father or other possible guardian.

PARENTAL DUTIES

GENERAL

The parents of children in the care of a local authority, though they may have been deprived of some rights, continue to have liabilities. They must ensure that the authority, in whose care the child is, is kept informed of the parents' address; penalty for non-compliance is a fine of £10.[23] This was formerly only the case as regards children up to the age of 16 but the age limit has been raised to 18.[24] Parents are also liable to make contributions towards the maintenance of children under the age of 16.[25]

LEGISLATION

Prior to the passing of the Children Act 1948, the assessment of parents of children in care of Poor Law Authorities was governed by the Poor Law Act 1930, but the Children Act repealed these provisions and aligned the procedure as regards children in care under s. 1 of the Act with that already in operation under ss. 86, 87 and 88 of the Children and Young Persons Act 1933, in respect of children committed to care. The 1948 Act also introduced important changes in so far as the only persons liable *under these sections* to contribute towards the maintenance of a child were to be the father (excluding putative fathers of illegitimate children) and the mother (including mothers of illegitimate children). Payments by parents are due only so long as the child is *under age of 16 years*; after that age he is liable to make contributions towards his own maintenance from his earnings, if any. Contributions under *this Act* are payable in respect of the following:

a Children in the care of a local authority under s. 1 of the Children Act 1948.

b Children committed to the care of a local authority, but not including children who are at home or those committed on interim care orders or remanded to care.[26]

ADOPTION

Contributions cease to accrue under (a) and (b) above where notice of intention to adopt a child is received by a local authority, but may be revived if the application to adopt is withdrawn or refused or if the application has not been made within twelve weeks from the date of notification.[27]

RECEIPT OF CONTRIBUTIONS

The "persons entitled to receive contributions" are the local authorities for the areas in which the parents reside. As the father and the mother are separately liable, more than one local authority may be involved if the parents are not living together.

AMOUNT OF CONTRIBUTIONS

Section 62 of the Act of 1969 amends the legislation relating to contributions under the Children Act 1948 and the C. and Y.P. Act 1969.

When a child is received into care or committed under a care order (except an interim order) and is under 16, the local authority must "propose" to the parents, known as the contributories, the amount of the contribution to be made. This amount may not exceed the weekly sum which the local authority would pay as a boarding out allowance, ignoring any "special" rate of allowance, for the child in question. In other words there is to be no payment in respect of the running costs of a children's home or community home.

If the authority and the contributory cannot agree on the amount proposed within one month, or if they agree but the contributory defaults in one or more payments, the authority may apply for a contribution order. The court may not make an order for a sum greater than that proposed by the authority in the first instance. If an application is made to the court for a variation of a contribution order, the authority must propose an amount, and the variation ordered must not exceed that amount.

As stated above, contributions are not payable in respect of interim or remand orders, nor for any period when a committed child is living at home while a care order is in force. Local authorities may consider whether any contribution should be payable while any child or young person is in care for the purpose of assessment on a voluntary basis (perhaps for up to four weeks).

TRANSFER OF PAYMENTS TO CARE AUTHORITY

Payments received by local authorities under agreements and under court orders in respect of children for whose maintenance other local authorities are responsible, are transferred to those local authorities half-yearly after the deduction of 10% administrative expenses.

AFFILIATION ORDERS

Where there is an affiliation order in force in respect of a child who falls in any of the classifications set out under "Legislation" above, the local authority for the area in which the *putative father* is residing may apply to a magistrates' court in that area for the affiliation order to be varied for payment to that council. If the child in respect of whom the order is payable ceases to be in care and then at a later date returns, the local authority may apply for the order to be revived.[28] An affiliation order does not lapse on the death of the mother.

If there is no affiliation order in force when a child becomes in any way chargeable to a local authority then the local authority for the area in which the *mother* resides may try to make a voluntary agreement with the alleged father, or make application to a magistrates' court in the area for such an order to be made.[29] The application is dealt with as if it were being made by the mother herself but there is no need for her to appear unless the application is contested. In this event her evidence must be corroborated in a material particular, *e.g.* the blood test provision of the Family Law Reform Act 1969 (Part III). If the mother is dead or cannot be found to give evidence, no order can be made in a contested application.[30]

Money received under varied affiliation orders and affiliation orders made on the application of a local authority is paid over directly or through the Clerk of the Court to the local authority entitled to receive it, in the same way as the money paid under contribution orders.

RESTRICTIONS

An application by a local authority for an affiliation order must be made within three years of the date on which the child last came into the care of an authority.

ENFORCEMENT

In order to enforce payments due under affiliation orders application must be made to the magistrates' court for the area in which the *putative father* resides.

ATTACHMENT OF EARNINGS ORDERS

Orders made under s. 87 of the Children and Young Persons Act 1933, and s. 26 of the Children Act 1948, are defined as maintenance orders within the meaning of the Attachment of Earnings Act 1971. It is therefore possible for a local authority to apply for an attachment of earnings order in these cases. Money due under the orders is deducted from the contributor's earnings by his employer and forwarded to the Clerk of the Court for eventual transmission to the local authority. This is a very convenient method of obtaining money from unwilling contributors but if the contributor changes his employment, the order has to be re-directed to the new employer, if known.

CANCELLATION OF ARREARS

Courts have power to write off arrears of contributions due under court orders, usually in respect of sickness or unemployment. If a contributor is sent to prison in default, the arrears are not discharged by the imprisonment but may be remitted by the court subsequently. Arrears due under agreements may be enforced through the county courts as a debt, but alternatively may be written off by the local authority.

MOVEMENTS OF CONTRIBUTORS

The requirement that parents and putative fathers should keep the local authority informed of their whereabouts is intended primarily to enable the local authority to preserve the link between parents and their children. A secondary purpose is to assist local authorities to keep in touch with parents for purposes of parental contributions.[31]

When a parent moves away from the area of a local authority it is necessary for responsibility for the assessment and collection of contributions to be passed to the new area. The second authority will usually accept a voluntary agreement as the basis of contributions until such time as particulars of the contributor's means can be obtained and a new agreement completed. A similar procedure is followed in respect of contribution orders.

The second local authority will not usually accept responsibility for the collection of arrears which have accrued under voluntary agreements but will accept arrears due and enforceable under justices' orders.

The importance of prompt notification of changes in parents' addresses will, therefore, be appreciated. If a contributor moves sufficiently often from one local authority to another without giving notice, it is possible for him to evade payments and contact for a long period.

MISSING PARENTS

Attempts are made with varying success to trace parents whose addresses are not known. The Chief Officers of Police, the Salvation

Army Bureau of Missing Persons, and in certain circumstances the Department of Health and Social Security are the chief avenues of enquiry. In addition, courts, but not local authorities, may obtain information from the Passport Office, the Ministry of Defence and the D.H.S.S., but only for the purpose of proceedings related to contribution orders.

RETROSPECTIVE CONTRIBUTION ORDERS

There is often unavoidable delay in obtaining contribution orders during which the contributor is able to evade payment. This is remedied to some extent by s. 30 of the Children and Young Persons Act 1963, which permits a court to make an arrears order with retrospective effect, provided the application for the order is made not less than three months after the end of the period of default. The period of default is defined as the period during which the person was liable to make contributions in respect of a child but no contribution order was in force. This provision for dealing with arrears covers the case of the contributor who defaults under agreement and an order is being sought against him.

MATRIMONIAL CAUSES ACT 1973
MATRIMONIAL PROCEEDINGS (MAGISTRATES' COURTS) ACT 1960
FAMILY LAW REFORM ACT 1969
GUARDIANSHIP ACT 1973, s. 2

Provision is made under these Acts for court orders to be made requiring parents to contribute in respect of children whose care is committed to the local authority. The amounts of contribution are at the discretion of the court.

CASE WORK APPLICATION

The view is widely held that the assessment and collection of parental contributions should be dealt with by administrative staff in the Social Services and/or Treasurer's Departments of the local authority, in the same way as other financial matters. It is also considered by some local authorities that social workers will achieve a better relationship with parents if they are not responsible for this work.

There is, however, a need for liaison between the officers responsible for assessment and collections on one hand and social workers on the other. The obligation of the parents to contribute towards the maintenance of their children in care is an important factor in the relationship between the parents and the local authority.

The Social Services Department is responsible for dealing with families on other financial matters such as charges for home help services and sometimes for the payment of rent where this falls under a departmental rent guarantee scheme. In some instances a family will be receiving financial assistance under s. 1 of the 1963 Act at a time when money may already be due to the Authority in respect of one or more of the services mentioned above.

The total financial position of the family can be considered by the department; authorities are in a position to integrate their procedures for assessment and collection (in respect of all services) in such a way as to support and reinforce their social workers in the best interests of the families concerned. This arrangement is mentioned as a possibility in Chapter 3.

FAMILY ALLOWANCES

It may be relevant here to consider the question of family allowances. For the purpose of the Act, a child is a person under the upper limit of school age, handicapped or under 19 and in full-time education or apprenticeship. The following children are excluded from any family however:

a those detained for certain grave offences;
b those committed under a care order not being an Interim Order;
c those in respect of whom a local authority has assumed parental rights by a resolution;

In these cases neither a parent nor any other person may claim a family allowance in respect of the child. In the case of other children living away from their parents, a Family Allowance may be claimed provided that the parent is contributing at least £1·50 per week towards his maintenance in cash or kind. In this way children in care under s. 1 of the Act and under the Matrimonial Acts or Wardship or Guardianship proceedings may be included in their own families for family allowance. Generally speaking the first four weeks of absence from the family are disregarded in considering entitlement.

Children subject to a care order or to a resolution may be allowed to live in the charge of their parents, guardians, relatives or friends, however, and in these circumstances may be included in the family for family allowance purposes for so long as they remain in the charge of the parent or other person.[32] There is an arrangement whereby local authorities notify the Ministry of the movements of children and of non-payment of contributions at certain intervals. This information is used by the Ministry to withdraw or re-issue entitlement to family allowances.[33] Delay in notifying movements of children may result in serious hardship to parents whose entitlement has been withdrawn, while re-issue is being considered.

CONTRIBUTIONS FOR 1973–74

In considering the question of parental contributions generally, it is of interest to note that the cost of child care to local authorities for the year 1973–74 was £77m, excluding administration, the average direct cost of maintaining a child in care was £18·79 per week, the total parental contributions amounted to £1,737,000, and the average weekly contribution by parents was 42p per child.[34]

It is obvious that the total amount contributed by parents is a very small part of the cost of the service, but it has to be remembered that in many cases a parent is assessed to pay a nil contribution, and that no payments are due in respect of children aged over 16. There has for some years been disagreement about the value of assessing parents in those cases where the child is in care under the Acts of 1948 and 1969. In other cases, of course, the order is made by the court, after representations by the care authority, and not by the "proposal" procedure described above.

The obligation of parents to maintain their children dates at least from the Poor Law of 1601, and failure to do this is still an offence under s. 1 of the Children and Young Persons Act 1933, while the parent has the charge and control of the child. It is therefore argued that the obligation continues even though the child is in care, and this view is expressed in the legal requirement that it is the duty of a parent to contribute, according to his or her means, while care continues, but only up to the age of 16.

In many cases there is no income apart from family allowances or state benefits, so that if an assessment is made the money will in effect be laboriously transferred from the D.H.S.S. via the parent to the local authority, at considerable cost of time and effort. In other cases, there is income from employment, often with the addition of family allowances, and this is all assessable according to whatever scale a local authority has adopted.

There are those who feel that parents must find it hard to understand why they should be required to contribute towards the maintenance of their children while they are in care, since they do not make any payment when they are being maintained in hospital, or in a special school (apart from pocket money and clothing). If the duty to maintain in one set of circumstances has been eroded, why not in another? Advocates of this point of view also consider that the administrative costs of assessing and collecting parental contributions are so high as to make it unprofitable, and they also point out that the process in itself can create friction with a family, with detrimental effects upon the plans of the social worker involved. Social workers themselves very rarely find themselves called upon to deal with the contribution aspects of a case, and probably prefer to leave this to administrative staff, in rather the same way as Mr Spenlow in *David Copperfield* left all the unpleasant work to his partner Mr Jorkins. Whatever the merits of these two opposing views, the position broadly is that the willing contributors pay, while others do not, there being very limited powers of enforcement by the courts even if an order is obtained.

That there is a "duty" to contribute is not in doubt, but it is for each local authority to decide whether to enforce the duty, and, if so, by what means and to what extent. It might be helpful in the first place to avoid any purely automatic assessment procedure on admission to care, so that the whole question could be considered along with other aspects, in conjunction with at least one parent. There may also be something to be said for allowing a period of several weeks to elapse in s. 1 care before an assessment is made. This will probably be made more acceptable under the Child Benefit Act 1975. This will have great effects upon the payment of family allowances which will be replaced by a child benefit payment; this is likely to continue to be paid for a period (at least eight weeks) after admission to care, and could probably be ignored by a care authority for that time. Child Benefit for the first child of a family will be payable in respect of "one-parent" families from April 1976, and for other families a year later. One great advantage of the present assessment method is that there are members of staff with a particular interest in the whereabouts of parents of children in care. They can be of great help to social workers in many ways, specially at periodical case reviews.

NOTES

1. Legitimacy Act, ss. 1 and 2.
2. Guardianship of Minors Act 1971, s. 14.
3. Children and Young Persons Acts, 1933, s. 107(1).
4. *Ibid.*, Children Act 1948, s. 59(1), Adoption Act 1958, s. 57 as amended.
5. Children Act 1948, s. 59(1), Adoption Act 1958, s. 57, Children Act 1958, s. 36, Nurseries and Child-Minders Regulation Act 1948, s. 13, all as amended.
6. Children Act 1948, s. 1.
7. Nurseries and Child-Minders Regulation Act 1948, Children Act 1958, as amended, Adoption Act 1958.
8. C. and Y.P. Act 1933, s. 17.
9. Adoption Act 1958, s. 8.
10. Children Act 1948, s. 6.
11. C. and Y.P. Act 1963, s. 25.
12. Guardianship Act 1973.
13. C. and Y.P. Act 1969, s. 21(2).
14. *Ibid.*, Schedule 1 and Home Office Circular 299/1970.
15. Children Act 1948, s. 2.
16. C. and Y.P. Act 1963, s. 48.
17. *Ibid.*, and Children Act 1948, s. 2.
18. *Ibid.*
19. Children Act 1948, s. 4.
20. Children Act 1975, Schedule 1, Part II.
21. Matrimonial Causes Act 1973, s. 42(3).
22. Family Law Reform Act 1969; Guardianship Act 1973.
23. Children Act 1948, s. 10; C. and Y.P. Act 1969, s. 24(8); Matrimonial Causes

Act 1973, s. 43; Matrimonial Proceedings (Magistrates Courts) Act 1960, s. 3; Family Law Reform Act 1969, s. 7; Guardianship Act 1973, s. 4(6).
24. C. and Y.P. Act 1969, s. 24(8).
25. Children Act 1948, ss. 23 and 24.
26. C. and Y.P. Act 1969, s. 62.
27. Adoption Act 1958, s. 36.
28. C. and Y.P. Act 1933, s. 88.
29. Children Act 1948, s. 26.
30. Affiliation Proceedings (Amendment) Act, 1972.
31. Home Office Circulars 204 and 206/1963.
32. Family Allowances Act 1965, s. 11.
33. Home Office Circular 222/1970.
34. *Children in Care 1974*, Cmnd. 6147.

GENERAL NOTE

The position of parents will in due course be greatly affected by the implementation of the Children Act 1975, especially as regards the various ways in which their parental rights may be diminished by the new measures; the more important of these are briefly commented upon in Chapter 17.

Chapter 11

METHOD OF TREATMENT OF CHILDREN IN CARE

The treatment of children in care is dealt with in Part II of the Children Act 1948, ss. 11–22 inclusive as amended by Children and Young Persons Act 1969, ss. 27 and 49 and the Children Act 1975. These sections apply to children however they may have come into care, whether through the courts or otherwise including those committed on interim orders or on remand warrants, but where the High Court is concerned, the local authority may be subject to decisions by that court. The underlying duty of the authority with regard to children in care under s. 1 of the Children Act 1948 when parental rights have not been vested in the authority, is to endeavour to secure that the care of the child is taken over by the parent or guardian or by a relative or friend (with safeguards regarding religious upbringing) if this is consistent with the welfare of the child. This implies that there should be a positive effort towards returning children to their families.[1]

A similar duty is conferred by s. 1 of the Children and Young Persons Act 1963, which requires the authority to provide advice, guidance and assistance to promote the welfare of children by diminishing the need for them to remain in care under either the Children Act or the Children and Young Persons Acts. This principle, therefore, applies to all children in care, whether the authority has parental rights or not, though obviously the local authority will not make positive efforts to return children to the care of their parents unless this would be consistent with their welfare.

PARENTAL RIGHTS RESOLUTIONS

Whenever it is felt that positive efforts should *not* be made to return a child to his parents, or whenever an immediate request for his return would be unwelcome, there may well be a case for consideration of a resolution under s. 2 of the 1948 Act, by which the rights of either or both parents might be assumed by the authority.

There is a wide variation between authorities in the use of this provision, and there is reason to suppose that many of those children who have been in care for considerable periods of time should have the protection that a resolution would afford. In the well-known study *Children who Wait*,[2] it is argued that most of the children in care with an uncertain future have family backgrounds which would justify the use of s. 2. The existing grounds are already very wide, but are not perhaps always understood in some authorities as they are in others.

Reluctance to take the necessary action may be due to an opinion that the passing of a resolution is punitive towards parents who are themselves in need of help; or it may be felt that a resolution will bar the way to rehabilitation; or, simply, that the decision is a hard one to take and tends to be deferred from one review to another. Possibly the resolution is viewed in the wrong way altogether, and is looked upon as a dramatic intervention against a child's parents rather than as a means of ensuring the creation of a plan of what will be best for both child and parents in the longer term. The effect of a resolution is to give to the local authority the care and control of the child in a way very similar to that of a care order, so that it can plan the future either towards rehabilitation into the family, or away from it, without the constant threat of parental intervention at the wrong time or for the wrong reason, for instance because of some concurrent action in connection with financial assessment or enforcement of arrears. There is no need for a resolution to remain in force for a long period if a shorter time is sufficient for the purpose; and even while it is in force, the child may be placed with his parents and live with them in a normal way, though still remaining in care. But its very existence, for either a short or long period, give protection to a child, and makes objective planning of the future possible. None the less, the use of s. 2 powers is not to be undertaken lightly; it is an administrative action by the local authority, but is subject at every stage to the scrutiny of the courts, and the rights of parents are fully safeguarded.

When the passing of a resolution is contemplated, there are a number of steps to be taken, the following being the suggested order.

1. Find out when and by whom a resolution will be passed. The powers rest in the local authority but are almost certainly delegated to the Social Services Committee, which may have re-delegated them to a sub-committee or to some specially constituted panel of officers and members. Any such delegations must be duly recorded in the minutes of the authority and may later have to be proved in evidence.

If the powers have *not* been delegated by the Social Services Committee only that Committee can pass a resolution, and there may therefore be delay until the next meeting. To overcome this difficulty, some authorities have instituted special panels which may be convened at short notice and have delegated powers to deal with certain urgent matters, such as this.

2. Consider the grounds on which a resolution may be passed (see Chapter 10) and decide which is to be used, that is to say which can be proved in the event of an objection.

3. Except in the case of (a) and (e), discuss with the parent concerned the needs of the child, the present parental circumstances, the need for unhurried planning of the child's future, and the long-term objectives, with a view to securing the agreement of the parent to the passing of a resolution on the appropriate ground. If agreement is obtained it must be in writing and contain an acknowledgement of a full explanation of the nature and purpose of a resolution, the parental rights which it would convey and those it would leave with the parent, and the possibility of its being rescinded or revoked at a later date. There are other matters such as continuing liability to maintain the child, but these are usually contained in a specially designed form of agreement for this purpose. The obtaining of parental agreement offers the best opportunity of planning long-term care of a child, with a parent who is fully aware of the views of the social worker and who can, at the same time, be offered help in arriving at the right decision for the child in all the known circumstances.

4. If, however, agreement is not obtained, the evidence for a resolution must be assembled, *e.g.* proof of death in (a), proof of abandonment in (b) and (e), medical evidence in (c) and possibly (g), and social worker evidence in (d) and (f).

5. Produce a report for the Committee or other body empowered to pass a resolution, stating the full names of the parent or parents concerned, date of reception of the child into care, the stated reason,

the present circumstances and relevant previous history, especially of periods in care.

6. After the resolution has been passed and recorded, no further action is necessary in cases in which there is no parent or guardian, or in which a parent has given written consent as in 3 above. In all other cases, a notification of the passing of the resolution and the grounds for it must be personally given or sent to the parent concerned by recorded delivery at the last known address. The notification must inform the parent of the right to object, in writing, to the authority within one month of the receipt of the notification, and of the action which will be taken if a notice of objection is in fact received. (It is usual for there to be a form of notification in these cases, but normally it will be accompanied by a less formal letter of explanation. The contents of this letter will vary according to the attitude of the parent when the possibility of agreement was being discussed.)[3]

7. If no notice of objection in writing is received within one month of the delivery of the notification, the resolution stands.

8. If a written notice of objection is received, immediate action must be taken by the authority to lay a complaint before a juvenile court (not before the clerk or a single justice). The complaint may be made in person or in writing, but if it is not validly made to a juvenile court within fourteen days of the receipt of the objection, the resolution will lapse and become null and void.

On hearing the complaint, the juvenile court will, if satisfied with the substance of it, fix a date for the hearing of the case and will issue summonses to the parent or parents concerned, but not to the child. It is then that the evidence in support of the resolution will have to be given on behalf of the authority, which will almost certainly be represented by a member of its legal staff.

The juvenile court at this hearing may either uphold the resolution by ordering that it shall not lapse, or refuse to make such an order. At any subsequent time, a parent may apply to the authority for the resolution to be rescinded by another resolution, or may apply to a juvenile court which may, after hearing the evidence, set it aside.

The emphasis of the Act, however, is clearly on co-operation with parents with a view to returning children to their care eventually and this underlines the need for the position of parents to be continually borne in mind even in those cases in which the authority has parental rights, unless a decision has been made that the child's future does not lie with the parents.

The assumption of parental rights by a local authority or the committal of a child to care, which were discussed in the previous chapter, do not generally authorise the authority to act directly contrary to the parents' wishes where these are reasonable, and there are certain matters in which the parents' rights are preserved. These are as follows:

RELIGIOUS PERSUASION

Each Act dealing with children and young persons in care contains provisions with regard to religious upbringing, though only in a negative way. A care order does not authorise a local authority to cause the person concerned to be brought up in any religion except that in which he may have been brought up but for the order.

So far as children in care under the Children Act are concerned, the authority would normally expect to arrange for a child to follow his own religious persuasion. This is normally the religion of the parents, particularly the father, but this is to be considered in conjunction with the welfare of the child himself. If, for instance, a child has been brought up, before coming into care, in a faith other than that of his parents it is considered that there should be no disturbance of the situation. It would also be possible for a child of mature judgement to decide to change his own religious persuasion, even if this was not in accordance with the wishes of his parents. In any event, however, parents who were available would be consulted on all matters of this kind. Even where a local authority has assumed parental rights in respect of a child in care the statute provides that a resolution shall not authorise the authority to bring up the child in a creed other than that in which he would have been brought up but for the resolution.[4]

MEDICAL TREATMENT

It is usual for parents to be asked to authorise the Social Services' Committee to give consent for any immunisation, operative or medical treatment which may be necessary while the child is in care. Some parents may have conscientious objections to a particular form of immunisation or treatment and even where the authority has parental rights these are not generally used to overrule the parents' wishes. Moreover, any authority having a child in care would make it the normal practice to inform the parent of any serious accident, illness or operative treatment which may be required and would normally endeavour to obtain parental agreement before giving the necessary authority. "Blood" cases are dealt with in Chapter 8. Under the Family Law Reform Act 1969 (s. 8), a minor over the age of 16 may himself consent to any surgical, medical or dental treatment and if he gives consent, that of his parent or guardian is not required.

EMIGRATION

Although the local authority is permitted, with the consent of the Secretary of State, to arrange for the emigration of any child in care (except those committed under the Matrimonial Acts or as wards of court or under the Guardianship Act 1973), the Act requires that the parents or guardian shall be consulted; in this context "parents or guardian" includes those who have been deprived of their parental rights.[5]

ADOPTION

Although the authority under a resolution is given the parental rights and powers of the parent, or parents, concerned, it is not required to give consent to the adoption of a child in care.[6] As we shall see, the only consents required are those of the parents of a child and if these cannot be obtained the court can either dispense with the consents on certain grounds or decline to make the order. The powers of the local authority cannot be used to overrule the wishes of the parents in this matter.

MARRIAGE

The powers of a local authority under a resolution are thought to include the power to give consent to the marriage of a child but, here again, it would be the normal practice for this consent to be obtained from a parent, if possible, before the authority exercises its powers (see Chapter 4).

GENERAL CONSIDERATIONS

It is desirable that a local authority should regard itself as exercising a trusteeship in respect of children in care and, in addition to consulting parents on the matters mentioned above, it is usual for them also to be consulted with regard to such things as choice of school, joining one of H.M. Services or taking part in flying, climbing, or any other hazardous pursuit.

As mentioned in the last chapter, it is essential that on the admission of a child to care full information should be available about the method of admission, the position of the parents with regard to custody, their views on medical treatment, their religious persuasion and their general wishes with regard to the child's upbringing. A local authority with parental rights must exercise them carefully, and the court will not usually interfere with their discretionary use of powers, *e.g.* to determine matters of access to parents.

It is also important that parents should be informed that they are required to keep the authority notified of their address[7] and that they should realise that while the child is in care the local authority will wish to make what arrangements it thinks best for the child, including the possibility of placing him with foster parents on either a short-term or long-term basis.

When compiling a case history for a child as much information as possible about the parents and their relatives and families should be included.

Although many children remain in care for only a short period and the authority has a duty to work for their return to the care of their parents, it is nevertheless true that any child in care is liable to remain in care until the age of 18 or 19 in some circumstances (see Chapter 13).

While a child is in care the authority must, in reaching decisions about him, give *first consideration* to the need to safeguard and promote his welfare *throughout his childhood*, and must as far as possible consider his wishes and feelings, but there are exceptions to this general duty.[8] The local authority is also required to make use of facilities and services which are available for children who are in the care of their own parents; this is necessary to avoid discrimination between children who are living in their own homes and children who are in care. This involves the use of such facilities as special schools or hostels for handicapped children (provided by the Education Department), youth employment service, hospitals, mental hospitals and any other form of treatment or service available to children living with their own families. Education Committees have certain welfare powers and in order to avoid conflict with these, there are regulations which lay down how they are to be applied to children in care; thus children in care do not receive free school meals, free milk or clothing provided by the Education Committee, as the authority is regarded as a parent having sufficient resources to pay for these services. On the other hand, a child in care who is placed in a special school or similar educational establishment is maintained there by the Education Committee, except as regards clothing and pocket money, which are provided by the local authority acting as parent.[9]

A CHARTER OF RIGHTS FOR CHILDREN IN CARE

The British Association of Social Workers has set out a proposed Charter of Rights containing the principles which it considers ought to apply to all children in care, wherever they are being brought up. They are obviously much more important for those in long-term care, either in a foster home or in a community home, or elsewhere. Briefly the Charter expresses the intention that the child in care has a right to:

1. individual respect and consideration, even though his rights and needs will be closely associated with those of others;
2. be looked after by skilled adults who have been specially selected and who have a commitment to the understanding and meeting of his individual needs;
3. live in an environment which is conducive to his emotional, physical, social and intellectual development;
4. individual attention which shows recognition of, and respect for, his unique identity;
5. information concerning his circumstances and participation in the planning of his future;

6. administrative standards and procedures within his caring agency which will protect him and promote his interests;
7. the protection of the law.

This Charter provides an excellent summary of the social work practice which is already implicit or explicit in the statutes and regulations relating to children who are in care. Section 59 of the Children Act 1975 (referred to on page 141) should make this Charter a reality.

The *physical* care of children consists largely of provision for their accommodation and maintenance. The alternative methods of providing this are laid down in the Children Act 1948, s. 13.

REVIEWS

In considering the various ways in which it may provide accommodation and maintenance for children in its care, the local authority and its social workers should always bear in mind what has already been said about co-operation with parents. As will be seen, there is a wide range of accommodation available to local authorities, including former approved schools and remand homes, as well as nurseries homes and hostels.

Although this whole range of accommodation may be used for any child in care, according to the assessment of his need for a particular type of care or treatment or training, there may well be prejudices for a time against the admission of a child or young person to a particular kind of establishment, such as a former approved school now functioning as a community home. It will be desirable to seek the co-operation and assent of a child and his parents before a decision is made on an issue such as this; otherwise the parents whose child is in care under s. 1 of the 1948 Act (no Resolution having been passed) might decide to withdraw the child from care altogether; the parents whose child is subject to either a Resolution under s. 2, or to a care order, could apply at any time to the court for revocation of the Resolution or Care order on what might appear to them to be the ground of the authority's abuse of its parental powers. It is therefore essential that in all cases, and specially those where long term care is likely, there should first be a proper assessment of the needs of the child, arrived at in co-operation with his parents as far as possible, and that the method of care should be carefully selected, again in consultation with the parents. The consultation should be a continuing process, taking into account the possibility of different forms of care at different times, and almost always directed towards the ultimate restoration of the child to his own home.

This principle is formally recognised in s. 27 (4) which requires the authority to review at least every six months the case of every child in its care. Previously the only required reviews were those of boarded-out children; it may be that in many of these reviews attention was directed towards the immediate welfare of the child, and rather less to the question whether or not he ought to remain in care. Some authorities have already been concentrating on this question and finding that with the imaginative use of other powers under the Act of 1963, discharge from care can be considered in cases where it has for some time seemed unlikely. Needless to say, such reviews are more useful, though possibly more difficult, when the child, if old enough, and his parents are actually involved in them, and are able to put their own point of view directly to the social workers concerned in the case.

It should be noted that under s. 27 (4) when a local authority is carrying out a six-monthly review of the case of a child in care *under a care order*, it is required to consider specifically whether or not it should apply for the order to be discharged by the court. The initiative rests with the local authority. Similarly, there would seem to be every reason for the authority to consider the possibility of discharge from care in reviewing all those cases when discharge is a matter for the parents and the local authority to determine without recourse to the court.

METHODS OF CARE

BOARDING-OUT

Foster parents range from the old-fashioned warm welcoming mother figure prepared to look after any child presented to her, to the more sophisticated foster parents living in a house provided and furnished by the organisation, and caring for a specified number of children in what is really a Home, but is called a foster home. This and many other experimental forms of foster care have been used during the last century. Diversity of method seems to be essential, as foster care is an important part of the service, though fortunately it no longer is the automatic first choice for any and every child and young person in care.[10]

Not surprisingly, foster parents like other groups of people feel the need to speak with one voice. In 1974, some of them formed the National Foster Care Association with members drawn from all over the country. The objects of this Association, as reported, are laudable, but they omit any reference to the parents of the children they care for. The parents themselves have not yet formed an association, but if they do, they might well press for a better understanding and use of the Boarding-out Regulations which, though issued in 1955, are still in force and lay down a procedure which could well improve the practices described in the literature.

Boarding out is governed by the regulations made under the Act.[11]

So far as social workers are concerned, the most important requirements are as follows:

a *"Boarding-out"* means living with foster parents as a member of their family (but does not include children placed for adoption).[12]

b *Foster parents.*—A child may only be boarded-out with:
  i husband and wife jointly;
  ii a woman only;
  iii a man who is a grandfather, uncle or elder brother of the child;
  iv a man who was acting jointly with his wife as a foster parent but whose wife has died or left the home.[13]

c *Conditions.*—Before a child is boarded-out a social worker must have visited the foster home and have reported, in writing, on the material conditions, stating that the home is likely to meet the needs of a *particular child*.[14] The officer must either know the child concerned or be fully informed about him. The officer must also make a written report on the reputation and religious persuasion of the foster parents and their suitability in age, character, temperament and health for the care of a particular child, and must further report whether any member of the foster parents' household suffers from any physical or mental illness or has been convicted of any offences which would make the placing of the child undesirable (see Appendix C for suggested all-purpose investigation).

(**Note**: In practice, the latter enquiries as to health and criminal record are made officially in writing, as there are certain difficulties about obtaining sufficient information).

Before a child is placed in a foster home which has been approved he must have been medically examined during the previous three months and a written report as to his state of health must[15] be available.

d *Medical care.*—Arrangements must be made for medical examination of the child within one month of boarding-out if under the age of 2 years. Thereafter six-monthly while under the age of 2 and annually[16] if over that age.

Arrangements must also be made for the child to receive medical and dental attention as required.[17]

e *Undertaking.*—The foster parents are required to sign a form of undertaking,[18] which may be modified if the child is over compulsory school age.[19]

f *Visitation.*—In addition to a visit within one month of the placing, the officer is required to visit a child under 5 years of age every six weeks for the first two years and thereafter once every three months. A child over 5 years of age at the time of the placing must be visited every two months for the first two years; thereafter every three months.[20]

With regard to children over compulsory school age, the regulations do not, in fact, require visits to be paid but state that the officer must *see the child* within three months of attaining school-leaving age and thereafter every three months.[21] (This provision can be very useful in certain cases if there should be any difficulties about visiting the foster home, though normally visits are paid as in the case of younger children.)

In addition to the periodical visits or interviews laid down above, an officer must visit the foster home or see the child within one month of any change of address and *immediately* if any complaint is received about or from the child himself.

The officer must make a written report on the child's welfare, health, conduct and progress after each visit and after each interview with the child.[22] (*It should be noted that the frequency of visits laid down in the regulations is to be regarded as a minimum.*) If the authority is of opinion that the boarding-out of a child with particular foster parents is no longer in his interest[23] it is required to remove him from the foster home and in emergency, an officer has the power to remove a child forthwith, though normally this would be done after consultation with a more senior officer.[24]

g *Reviews.*—The case of each child should be reviewed before placing with foster parents, within three months of the placing and thereafter not less than every six months, and such reviews are to be made by persons not acting as visitors.[25]

h *Short-stay boarding-out.*—Short-stay boarding-out is still extensively used in the cases of children who come into care for a short period, for instance, during mother's confinement, operation, etc. The principles of the regulations apply but there are certain modifications if the period of stay is expected to be less than eight weeks; these are[26] as follows:

   i the report on the foster home must be made in writing by the officer indicating that this placing is likely to be suitable for a particular child; [27]

   ii the foster parents need not complete a form of undertaking but they must be informed of the child's religious persuasion and their obligations as foster parents;[28]

  iii visits must be made within two weeks of the placing and thereafter not less than every four weeks;

  iv in the case of children over compulsory school age visits must be made every four weeks;

   v in all cases a visit must be paid on receipt of any complaint about or from the child.[29]

If the short-stay boarding-out lasts for eight weeks and is then expected to exceed a further four weeks, the boarding-out must be treated as long-stay and will come under the full scope of the regulations.[30]

i *Child already in foster home—Reception into care.*—It sometimes happens that a child is received into care while living in what amounts to a foster home. Such cases include those where an uncle or aunt, or other person, is caring for the child without financial assistance and applies for the child's reception into care so that an allowance may be paid. In such instances, the regulations provide that the child shall *not* be removed from the home in order that the necessary enquiries can be made.[31]

j *Children boarded-out by other authorities or voluntary societies.*—The regulations apply to such children and a local authority officer may be required to visit them on behalf of the authority or society concerned.[32]

k *Boarding-out allowances.*—Each authority has its own scale of boarding-out allowances payable to foster parents, and there were wide variations when a survey was conducted by B.A.S.W. in 1973. These are graded according to the age of the child and include payments in respect of maintenance, pocket money, clothing, holidays, etc. When a foster parent is receiving a Guardian's Allowance, Family Allowance, Pension, or other payment in respect of a child, it is usual for the amount in question to be deducted from the authority's own allowance.

Though boarding-out allowances are usually paid to foster parents they are not governed by regulations and in rare cases foster parents do not wish to receive them. The payment or non-payment of the allowance does not, however, affect the foster parents' position and responsibility, which are based on the form of undertaking (see para. **e,** *ante*).[33]

l *Application.*—By definition the regulations do not apply to children in care who are:

> **i**   in lodgings and not living as a member of the family;
> **ii** in residential employment;
> **iii** staying with a family for a holiday not exceeding three weeks;
> **iv** living in a hostel, for example, one provided by the Y.M.C.A. or Y.W.C.A.

Such children and young people obviously require supervision while they remain in care but this is not exercised under the Boarding-out Regulations.[34]

m *Contact with parents.*—Bearing in mind what has been said previously about the position of parents, it will be obvious that in many cases they have a right to see their child who is boarded-out. This creates a rather difficult situation in which it is necessary for the foster parents, the child and the parents to be treated with every possible consideration. Some foster parents, particularly those taking children for short periods, are willing for parents to visit but in other cases it may be necessary for meetings between parents and children to be arranged at some neutral point, such as a children's home, at least until the emergence of the truly professional foster parent.

Parents should, in general, be informed that the local authority may decide that a child should in his own interests be placed in a foster home and they should be helped to avoid the wrong impression which they have sometimes formed from reports appearing in the press.

Many parents feel that boarding-out and adoption are indistinguishable and, because of their own failure to provide for their children, are inclined to be hostile towards boarding-out; but with understanding on all sides it is frequently possible to use this method of care for the benefit of all concerned, always provided that the local authority pays full regard to its duties towards the parents of the child in care.

Clearly these attitudes to care should be examined before placing occurs; in this the regulations can be seen to serve the interests of the child.

First, they differentiate between short- and long-term foster care (para. **h** above). Obviously, if a placing is known to be for three or four weeks, the long-term considerations will not arise in such an acute form. All the parties will know what the position is and the short-stay foster parent will probably accept parental visits (especially if she knows the parents and has been recruited on that basis). There is therefore a need for a decision by the social worker as to whether or not this is a short-stay case, not expected to remain in care for more than twelve weeks at the most. If it is said that this is sometimes an impossible decision at the outset, para. **g** above provides for a review within three months, and this gives the opportunity to review the whole circumstances before deciding that the conversion to long term is inevitable. The question then is whether the existing foster mother is prepared to maintain her attitude for a longer period, or whether in fact she can continue at all. If not, then other arrangements must be made, and if they involve foster care, that must be provided on a long-term understanding. Long-term fostering should be based on a conscious decision that it will meet the needs of the child, rather than simply allowing it to develop from a short-stay situation. In both short- and long-term placements, the regulations require a report including a statement that the placing is considered suitable for *a particular child* (para. **c** and **h** (i)) and this is obviously more important for the long-term placement.

There is evidence that in this respect, practice, even in the former Children's Departments, has left much to be desired.[35] In considering whether a placing is suitable for a particular child his relationship with his own family is obviously a very important factor which must be taken into account. Rosamund Thorpe in her study looked at the situation of a number of long-term foster children and suggests that their well-being is enhanced by (a) a clear understanding of the placing in the foster home, (b) continued identification with the actual parents, and (c) real contact with the parents.

George's study concerns the relationship of social workers and foster parents (in the days when there were child care officers and children's departments). He suggests that the social workers mainly looked upon foster parents as "colleagues", but half the foster parents saw the social workers as "friends", and some of the others as "colleagues". In neither group did many see the social worker as "supervisor", and neither thought it at all necessary to inform a child's parents about any incident, such as stealing, even if the social worker had been informed, which was not by any means always.

While there are foster parents who think of their role as professional, in this study most of them considered themselves as parents in effect, and were naturally not keen that real parents should visit. Visits by the social worker served to remind them of what they did not want to know—that the child was not a part of the family. George suggests that this is the essence of the "lay" foster parent, and that it is the "professional" who should be able to improve the child's relationship with his own family in spite of difficulties. But there was little commitment to this, even by the social workers concerned.

So here again there is a stimulus to find a foster parent (perhaps a relative or friend) who knows the child and the circumstances of the family and is willing to give the help required. If this is not possible, a foster home will be chosen from those which have already had general approval by the department. But in choosing the foster home for the "particular child", several points have to be considered:

1. Is it intended that the child will eventually return to his family? If so, after how many years? (This is the basic hard question referred to in an earlier chapter.)
2. If so, do his parents understand what fostering means?
3. Does the child understand the position?
4. Are the chosen foster parents willing to meet the parents before the placing? And the child?
5. Will they accept a refusal of the placing by the parents?
6. If the child is placed, will they allow the parents to visit, welcome them, and even inform the social worker if visits are not made?
7. Do they recognise the importance of keeping parents informed directly about any events, good and bad, in the life of the foster child?

If they cannot accept a code of this kind, can they implement the policy to which the social worker is committed by decision 1 above? George thinks not.

After a child is placed he must be visited at stated intervals (as a minimum) and in emergency (paras **f** and **h**). What is the purpose of the visit? Is it for a social chat with the foster parents? According to the regulations, it is to visit the child and to write a report on a number of matters, including progress. The word implies forward movement towards some goal—in this case the child's return to his parents. What has happened in the way of parental contact, or visits to or from brothers and sisters of the family? Are there any significant events which ought to be related to parents? How is the child himself dealing with the possibly long drawn out difficulties which are keeping him away from home? Questions of this kind give pointers to the work which still has to be done to reach the goal. Always there is the fundamental question as to whether this placing is in the interests of the child: should he be removed from it if it obstructs the long-term plan, and if so, to where? This is one of the matters to be dealt with at the review (para. **g**) every six months, when the social worker must have the advice of someone not dealing with the case, for instance a team leader. The review should be first of the file, to see that all the requirements of the regulations have been carried out, and then of the situation bearing in mind the original decision. When more than one child of a family is in care, there is much to be said for arranging the reviews to coincide with the six-monthly review of all children in care, boarded out or not. It has been found profitable for parents and children to attend these reviews and for foster parents to be present, or if they cannot, to prepare a brief report on the position as they see it.

Foster parents who can fulfil the demanding task described can claim to be acting professionally, and this should be taken into account during the continuing debate about rates of allowances, whether there should be a payment over and above the cost of maintenance, and similar matters, which seem to attract more attention than training for the vital work of helping to carry out the planned restoration of a child to his family. Perhaps this should receive urgent consideration.

Those long-term foster parents who look upon themselves as "parents" and who cannot subscribe to the idea of restoration will be affected by the Children Act 1975. This is discussed in Chapter 17. It is probable that the D.H.S.S. will be preparing and issuing a comprehensive guide on foster care, similar to the *Guide to Adoption Practice*. In the meantime, strenuous efforts are being made by many local authorities to recruit more foster parents and to support those already known to them. Similar efforts are being made by the larger voluntary societies, and it is clear that foster homes are needed as greatly as ever before. It is essential, however, that the function of foster parents should be clearly understood, and in this there still appears to be some confusion which the proposed Guide may help to resolve.

RESIDENTIAL CARE

Under the heading "resources" in Chapter 2 are set out the various types of residential establishment which are now community homes under the Regional plan. The local authority should be able to accommodate in any appropriate community home any child or young person in its care but in practice this only relates to an authority's own community homes (see under "Community homes with education on the premises", *post.*)

All community homes which were formerly directly provided by *a local authority* (including any observation centres, remand homes or approved schools publicly owned) are subject to the control of the authority which is known as the "responsible body", and may or may not appoint "managers". Broadly speaking the responsible body, or the managers if there are any, are responsible for the administrative arrangements, but the day-to-day care and discipline of each child or young person are under the direct control of the person appointed to be in charge, in consultation with the Social Services Department which has the child in care.[36]

Although social workers may not be concerned in the actual conduct of these homes, which include nurseries, they have many opportunities of co-operating with the staff in them, and it is therefore important that they should have some understanding of the principles and methods involved.

These principles are as suggested in para. 427 of the Curtis Report, which reads as follows:

"If the substitute home is to give the child what he gets from a good normal home it must supply:
i Affection and personal interest;understanding of his defects; care for his future; respect for his personality and regard for his self-esteem.
ii Stability; the feeling that he can expect to remain with those who will continue to care for him till he goes out into the world on his own feet.
iii Opportunity of making the best of his ability and aptitudes, whatever they may be, as such opportunity is made available to the child in the normal home.
iv A share in the common life of a small group of people in a homely environment".[37]

Though ideas on the purpose of residential care may have changed, and it is now thought of primarily as a form of treatment for children who cannot for some reason live in their own homes, these principles still need to be borne in mind. But in most cases there is no question of a child being cared for until "he goes out into the world on his own feet". Residential care should be preparing him in most cases for his return to his own family and should be involved in contact with families to this end.

LOCAL AUTHORITY COMMUNITY HOMES

Advice on the daily running of homes was contained in a Home Office Memorandum on the Conduct of Children's Homes of 1951, which no longer applies to community homes, but some of its ideas are mentioned here, together with a reference to the relevant new regulation. It is doubtful whether all homes have yet reached the standard expected in 1951.

a *Type and Size of Children's Homes*

Before 1948 many children's homes were annexes to workhouses or were very large institutions, sometimes accommodating hundreds of children. Since then there has been a move towards the provision of much smaller homes, including what were known as "family group homes" accommodating between eight and twelve children. Some authorities provided homes of this kind on housing estates so that the children lived in a normal housing environment. The type of home provided, however, is a matter for each local authority and there is usually a combination of very small homes, larger homes accommodating up to about twenty-five children, and in places where they exist, cottage homes, which are in effect a group of family homes placed together and under the supervision of a superintendent and matron. There is as yet little specialist provision of homes to deal with children with special difficulties, for instance, those who are mentally or physically handicapped, but this is now a matter for the Regional Plan.

Each home, whatever its size, is to be conducted in such a way as to secure the well-being of the children in it, both physically and emotionally.[38] Local authorities have made great efforts to create a reasonable, not luxurious, standard of comfort within the homes, by providing brighter decorations, furnishings and facilities for hobbies and handicrafts, but the more important factors affecting the child's happiness depend as they always did on the attitude of the residential staff. Residential work is now therefore firmly regarded as a part of social work, and a single pattern of training for both field and residential social workers is being implemented as recommended by the Central Council for Training and Education in Social Work.[39]

b *Daily Life in the Home*

The larger home particularly has to be run by a daily routine which avoids institutionalism. This does involve, however, regular mealtimes, bedtimes and activities, from all of which children tend to acquire a sense of security. Much can be done by the staff in the normal course of everyday life, especially at mealtimes, to give them ideas about citizenship and about the world and events outside the home.

Apart from the routine arrangements, it is necessary for children to have every opportunity for recreation, both indoor and outdoor, and in this connection organisations, such as Scouts and Guides, are used for those children who are interested in them. Many children, however, prefer to follow their own interests within the home and it is important that facilities should be available, and also that money should be available for outside outings and visits.

The children in such homes attend normal schools and thus spend a large part of their life in the company of other children who are living at home with their parents.

The regulations provide that a child must have the opportunity of following his own religious persuasion.[40]

c *Personal Possessions*

It is important that children should have their own personal clothes, shoes and toys. They should also be responsible for their own pocket money, which is given to them on a scale according to age, and in the case of older children it is desirable that they should have some say in the expenditure of the allowance which is provided for clothing.

d *General Care*

The Regulations provide that a medical officer may be appointed for each home and that the children, while they remain there, must be provided with medical, psychiatric and dental care.[41]

There is now no regulation concerning punishment. Control of homes is to be on the basis of good relationships between staff and children, but the responsible body has power to introduce further measures for control at its discretion. It may in this way make rules for the administration of those additional measures, if any.[42]

The most important matter for residential staff, in which field officers are involved, is the question of contact with relatives and friends. It is the general intention that a child's link with his own family should be preserved wherever it is possible and this may often involve visits to parents in order to encourage them to keep in contact with the children. The new regulations provide that there must be facilities in the home for visits by parents, relatives and friends of the children.[43] Where there are no parents or relatives or contact is undesirable, it is possible for children to form friendships with older people who will invite them out occasionally, and in this way such bodies as the Round Table, W.R.V.S., etc. may often prove to be helpful.

e *Administration*

The regulations prescribe that records must be maintained in each community home, and they also provide for visitation by either members of the staff or members of committee, so that a report on each home may be made, in writing, once a month.[44] There is a regulation concerning precautions to be taken against fire and accident.[45]

f *Ages of Children*

There are no definite ages laid down but it is usual for local authority community homes to accommodate children from about the age of 3 up to 16 years of age or older. Nurseries are, for the purpose of the regulations, community homes and although they normally have children from 0–5 years, some of them accommodate older children; conversely, not all children under the age of 5 need to be in a nursery. Nor is it necessary for a child to leave a home at school-leaving age; it has been the general practice to try to arrange for children either to be boarded-out before they leave school or to remain at the home after starting work until such time as a suitable placing can be made for them or they can return to their parents.

g *Contact with field officers*

As will be seen there is every reason for field officers to work in co-operation with residential staff. This is especially so in the maintaining of contact between a child and his parents. It should be possible for this to be shared by both field and residential social workers, visits being paid by either according to the circumstances, and the impressions of the situation being shared without reservation. It must be remembered, however, that the people responsible for running the home are the residential staff, and if this is borne in mind a good deal of unnecessary friction can be avoided. On the other hand, the whole period of care, whether in foster homes or homes, must be seen as a continuous process, the two forms of care being complementary to each other.

h *Observation and Assessment*

In addition to other facilities for assessment which may be carried out in a variety of ways, the residential accommodation provided by a local authority must include separate accommodation for the temporary reception of children, with the necessary facilities for observation and assessment. It is not necessary for each authority to set up its own reception home so long as they have an arrangement for the use of premises provided by another authority. In some authorities reception accommodation may be part of an existing children's home or one of a group of cottage homes, but the larger authorities normally have a home set aside for this particular purpose known as a "reception centre". To this home children are normally admitted when they first come into care for a long period, for instance, having been committed by the juvenile courts. Sometimes children are admitted as a family during a short-stay emergency but this use is becoming less frequent and there is more need for the reception of long-stay children. Although as a home this is subject to the regulations, it is run in rather a different way, with more generous staffing, because of the particular demands of the work, and in some authorities the home includes a school with teachers experienced in remedial work with backward children. The main object of the reception centre is, however, to observe children; to collect from social workers and others information about them and their family backgrounds. After a period of observation, lasting for some weeks, the staff report on each child, normally to a Case Conference which meets periodically, and by that time it is usually established that a particular form of care is necessary for each child. This may, of course, take the form of boarding-out, return to parents or transfer to a community home or, occasionally, to a voluntary society home which is not a community home.

As well as the former local authority observation homes, a number of former remand homes and approved schools have been designated under regional plans as community homes for the specialist work of observation and assessment, so that there is now a wider range of facilities, including the non-residential types of assessment referred to elsewhere.

RESIDENTIAL CARE — COMMUNITY HOMES WITH EDUCATION ON THE PREMISES

The former approved schools provided by bodies *other than local authorities* are now included in regional plans, and are community homes, subject to the regulations, though they are usually referred to as having "education on the premises", to distinguish them from the more numerous small homes from which children normally go out to near-by schools. These are called either controlled community homes or assisted community homes, depending on the number of managers appointed by a named local authority, and whether or not its nominees are in a majority. Here again, the managers are only concerned with administration, control of care and discipline being vested in the person appointed to be in charge. The regulations otherwise apply in just the same way as to any other community home.

Although courts have no power to commit a child or young person to any particular place, but only to the care of the local authority, there is a marked tendency for local authorities to place in these homes those young persons who have been committed following an offence, and they are thus carrying out broadly the same function as they did when they were approved schools. This type of community home expects admission to be arranged as a result of a recommendation from the more sophisticated kind of assessment centre or unit, so that in fact the present practice differs little from the old, the route being court—assessment in special unit—recommendation—consideration—acceptance or rejection. In addition, there is quite rightly a growing expectation that young persons will have some choice of placing in order to avoid the idea of a sentence to some kind of penal establishment. For these reasons, local authorities do not in fact have ready access without question to all the facilities set up under the regional plan, as seemed to be the original intention.

The big difference between the old system and the new is that, once admitted, the young person is clearly in the care of the local authority to which he was committed, and not in any way under the control of the managers of the community home. The person in charge of the home is responsible for the day-to-day care, but the long-term planning in the case is the province of the authority. This includes such matters as home leave, parental contact, suspension of privileges, dealing with absconding, review of progress, and the form of care to be used after discharge from the home.

As a consequence of this, there is great concern about numbers of young people who are recommended for placement in a community home with education on the premises, but who for one reason or another are not accepted. As they are still in care and the local authority has clear responsibilities towards them, they are sometimes placed in their own homes, though this is not considered appropriate, or they may be placed in a smaller community home, even one of the very small family group homes, which may well be inadequately staffed, and in any case has no really effective way of providing "control".

RESIDENTIAL CARE — SECURE ACCOMMODATION

With the approval of the Secretary of State, a "responsible body" may provide secure accommodation within a community home, usually in a home with education on the premises. The regulations carefully prescribe the conditions for its use by the person in charge, and the time limits which apply. When a community home has no secure accommodation of its own, application may be made for a young person to be admitted to secure accommodation elsewhere, but there are various safeguards against the wrong use of this type of treatment.[46]

All community homes may be used as places of safety, for the reception of children moved in emergency by the police, for those on remand or committed under interim orders. Community homes provided by a local authority, or controlled community homes, but not assisted community homes may also be required by the Secretary of State to detain a young offender convicted on indictment of a grave crime. Such a person would not in this way enter the care of a local authority, and the expenses of his maintenance would be recoverable from the Secretary of State.

RESIDENTIAL CARE — HOMES PROVIDED UNDER S. 64

This section empowers the Secretary of State to provide, equip and maintain homes for children in the care of local authorities who need facilities and services which are considered to be unlikely to be available in community homes. A local authority may apply for the admission of a child in its care on terms to be determined by the Secretary of State. A very detailed history will be required.

Such homes will also be available for the accommodation of young persons convicted of grave crimes and sentenced to detention during Her Majesty's pleasure, or sentenced to detention for a specified period. Such a sentence is not to imprisonment, but is intended to provide suitable education and training. Sentencing to detention however need not always be the decision of the court, as there will be power to make a care order if this appears appropriate. Section 64 will however provide the local authority with an alternative method of accommodation in such cases, or other cases, if this seems necessary.

RESIDENTIAL CARE — VOLUNTARY HOMES, ETC.

Many voluntary homes, including some which were formerly voluntary approved schools, came into the regional plan for community homes, either as controlled, or as assisted homes. They are under no obligation to do so however, and notwithstanding the community home system, may continue as voluntary homes under the Children Act 1948.

Voluntary homes are those provided by such societies as the Church of England Children's Society, the National Children's Home, Dr. Barnardo's, the Catholic Rescue Society, etc. Except for those which are community homes, they are subject to the 1951 Regulations and it is always open to an authority to decide to place a child in a voluntary home for some particular reason. This may be in order to facilitate visits by parents or to provide some special form of education or training available at a particular voluntary home.

Where a child in the care of a local authority is placed in a voluntary home payment is made by the authority for his maintenance and it is the authority, and not the voluntary society, which is responsible for visiting him and for all decisions affecting his welfare and future treatment.[46]

In addition to community homes, authorities may of course accommodate children in care in other establishments within the control of the Director of Social Services, such as hostels for the mentally sub-normal, or in other accommodation such as schools for handicapped pupils, or in hospitals, or in any other accommodation which seems appropriate to the child's needs.

Children in care may also be placed in residential employment or in bed and breakfast accommodation, or in lodgings, or may provide for themselves, for instance by joining one of the Services.

OTHER ACCOMMODATION — IN OWN HOME

Section 49 contains an important provision by which any child in care may be allowed to be in the charge and control of a parent guardian relative or friend. This is to apply to children subject to care orders (interim or full orders) subject to s. 2 resolutions passed by the authority, or remanded to care. It does not apply however to a child detained on an interim order if he has applied to the High Court for release and has been refused, unless the High Court consents and makes any directions which it thinks fit. This provision is intended to enable a department to make a deliberate decision to use its parental powers to allow a child to live with his parents or other relatives for a fixed period or indefinitely, while still remaining in care. It was not intended primarily to be used simply because there is no other accommodation available, either for remand or other purposes.

ACCOMMODATION GENERALLY — LIMITATIONS ON THE EXERCISE OF POWERS BY A LOCAL AUTHORITY

The High Court may commit to a local authority the care of a child who is a ward of the court, or a child whose parents are before the court in guardianship or divorce proceedings.

In such cases, the child is to be treated as being in the care of the authority, but *not* under a care order.

The authority must exercise its powers with regard to the accommodation and welfare of the child subject to any directions given by the court.

COMMITTAL TO BORSTAL

When a person aged 15 or over who is committed to the care of a local authority *and* is detained in a community home, the authority may bring him before a court, with the consent of the Secretary of State, in order to apply for his removal to a borstal institution. This step is only to be taken as a last resort, and the court has to be satisfied that his presence in a community home is detrimental to the other persons accommodated there with him, because of his "behaviour".

If the court makes an order for removal under this section, the care order ceases to have effect.

Before making such an order the court may make an order for detention in a remand centre, but not a prison, for a period of up to twenty-one days, which may be extended from time to time but not so as to exceed eight weeks in all. If there is no remand centre available, the court may only adjourn the case, and care will continue. The period of detention in a borstal institution if ordered may not run beyond the date on which the original care order would have expired, *i.e.*, at the age of 18, or 19, according to the person's age at the time when the care order was made.

There is provision for appeal against a removal order, and for legal aid to be provided.

THE APPLICATION OF "CARE"

The provision of accommodation and maintenance (physical care), though important, is only a part of the local authority's duty; in behaving towards the children in care as a good parent would, it has a duty to ensure the mental, emotional and spiritual well-being of each child. An authority, however, is a corporate body, not a person, so that its functions as a parent must be carried out by *people*—that is, by its social workers in residential establishments or "in the field".

The Curtis Report[47] envisaged a child care organisation in which each child would ideally have one person to whom he could look for continuous care. This person would receive the child into care, keep in touch with him wherever he might be, advise and befriend him, and finally see him safely out of care at the age of 18 or, if he could return home, as soon as this became possible. In the event such a system has not generally been practicable because of changes of staff, travelling difficulties, especially in county areas, and other circumstances.

The whole concept of child care work has changed since 1948 and the emphasis is now towards preventing the admission of children to care at all. None the less, for those children who are likely to remain in care for a considerable period the ideal of continuity should be preserved so that each child may know who is responsible for planning his life in care for him, and with him and his parents. The whole process of care, wherever he may be living while in care, should be seen by the child and his family as *one*. Though social workers may come and go their written records will remain to take the place of their accumulated knowledge, memory and forethought.

It is essential for every child in care to know that "somebody cares". This is the essence of the Charter of Rights for children in care which was mentioned earlier in this chapter.

METHOD OF TREATMENT OF CHILDREN AND YOUNG PERSONS IN NEED OF CONTROL

The White Paper *Children in Trouble* on which the Act of 1969 is based suggested in para. 6 that delinquent behaviour may frequently be "not more than an incident in the pattern of a child's normal development. But sometimes it is . . . a symptom of a deviant damaged or abnormal personality". Later, the same paragraph speaks of a variety of facilities for "long-term care, treatment and control, including some which are highly specialised". Again in para. 20, it states that "effectiveness (of the measures taken) means helping children . . . in some cases it also means firm control of anti-social behaviour", and again mentions the need for a variety of facilities. Yet again, para. 49 states that "firm and consistent discipline is a normal and necessary part of a child's upbringing. Children may require control as well as help . . . and society may have to provide this control for its own protection and for the sake of the child, where the parents are unable to do so". These passages from the White Paper have perhaps received less attention than those which advance the more generalised aims of dealing with young persons who commit offences by the same methods as are applied to those who are in need of care.

But the Act itself seems to recognise that there are differences, and in the first instance states that "care" includes protection and guidance and "control" includes discipline (s. 70(1)). Section 5, if and when it becomes operative, provides that in certain circumstances prosecution for an offence will be authorised, notwithstanding care considerations. Sections 22 (5) and 23 (2) and (3) envisage a situation when, even before a final order has been made, a young person is "of so unruly a character that he cannot be safely committed to the care of a local authority" and may be sent to a remand centre if one is available.

Section 24 empowers a local authority acting under a care order to restrict the liberty of the person committed to its care, and s. 27 (2) authorises the authority to exercise its general powers in a way which may not be consistent with its general duty, if this is necessary for the protection of the public. Section 27 (3) enables the Secretary of State to direct a local authority with regard to the exercise of its powers if he considers this necessary for the protection of the public. Finally, s. 31 deals with the procedure for bringing about the removal of a person aged 15 from a community home to borstal, but only with the consent of the Secretary of State and an order of a juvenile court.

These sections of the Act imply that there are some young people for whom "control" including discipline is almost the overriding consideration, even though the principles of care should of course also apply to them. The great majority of such young people will have been committed to care following the committing of an offence, and will probably be known as persistent delinquents. They form a comparatively small proportion of all children in care, but a much higher proportion of those in long-term care. They will almost invariably be placed at some stage in a community home (with education on the premises) in very much the same way as their predecessors were sent to the former approved schools. They present a powerful challenge to the "responsible body" which may also be required to detain in a community home young offenders convicted on indictment of certain grave crimes, though not being in the care of a local authority.

This is the difficulty which gives rise to the demand for secure accommodation,[48] and to other problems associated with the use of community homes within the regional plan. It may possibly spring from serious misconceptions of the very nature of delinquency (meaning persistent and repeated law-breaking) and of the young persons concerned. Although deviant, are they necessarily damaged or abnormal personalities, as suggested in the White Paper? Or are they delinquent because offending has become habitual, and after a time provides an acceptable status? These questions are discussed in

"Delinquency: the problem for treatment"[49] which merits close study.

There has also been a suggestion (at a conference organised by the Institute for the Study and Treatment of Delinquency) that there may be a case for the addition of a security provision to a care order. This would have the purpose of providing for boys aged 13 and over intensive therapy within perimeter security. Remission of detention would be possible.[50]

From another angle, the closure of all juvenile institutions in Massachusetts in 1972 offers an interesting commentary. It is reported that all the boys in the juvenile institutions were placed either in foster homes or small residential units within their own local community, where treatment on the lines of "intermediate treatment" was applied. The essential element was that no child was sent away, but was placed within his own locality. It was then found that for the whole State, there was a need for *one* small secure unit for those young people who were disturbed, dangerous or a social threat.[51]

There is of course a great deal of writing on the whole question of residential care or treatment for children and young persons,[52] but in the wider context of residential care as a whole, there are problems of communication and of management which are of the utmost importance to social workers, and departments. Some of the issues are dealt with in *Social Work Today* for 17 April 1975, summarised in the phrase "residential care is not a package deal".

VISITORS

Unfortunately there are still some children in care who either have no parents or guardian or have little contact with them. In such cases the local authority will usually endeavour to ensure that the child has the benefit of a foster home, or that if he is in residential care he has contact with both children and adults in the world outside. Contact with other children will be provided in most cases at school and in leisure activities; contact with adults will often be provided by relatives, or by relatives of the residential staff, or by "unofficial aunts and uncles" who are encouraged to take a continuing interest in a particular child.

The Act envisages however a situation in which a child over the age of 5, *who is the subject of a care order*, is accommodated in a community home or other establishment such as a school or hospital where he may spend practically all his time and have little contact with anyone outside.

Section 24 of the Act requires a local authority to appoint a visitor for such a person if:

a The child has not been allowed to leave the home or other establishment during the previous three months for the purpose of attending school or work.

b The authority considers that contact between the child and his parents or guardian is so infrequent as to call for this step to be taken. The appointment of a visitor will be called for if the child has not lived with, visited or been visited by either parent or guardian for a period of twelve months.

The visitor appointed must be independent of the local authority, must be a voluntary worker, whose expenses may be claimed from the local authority, and has the duty of visiting advising and befriending the child concerned, in the same way as would be expected of his parents.

In addition, the visitor has the legal right to apply to the court on behalf of the child for the care order to be revoked.

NOTES

1. Children Act 1948, s. 1(3).
2. *Children Who Wait*, A.B.A.A., 1973.
3. For a suggested form of notification, see J.P. Vol. 136, p. 75.
4. Children Act 1948, s. 3(7).
5. *Ibid.*, ss. 17 and 9.
6. Adoption Act 1958, s. 4(3).
7. See previous chapter.
8. Children Act 1948, s. 12, as amended by the Children Act 1975, s. 59.
9. Local Authorities and Local Education Authorities (Allocation of Functions) Regulations 1951.
10. Children Act 1948, s. 13, as amended.
11. Boarding-Out of Children Regulations 1955.
12. Regulation 1
13. *Ibid.*, 2.
14. *Ibid.*, 17.
15. *Ibid.*, 6.
16. *Ibid.*, 7.
17. *Ibid.*, 8.
18. *Ibid.*, 20.
19. *Ibid.*, 27.
20. *Ibid.*, 21.
21. *Ibid.*, 23.
22. *Ibid.*, 9.
23. *Ibid.*, 4.
24. *Ibid.*, 5(1).
25. *Ibid.*, 22.
26. *Ibid.*, 24.
27. *Ibid.*, 25.
28. *Ibid.*, 27.
29. *Ibid.*, 28.
30. *Ibid.*, 30.
31. *Ibid.*, 1(4).
32. *Ibid.*, 13 and 14.
33. Children Act 1948, s. 13(1), as amended.
34. Boarding-Out Regulation 1(1).
35. Studies by R. Thorpe and V. George. "Mum and Mrs So and So", S.W.T. 7 February 1974, and "Foster care workers" 2 December 1971.
36. Community Homes Regulations 1972, Regulation 3.
37. Report of the Committee on the Care of Children 1946.
38. Community Homes Regulations 1972, Regulation 3.

39. *Residential Work is Part of Social Work*, C.C.E.T.S.W. No. 3.
40. Regulation 8.
41. Regulation 5.
42. Regulation 10.
43. Regulation 9.
44. Regulation 3.
45. Regulation 7.
46. Children Act 1948, s. 54(4).
47. Report on the Care of Children 1946.
48. Community Homes, Regulations 11–14.
49. Rod Ryall, *Social Work Today*, 16 May 1974.
50. J.P. 1973, p. 138.
51. *Ibid.*, p. 131.
52. Notably "Care and Treatment in a Planned Environment", D.H.S.S.

GENERAL NOTE

When security for a child in a foster home is a deliberate choice, new ways of ensuring it will be made available by the Children Act 1975 when it is fully implemented. These are commented upon briefly in Chapter 17. Another important change is likely to be the introduction of Regulations prescribing the way in which the periodical reviews of children in care are to be conducted. These will presumably stress the need to give first consideration to a child's welfare in accordance with s.59.

Chapter 12

SPECIAL PROVISIONS FOR
CHILDREN IN CARE

SUMMARY

As children may come into care at any time from early infancy to the age of 17 (exceptionally 18) and may remain in care until the age of 19, the time spent in care in some cases will be considerable. During this period the authority is responsible for all aspects of the child's upbringing and many eventualities may arise; special provision for some of these situations is made in the Children Act and other legislation.

It should be remembered that Part II of the Act applies to all children in care irrespective of the method of admission. But in committing the care of children to a local authority the High Court or divorce court may give directions to the authority as to the exercise of care in accordance with the legislation covering divorce, wardship and guardianship dealt with in Chapter 9.

SERVICES AVAILABLE TO CHILDREN

ADOPTION

A local authority has power to make, and participate in, arrangements for the adoption of children and, as we shall see in a later chapter, this includes the power to place for adoption children who are not in care.[1]

With regard to children *in care* who are boarded-out with foster parents the question of adoption by the foster parents sometimes arises. This is particularly so in the case of young babies whose mothers decide that they will be unable to provide for them, and in the occasional cases of abandoned or orphaned children who have been received into care or committed to care. There is, however, no age limit for adoption so long as the child is under 18 and has never been married; it therefore happens that children who have been boarded-out with foster parents even for a number of years may be the subjects of adoption applications. Foster parents and the local authority in such cases have to comply with the Adoption Act 1958, and the Adoption Agencies Regulations, which will be dealt with in a later chapter. There are, however, certain provisions of the Adoption Act relating to children who are already in care.

The prospective adopters do not have to obtain the consent of the local authority to notify their intention to adopt and they may, therefore, decide on this course without the authority's agreement or permission, though this is rarely the case. On receipt of the notification of intention to adopt, the child remains subject to the Boarding-out Regulations,[2] except that the authority cannot demand the return of the child under the terms of the Foster Parents' Undertaking and must instead demand his return by notice given under the Adoption Act.[3] If, at the time, the application has already been lodged with the court the notice cannot even be given unless the court consents. Subject to this, however, the foster parents may be required to return the child to the authority within a period of seven days.

Further provisions of the Act in such cases are that no contributions are payable by the parents for a period of at least twelve weeks and the child's foster parents may become eligible for family allowances.[4] It is usual though not essential, for boarding-out allowances to be stopped when notification of intention to adopt is received, so that the foster parents become fully responsible for the child's maintenance.

When an adoption order in respect of a child in care is refused by the court or the application is withdrawn, the child need not be returned to the local authority unless his return is demanded by them.

Adoption is more fully discussed in Chapter 15.

APPOINTMENT OF GUARDIAN

When a child in care has no parent and no properly-appointed guardian, or other *person* having parental rights, the High Court, a county court or juvenile court may on application appoint any person as guardian.[5] This is a useful provision when it is desired to provide a child with a guardian, for instance one of his own relatives who may be acting as a foster parent.

Where a child has no parent or guardian but a *local authority* has parental rights under the Children Act, the court may still appoint a guardian but the resolution in such cases is terminated.[6]

EDUCATION

Among the facilities and services available to children is the full range of the local authority's educational system, including special schools, technical schools, grammar schools and grants for university or other higher education. So far as higher education is concerned, the child in care is normally regarded by the Education Authority as eligible for full grant aid. The Social Services Committee has power to assist persons over 17 who were formerly in care.[7]

It sometimes happens that foster parents wish to arrange for their foster child to attend a private school but this is normally regarded as a matter of personal preference for which, if they wish, they are expected to meet the costs involved.

EMPLOYMENT

The advice of the Youth Employment Service or Careers Advisory Service is available to children in care and a member of the social work staff normally attends interviews. When a child is handicapped, for instance by mental sub-normality, he may be eligible for treatment as a disabled person and for admission to an Industrial Rehabilitation Unit. It is always open to the authority to arrange for special training not provided by the Youth Employment Service or the Ministry, for instance at a voluntary establishment such as a voluntary home. In the matter of employment it is, of course, important that any child in care should be placed in work or training suitable to his abilities and ambitions.

APPRENTICESHIP

In the past local authorities have, in some cases, been required to enter into apprenticeship agreements, acting as parent of the boy or girl concerned. This was not very satisfactory as the period of care ends at 18 and after that the authority had no lawful responsibility or power. It is now provided that where an authority enters into a guarantee under a Deed of Apprenticeship or Articles these shall be valid until they expire, irrespective of the fact that the child may no longer be in care.[8]

EMIGRATION

A local authority may arrange the emigration of a child in care subject, however, to the consent of the Secretary of State.[9] This consent will not be given unless the Secretary of State is satisfied that emigration would benefit the child, that suitable arrangements have been made for his reception in the country to which he is going and that his parents or guardian have been consulted, or cannot be consulted.

The Secretary of State may consent to emigration even if the child is too young to express an opinion, provided that the emigration is to be in company with a parent, guardian or relative or for the purpose of joining a parent, guardian, relative or friend.

It will be remembered that in this sub-section "parents" or "guardian" include all actual parents or guardians.[10]

The Secretary of State has sometimes refused consent for emigration because of the prohibition contained in s. 52 of the Adoption Act 1958, against sending a British subject under 18 out of the country with a view to adoption in law or in fact. This difficulty has been overcome in the Act of 1963 so that the Secretary of State may now give consent to emigration in any case where it would benefit the child and the other conditions of the Children Act have been fulfilled.[11]

Although children whose care has been committed to local authorities under the Matrimonial Acts or under the Family Reform Act 1969 or Guardianship Act are to be treated generally in the same way as other children in care, there is a specific exception in that the authority may *not* arrange for their emigration.[12]

TREATMENT IN MENTAL HOSPITAL

Where a child in care is mentally disordered and is compulsorily admitted to hospital he does not cease to be in the care of the local authority. If the child is in care under a care order the authority is deemed to be his nearest relative—except for husband or wife. If the authority has assumed parental rights by resolution it is deemed to be the nearest relative, except for husband or wife, or a parent whose parental rights have not been assumed by the authority.[13] The authority is to be regarded as the nearest relative for the purpose of making application for the child's admission to hospital in view of the Social Services Committee's powers under Parts II to VI of the Mental Health Act 1959.

On the admission of a mentally disordered child in care to any hospital, if the authority has parental rights it must arrange for him to be visited and must take such other steps in relation to him as would be expected to be taken by his parents.[14] See also note under "VISITORS" in Chapter 11.

CRIMINAL PROCEEDINGS

Children in care, like other children, may commit offences. Normally the police will consult the authority as to whether proceedings should be taken and in some cases it is decided that a caution should be administered or that the authority should make different arrangements for care. The police may decide, however, to take proceedings, in which case the local authority and probation officer will be notified in the usual way.[15] Although probation officers normally undertake home surroundings enquiries it is the usual practice for them to leave this to the local authority which has the child in care and which is in a better position to make a report to the court. It may sometimes be desirable for the probation officer to make a completely independent report. There is great need for liaison with the probation service in such cases.

A child in care is liable to the same treatment by the juvenile court as any other child and may, therefore, be given an absolute or conditional discharge, be fined, remanded, sent to an attendance centre or detention centre (if a boy aged 14 or more), be placed under supervision, be committed to care, or if over 15 be sent to Borstal under certain circumstances. If he is in care under a previous care order, however, there is no point in the making of a second such order.

COMPENSATION

There are, however, cases in which a young person may have absconded, and during his absence have committed serious offences, with which he may be charged. If he is found guilty, the question of a fine or compensation may arise. Under s. 55 of the Children and Young Persons Act 1933, the court may order that the payments should be made by the parent (if he has conduced to the commission of the offence by neglect or otherwise); if the young person is in the care of a local authority by virtue of a care order, or if a s. 2 resolution is in force in respect of him, then the local authority has parental rights and *duties*, and may be liable to make payments in the same way as a parent.

There have been several cases on this point. Some authorities have already had payment orders made against them for quite large sums (£400 is the limit in criminal proceedings), but the question of "neglect of duty" is a wide one, in view of certain features which do not apply to a local authority in quite the same way as to a parent. The position was most recently set out in the judgement given by Lord Widgery, C.J., in *Somerset County Council* v. *Kingscott* 1975.[16]

This does not appear to mean however that there may not be cases in which the local authority would be liable. For this reason it has been laid down that in cases of this kind, it is not enough for a social worker to attend the court. It is essential that the local authority should be legally represented, as an order for payment of fine or compensation is a legal, rather than a social, matter.

When a supervision order is made naming a probation officer, it is necessary for there to be some working arrangement between the authority and the probation officer whereby he can exercise supervision without unnecessary duplication of visiting.

(It may be mentioned here that if a child is already subject to a probation or supervision order when admitted to care, the order remains in force but, in view of the changed circumstances, the court may be recommended by the probation officer to revoke it.)[17]

ILLNESS, ACCIDENT AND DEATH

When a child in care dies the local authority may arrange for his burial or cremation, provided that cremation is not contrary to the child's religious persuasion.[18] The authority may in such cases claim a death grant and may recover from the parent of a child under 16 the balance of expenses incurred. The authority must be notified of the death of any child living in one of its homes and of the circumstances. It is usual for the authority to notify the Secretary of State of the death of other children in care, for instance boarded-out, though this was not required by the regulations but by Home Office Circular 28/1964. Parents and guardians must also be informed if a child in a home has an accident, or a serious illness, or dies. This practice, though not obligatory, is also followed as regards children in care and accommodated elsewhere.

CONTACT WITH PARENTS

Much has been said about the need for preserving the link between a child and his parents and the authority has power to meet the expenses of parents in travelling to see their children or in attending the funeral of a child in care. This power may also be used with regard to other persons, for instance relatives, but is always subject to the proviso that assistance should only be given when the visit would be otherwise impossible without causing undue hardship.[19]

There is no specific power to pay the expenses of a child visiting parents, relatives or friends but these can now be provided under the general powers contained in the 1963 Act, if the visit will promote his welfare by diminishing the need for him to remain in care.[20]

MARRIAGE

It sometimes happens that a child in care, usually a girl, wishes to marry while under the age of 18. The law relating to the marriage of minors is contained in the Marriage Act of 1949. The main points are:

a That a marriage solemnized between two persons either of whom is under 16 is void.

b An infant aged between 16 and 18 requires consent in order to marry. The consents required are set out in the second schedule to the Act, which is as follows:

"I. WHERE THE MINOR IS LEGITIMATE

Circumstances	*Person or Persons whose consent is required*
1. Where both parents are living:	
a if parents are living together;	Both parents.
b if parents are divorced or separated by order of any court or by agreement;	The parent to whom the custody of the minor is committed by order of the court or by the agreement, or, if the custody of the minor is so committed to one parent during part of the year and to the other parent during the rest of the year, both parents.
c if one parent has been deserted by the other;	The parent who has been deserted.
d if both parents have been deprived of custody of minor by order of any court.	The person to whose custody the minor is committed by order of the court.
2. Where one parent is dead:	
a if there is no other guardian;	The surviving parent.
b if a guardian has been appointed by the deceased parent.	The surviving parent and the guardian if acting jointly, or the surviving parent or the guardian if the parent or guardian is the sole guardian of the minor.
3. Where both parents are dead.	The guardians or guardian appointed by the deceased parents or by the court under section four of The Guardianship of Minors Act 1971, s. 3 or 5.

II. WHERE THE MINOR IS ILLEGITIMATE

Circumstances	*Person whose consent is required*
If the mother of the minor is alive.	The mother, or if she has by order of any court been deprived of the custody of the minor, the person to whom the custody of the minor has been committed by order of the court.
If the mother of the minor is dead.	The guardian appointed by the mother."

c Where a local authority has parental rights by a Resolution its consent should be obtained additionally, but we have already seen in an earlier chapter that the consent of the authority should normally only be given after consultation with any parent who is available to give consent.

d If any required parental consent cannot be obtained because of the parent's absence, inaccessability or disability the Registrar General may dispense with consents altogether or, alternatively, an application may be made to a court for consent, which then has the same effect as the consent of a parent.

Finally, it should be noted that if the child in care is a Ward of a High Court the consent of the High Court must also be obtained.

The fact that a boy or girl in care marries does not appear to invalidate any care order or resolution assuming parental rights.

PARENTHOOD

Young people in care sometimes become parents and in this event the child concerned has to be dealt with as a separate individual and, for instance, the question of need for his admission to care has to be considered separately, the young person in care already being regarded for all purposes as the parent.

BEHAVIOUR DIFFICULTIES

We have already dealt with the question of children in care who commit offences and may appear before the juvenile court. There are, however, a number of behaviour difficulties which may not result in criminal acts but which require serious consideration by the local authority.

Children in residential care particularly may show the effects of their deprivation by aggression or by such symptoms as pilfering, lying, dirty habits, inability to form relationships, wandering or absconding. As we have seen, it is essential that the staff of children's homes should be able to understand these difficulties and to relate them to the child's previous history.

With regard to children in foster homes or lodgings; there may be similar problems but here it is the duty of the social worker to interpret the behaviour problem to the foster parents and to endeavour to obtain their understanding and co-operation. If this cannot be done there is likely to be a breakdown of the placing and when this seems to be inevitable and the child is in a foster home it is necessary for the child to be removed under the Boarding-out Regulations.[21]

A similar difficulty may arise in the case of children who are in care but living with their parents by permission of the local authority.

Any behaviour problems manifested by children in residential care or elsewhere require investigation and serious consideration of the suitability of the placing. If the difficulties are serious and persistent they call for a review of the child's whole history and for reconsideration of his relationship with his family and home. In situations of this kind it is usually helpful to refer the problem to the Child Guidance Service for assessment and to follow any recommendations which may be made. To deal with the immediate problem, however, it will often be necessary to move the child from his foster home or children's home for a period of observation and assessment, which may be provided by the authority in the most suitable way, either residentially or on a daily basis.[22] The authority will of course be able to apply for admission to any home of any kind provided under the Act which is considered suitable as a result of the assessment (see Chapter 6).

The final sanction is for an application to be made by the local authority to a juvenile court for a care order if this is essential for ensuring control. Such an application could also be made by the police (in cases of an offence), the local education authority (in cases of non-attendance at school) or the N.S.P.C.C. in other cases, but there would first be consultation with the care authority, and the care or control test would have to be satisfied, except of course in the case of a charge for an offence.

If however a care order is already in force, and the local authority cannot otherwise provide for the accommodation of the child concerned, it could consider applying to the Secretary of State for the child's admission to a special home under s. 64, or for permission to bring him before a court with a view to his removal to borstal, if he is already in a community home. (See Chapter 11.)

ABSENTEES

CHILDREN IN CARE BUT IN CHARGE OF PARENTS

Under s. 13(2), of the Children Act 1948, as amended, as we have seen, a local authority may allow a child in care who is subject to a resolution to be in the charge and control of a parent, guardian, relative or friend, either for a fixed period or indefinitely.

A position may arise in which the authority considers that the child should be returned at the end of the fixed period, or, if there was no fixed period, at once. In this event the authority must serve a notice in writing requiring the person who has the charge of the child to return him at a specified time. Anyone harbouring or concealing the child after that time, or preventing him from returning as required is liable on summary conviction to a fine of up to £100 or imprisonment for two months or both.

There is a greater penalty for any person taking such child out of the care of the authority, assisting him or inducing him to run away, or harbouring or concealing him after he has run away.[23]

So far as children in the care of a local authority under a care order are concerned, if they are for the time being in charge of a parent, guardian, relative or friend, they may be required by the authority to return to live at premises specified by the authority, and if they fail to do so would be dealt with as "absentees" under

s. 32 of the 1969 Act. This is a general section dealing with absentees from any place where they are required to live for the time being, and applies to persons subject to care orders, interim orders, remand warrants or to arrangements made by the police and the local authority under s. 29(3) in respect of a person who has been arrested but not released. The section also relates to children in places of safety whether detained in a community home or elsewhere.

If it is believed that a specified person is able to produce an absentee, a magistrates' court may issue a summons requiring this to be done. Failure to comply with the requirement is an offence carrying a penalty of a fine of £100.[24]

Any person knowingly compelling, persuading, inciting or assisting a child to become or remain an absentee will be guilty of an offence carrying a penalty of a fine of £100 or up to six months' imprisonment, or both.

As absentees may well abscond from England and Wales into other parts of the United Kingdom, there are provisions for their recovery. These are referred to in paras 242–246 of the "Guide".[25]

FAMILY ALLOWANCES

It may be noted that during such time as a child is allowed to reside with his parents he may *lawfully* be included in the family for the purpose of obtaining family allowances.[26]

TRANSFERS WITHIN THE UNITED KINGDOM

By s. 25 arrangements may be made for a person subject to a Care Order (made in England or Wales) to be transferred to Northern Ireland if his parents or guardian go to live there. There are reciprocal arrangements in respect of persons subject to similar Orders made in Northern Ireland.

Transfers to and from Scotland are provided for in the Social Work (Scotland) Act 1968—see Home Office Circular 78/71.

Section 26 deals with persons subject to "relevant orders" made in the Isle of Man or the Channel Islands, and admitted to accommodation (*e.g.* a community home) in England or Wales. Such a person may be deemed to be subject to an order committing him to the care of the local authority in whose area he is accommodated for the time being. Such cases are not subject to the statutory review.

NOTES

1. Adoption Act 1958, s. 1.
2. *Ibid.*, s. 36(2).
3. *Ibid.*, s. 35.
4. *Ibid.*, s. 36(2).
5. Guardianship of Minors Act 1971, s. 5 (such a guardian is not only the guardian of the person, but also of the estate, *i.e.* property).

6. *Ibid.*
7. Children Act, s. 20, Children and Young Person's Act 1963, s. 46, and Table, Chapter 13.
8. Children and Young Persons Act 1963, s. 47.
9. Children Act 1948, s. 17.
10. *Ibid.*, s. 9.
11. Children and Young Persons Act 1963, s. 55.
12. Matrimonial Causes Act 1973, s. 43; Matrimonial Proceedings (Magistrates' Courts) Act 1960, s. 3(2); Family Reform Act 1969, s. 7; Guardianship Act 1973, s. 4.
13. Mental Health Act 1959, ss. 10 and 50.
14. *Ibid.*, s. 10.
15. Children and Young Persons Act 1969, ss. 9 and 34(3).
16. [1975] All E.R. 326.
17. Children Act, s. 6(1).
18. Children Act 1948, s. 18, Community Homes Regulations 1972, Regulation 6.
19. Children Act 1948, s. 22.
20. Children and Young Persons Act 1963, s. 1.
21. Boarding-Out Regulations, Regulation 4.
22. See Chapter 6.
23. Children and Young Persons Act 1963, s.49 and Children Act 1948, s. 3(8).
24. Children and Young Persons Act 1969, s. 32, and Children Act 1975, s.68.
25. *Ibid.*
26. Family Allowances Act 1965, s. 11.

GENERAL NOTE

The Children Act 1975 will in due course provide additional provisions for children in care, notably the possibility of custodianship, and a greater prospect of adoption if that is considered to be the right way to promote and safeguard welfare. These changes are commented upon briefly in Chapter 17.

Chapter 13

PROVISIONS FOR DISCHARGE
AND AFTER CARE

SUMMARY

DISCHARGE

As there are various ways of coming into care so there are various ways of being discharged from it. These are as follows:

1. ATTAINMENT OF THE AGE OF EIGHTEEN

At this age care under s. 1 of the Children Act 1948, expires, as does care under either of the Matrimonial Acts, the Family Law Reform Act 1969, and the Guardianship Act 1973.[1]

Resolutions in respect of children in care under s. 1 also cease to have effect. Care orders made under the Children and Young Persons Act 1969, expire at the age of 18, unless previously revoked or extended to the age of 19 by a court. (A care order made after the age of 16 is in force until the 19th birthday unless previously revoked.)[2]

2. CARE ASSUMED BY PARENT, GUARDIAN, RELATIVE OR FRIEND

So far as a parent or guardian is concerned, there is a *right* to take over the care of a child who is in care under s. 1 and in respect of whom no resolution has been passed,[3] provided that the parent seeking to take over the care of the child has not been deprived of custody by a court. This is not an absolute right, however. The authority cannot keep the child in care, but has no absolute duty to return a child from foster parents to the care of a parent (*Krishnan* v. *London Borough of Sutton* (1970).) In some cases arising from such circumstances an application has been made for the child to be made a ward of court but this is a step which should only be taken on legal advice in view of decisions already made by the Court of Appeal in *Re(T), an infant,* (1970) and in other cases where the Family Division of the High Court has been asked to use its wardship powers for the protection of children. Though the court will not usually interfere with the exercise of statutory powers by a local authority, it might in an exceptional situation make the child a ward of court as an extra protection for a child already in care. It has been held that a child in care may be made and remain a ward of court. In rare cases of great complexity, it is open to the local authority to seek the guidance of the Family Division.

So far as relatives or friends are concerned, they have no *right* to demand the discharge of a child from care unless, of course, they happen to be duly appointed guardians.[4]

It will be remembered that the authority has a duty to secure that the care of the child is taken over by a parent, guardian, relative or friend if this is consistent with the child's welfare. In this section the word "child" refers to anyone under the age of 18 and there may be cases of older children particularly who refuse or do not wish to be discharged from care. In such cases there will probably have been a long period of separation or estrangement affecting both the child and his parents and the situation must be dealt with having regard to their understanding of the position. and their genuine wishes. It is to be hoped that situations of this kind will arise less frequently in future, as local authorities look more closely at the possibility of assuming parental rights where this is justified and at the same time examine the desirability of involving both parents and children in the six-monthly review. Some children in long-stay foster homes will be affected by the Children Act 1975 which is discussed in Chapter 17.

3. RESCISSION OF A RESOLUTION

A resolution of a local authority assuming parental rights in respect of a child in its care may be rescinded by the authority if this action appears to be for the benefit of the child.[5]

Or, a parent or guardian in respect of whom a resolution has been passed may make a complaint to a juvenile court at any time while the resolution is in force, asking that the resolution be determined, and the court after considering the facts may determine the resolution. On the rescission or determination of a resolution, but not otherwise, the child will cease to be in the care of the authority. Legal aid is available in such applications.

Older young people in care may wish to be discharged from care without returning to a parent or guardian. The authority may discharge if this is in the interest of the welfare of the child—an all embracing term. For instance, a young person discharged from care should be able to maintain himself.

4.   REVOCATION OF A CARE ORDER

A person subject to a care order, or the local authority concerned may apply to any juvenile court in the authority's area, or in the area of the child's residence for the discharge of the order. Legal aid is available. A parent or guardian does not have a right to apply for revocation, but may do so on behalf of the child or young person. This appears to imply that the child wishes the order to be revoked, or that the parent must prove that revocation is in the interests of the child, even if he himself does not seek the revocation. He should give evidence accordingly and be represented independently of the parent. (See Chapter 17 referring to provisions in Children Act 1975.)

If satisfied as to the "care or control test", the court may discharge the care order and may, not must, make a supervision order, provided that the person concerned has not attained the age of 18.

If the order is not discharged, no further application may be made without the consent of the court during a period of three months.

If the order is an interim order, and is discharged, a supervision order may not be made. If it is not discharged no further application may be made without the consent of the juvenile court, but an appeal may be made to the High Court.[6]

5.   ADOPTION

As an adoption order vests the parental rights in the adopters, the child concerned is obviously discharged from the care of the authority and a resolution or care order in respect of him ceases to have effect.

6.   EMIGRATION

Emigration does not automatically terminate care, as if the child emigrates with the foster parents he is still in care and the Boarding-Out Regulations still have to be observed by arranging for supervision through an agency such as International Social Services (or in H.M. Forces Families, S.S.A.F.A.). There are cases, however, in which a child may emigrate with a parent, guardian or relative or for the purpose of joining a parent, guardian, relative or friend and in such cases the child would be discharged from care, as under s. 1 (3).

7. DEATH

8. REVOCATION

Revocation of a committal order made under the Matrimonial Causes Act 1973, s. 43, the Family Reform Act 1969, s. 7, or the Guardianship Act 1973, s. 2 (2) or under the Matrimonial Proceedings (Magistrates' Court) Act 1960, s. 10 (1) terminates care. The application may be made either by the local authority, by any person having the legal custody of the child, or by any person who is applying at the same time for the custody of the child.

9. LAPSE

With minor exceptions, there is no provision for care simply to lapse, except by reason of age. It should usually be brought to an end by some positive act such as a court order, or by a decision by the authority to discharge, as under s. 1 of the Children Act 1948.

10. REMOVAL TO A BORSTAL INSTITUTION

When this is ordered by a court in respect of a person aged 15 who is subject to a care order, and accommodated in a community home, the care order is discharged (see Chapter 10). In any other case of a child in care, the care order does not lapse and if it is superfluous it should be revoked by the juvenile court on application. Committal to a detention centre does not revoke a care order, and application must be made if it is thought that the care order should cease. If there is a s. 2 resolution, care will continue, as will parental rights, unless the resolution is rescinded, or set aside.

AFTER CARE

It will be clear that there are cases of children who are discharged from the care of the authority but who require supervision, advice and possibly assistance after their discharge. There are various provisions in the Acts to meet this situation:

a When a child is in care under the Children Act 1948, and is discharged from care when over compulsory school age, the authority has a duty to continue to advise and befriend him unless they are satisfied that his welfare does not require it.[7] If at the time of discharge he goes to live in the area of another authority that authority must be informed, but the decision as to whether to exercise supervision is for the authority in whose area the child resides and not for the authority which has discharged the child from care. There are no requirements or regulations as regards the extent of the supervision, except that it may continue until the age of 18, and there is no power under this section to give financial assistance. The Children Act contains no provision for the after-care of children who are discharged while of compulsory school age, or below school age, but supervision may now be exercised, with the consent of the parents, under the general powers of the 1963 Act, s. 1.

b When children are in care under a care order this remains in force, as we have seen, until the age of 18 or 19 unless before that time it is revoked by a juvenile court.[8] In such cases a supervision order *may* be made for a period of not more than three years. It is important to note, however, that no supervision order in care proceedings is now to have effect over the age of 18. Supervision orders are dealt with in Chapter 14.

After a care order has been revoked the local authority has no duty to exercise after-care supervision unless named in the supervision order and has no power under the supervision order to give financial assistance, except to meet the cost of any facilities which may be provided under the order.[8]

c In certain circumstances the authority has power to give financial assistance by supplementing the earnings of young people under the age of 21 who have been in care at any time since ceasing to be of compulsory school age, and are aged 17 years or more. Moreover, the financial assistance may be continued after the age of 21 for the purpose of enabling a boy or girl to complete a course of education or training already entered upon.[9]

The giving of financial assistance is not to be confused with care and is quite independent of any duty to advise, supervise or befriend. Such financial assistance may now be available to both the more successful young people, such as apprentices or students in training college or universities, and to the less successful who after the age of 17 pass out of care into borstal, prison, mental hospitals, etc., but in such cases financial aid is only to be given in exceptional circumstances.

The Children and Young Persons Act 1963 considerably amended and expanded the powers and duties of a local authority with regard to children formerly in care. The Act of 1969 in effect makes the local authority the sole substitute parent for all the purposes of the Act. In this way it provides a continuing responsibility for care up to the age of 18, or in some cases 19, thus making the former "approved school after-care" unnecessary.

The Table on page 180 sets out the functions of local authorities in regard to persons formerly in care whether under care orders or otherwise.

It will be noted that these functions may now be exercised by any local authority, not only by the authority in whose care the person has been.

NOTES

1. Children Act 1948, ss. 1 and 4(1); Matrimonial Causes Act 1973, s. 43; Matrimonial Proceedings (Magistrates Courts) Act 1960, s. 3(4); Family Law Reform Act 1969, s. 7; Guardianship Act 1973, s. 4(1).

2. Children and Young Persons Act 1969, ss. 20 and 21.
3. Children Act 1948, s. 1(3) and s. 6.
4. See Chapter 10.
5. Children Act 1948, s. 4.
6. Children and Young Persons Act 1969, ss. 21 and 22(4).
7. Children Act 1948, s. 34.
8. Children and Young Persons Act 1969, ss. 18(4) and 19(6).
9. Children Act 1948, s. 20, Children and Young Persons Act 1963, ss. 46 and 58.

GENERAL NOTE

The Children Act 1975 will in due course affect the contents of this chapter,' first by the provision to a local authority to require notice of removal of a child from s.1 care, and secondly by limiting the power of a parent to act on behalf on a child in applications for discharge of a care order (see Chapter 17).

FUNCTIONS OF LOCAL AUTHORITIES IN REGARD TO PERSONS FORMERLY IN CARE

Qualifying conditions	Relevant enactment	Function exercisable by	Nature of power or duty to befriend, etc.	Nature of power to give financial assistance	Function exercisable while person concerned is
That the person concerned ceased to be in care when over compulsory school age	Children Act 1948, s. 34	Local authority in whose area the person is	Duty to advise and befriend him unless his welfare does not require it	—	Under the age of 18
	Children Act 1948, s. 20(1)	Any local authority		Power to make contributions to cost of accommodation and maintenance near place where employed, seeking employment or receiving education or training	Aged 17 and under 21
That the person concerned ceased to be in care when aged 17 or on attaining the age of 18	Children Act 1948, s. 20(2)	Any local authority	—	Power to make grants towards expenses of receiving suitable education or training	
	Children and Young Persons Act 1963, s. 58	Any local authority	Power to cause him to be visited, advised and befriended, at his own request	Power in exceptional circumstances to cause him to be given financial assistance	

Notes:
1. This table is only a guide to the statutory provisions and does not reproduce their exact wording.
2. The same person may fulfil more than one of the conditions mentioned in the first column of the table.
3. Section 34 of the Children Act 1948, applies only to children who have been in care under s. 1 of that Act. The other enactments mentioned in the second column of the table apply also to persons who have been in care under orders or matrimonial orders or orders under the Family Law Reform Act 1969.
4. The powers conferred by sub-ss. (1) and (2) of s. 20 of the Children Act 1948, are exercisable in regard to a person aged 21 or over in the circumstances mentioned in sub-s. (3).
5. Where a local authority has acted as guarantor under a deed of apprenticeship or articles of clerkship entered into by a child in their care, they may assume the same obligation under any supplemental deed or articles even if he is no longer in their care. (Children and Young Persons Act 1963, s. 47.)

Chapter 14

OTHER SERVICES

SUMMARY

1. SUPERVISION

The elements of prevention-protection and care are compounded in that most important duty of the Social Service Department—supervision.

As we have seen, "voluntary" supervision may be offered to families and children in their own homes, and supervision with statutory authority may be exercised in respect of children living in privately arranged foster homes, local authority foster homes, prospective adoptive homes, or in residential care.

SUPERVISION IN MATRIMONIAL, WARDSHIP AND GUARDIANSHIP CASES

Another type of supervision is that exercised under the authority of court orders.

There are some cases in which children are already being supervised under orders made in divorce or matrimonial proceedings; to these may be added those wards of court who may now be placed under supervision under the Family Law Reform Act 1969 and those supervised under the Guardianship Act 1973. In all such cases, the court has had power to make an order for the custody of a child, but has considered that there are exceptional circumstances which make it desirable that the child should be under the supervision of an independent person. A supervision order has therefore been made nominating either a probation officer, or a local authority to undertake the supervision of the child; the court making the order retains the power to vary or discharge it. Such orders will continue to be made probably more frequently, in the future. They are not to be confused with the supervision orders which can be made under the Children and Young Persons Act 1969, in either care or criminal proceedings brought under its provisions. The main differences are set out in question and answer form in the following pp. 183–193.

SUPERVISION ORDERS UNDER THE 1969 ACT

Such supervision orders succeed the former type of supervision order which was made by juvenile courts in care protection or control proceedings under the 1963 Act, or following the revocation of a Fit Person Order; they also succeed the former probation order in respect of a person under the age of 17, and may therefore be made by a juvenile court, or by a crown court.

These supervision orders are dealt with extensively in the Guide to Part I of the Act, in paras 108–150. Some of these paragraphs are referred to by number in the notes which follow.

Supervision orders follow either criminal or care proceedings before a court, in the same way as care orders. When made in criminal proceedings, a supervision order is a sentence, unlike a probation order (para. 81). It does not contain a minimum period of supervision, but there is a maximum period of three years, which means that in some cases supervision may continue until the person supervised is well over the age of 18. After that age, only an adult court has power to vary or discharge the order, and may impose punishments (fine, attendance centre order) whether allowing the supervision order to continue in operation, or not. The court may order fine or imprisonment if it decides to discharge the order (142/143).

A juvenile court has power to deal with applications for variation or discharge of a supervision order while its subject is under the age of 18, and unlike the adult court may make an interim care order while considering what action to take upon the application before it. Where the person supervised is over 17, but not yet 18, the juvenile court may elect to use the powers of the adult court referred to in the last paragraph.

It may be thought that supervision orders made in criminal proceedings have much in common with the probation orders they replaced, but as will be seen, they may not include a condition of

SUPERVISION UNDER ORDERS OF COURT (ENGLAND)

CONTENTS

These notes relate only to supervision carried out under court orders.

They do *not* cover supervision under statute, such as the Adoption Act 1958, the Children Act 1958, or the Boarding-Out of Children Regulations.

Nor do they refer to:

(1) Duties to advise and befriend under s. 34 of the Children Act 1948 or other statutes.

(2) The provision of advice, guidance and assistance under the Children and Young Persons Act 1963.

(3) The supervision exercised in respect of children in the care of other local authorities.

	CHILDREN AND YOUNG PERSONS		ORDERS FOR SUPERVISION IN:			
QUESTION	Criminal Proceedings	Care Proceedings	Matrimonial Proceedings	Divorce Proceedings	Wardship Proceedings	Guardianship Proceedings
Statute	C. and Y.P. Act 1969, s. 7(7) Also under s. 21 (2) following discharge of a care order provided that, from January 1976, the "care or control" test is satisfied.	C. and Y.P. Act 1969, s. 1(3)	Matrimonial Proceedings (Magistrates' Courts) Act 1960 Supervision may be ordered as part of matrimonial order under s. 2(1) and s. 4	Matrimonial Causes Act 1973, s. 44	Family Law Reform Act 1969, s. 7(4)	Guardianship of Minors Act 1971, extended by the Guardianship Act 1973 **1**
Court	Juvenile court or crown court	Juvenile court	Magistrates' Court (Domestic Proceedings)	Family Division of High Court or County Court with Divorce jurisdiction (Matrimonial Causes Act 1967)	Family Division of High Court	High Court, County Court, Magistrates' Court (Domestic Proceedings) **2**
Rules	Magistrates' Courts (Children and Young Persons) Rules 1970		Magistrates' Courts (Matrimonial Proceedings) Rules 1960			Magistrates' Courts (Guardianship of Minors) Rules 1974 **3**
Age at which orders may be made	Under 17 at the date when proceedings are commenced, s. 1(5) provides that no person aged 16 who is or has been married may be made subject to care proceedings C. and Y.P. Act 1963 (s. 29 as amended)		Under 16 (s. 2(1) (d1))	Under 18	Under 18	Under 18 **4**
Are enquiries made prior to the order?	Yes—Under C. and Y.P. Act 1969, s. 9, by local authority, but the home surroundings part of enquiry may be made by the probation service under arrangements under s. 34(3). for children of a specified age which may not be higher than 14. It is now 13 (1974) Rule 10	Rule 20	Court may call for a report from the probation officer or from local authority. S. 4 (2). The ten days' notice is not required (r. 1)	A court may request a probation officer to make enquiries and a report with a view to helping in the making of a decision. Rule 31 of the Probation Rules requires probation officers to make such reports on request. There is a memorandum regarding consultation with local authorities in divorce proceedings		**5**

In what circumstances may the order be made?	Person has been found guilty of an offence s. 7(7) Note that unless the offence is homicide proceedings may be care proceedings, using condition (f)	Court has found that one of the conditions (a) to (f) in s. 1 is satisfied, *and* that necessary care or control is not likely to be provided unless an order is made. The order made must be for the welfare of the child or young person (C. and Y.P. Act 1933, s. 44). Note that "care" includes protection and guidance, and "control" includes discipline (C. and Y.P. Act 1969, s. 70(1)) A supervision order may also be made by the court which discharges a care order (but not an interim care order) s. 21(2). See Note 1, *ante.* In making a supervision order the court must be satisfied that the person concerned will reside in the area of a local authority (s. 18(1))	In an application by one spouse for a matrimonial order, a child of the family has been committed to the custody of a parent, or other person, and there are exceptional circumstances making independent supervision desirable. S. 2(1) (f)—See s. 16 for meaning of "child" of the family	The court has jurisdiction to make an order for custody of a child and there are exceptional circumstances making independent supervision desirable, the child having been committed to the care of a person. (Not custody)	The minor is a ward of court (not already committed by the Family Law Reform Act to the care of a local authority) and there are exceptional circumstances making independent supervision desirable	The court has made an order under the Guardianship of Minors Act 1971 (s. 9) giving the custody of a minor (under 18) to a person, but there are exceptional circumstances making independent supervision desirable. (Such an order may be made if the child is illegitimate (s. 2(6))
Can other orders be made at the same time?	No, except that in making a supervision order, the court *may* discharge any previous existing care or supervision order (s. 7(7)) (s. 1 (4)) But there is power to make a separate order for compensation in criminal or care (offence condition) proceedings. (Criminal Justice Act 1972 and C. and Y.P. Act, ss. 3 and 6(3))	No, apart from the principal order referred to above. That is to say, a supervision order cannot be made at the same time as a committal to the care of a local authority (s. 2(4) (c)) (s. 44(3)) (s. 7(3))		Orders for payment or in respect of financial arrangements may be made separately as appropriate		
Can an order for supervision be made if the child is in care?	Yes, if charged with and found guilty of an offence in respect of which a supervision order can be made. The court may at the same time discharge any existing care order, supervision order or parental recognisance s. 7(7)	Yes, if the "care or control" test is satisfied. In s. 1(2) (a) the present tense "is" may be taken as applying to the situation as it would normally be; a child may in this event be brought before a court under s. 1(1) even though in care under the Act of 1948	No—s. 2(4) (b)	Yes, unless in care as a result of an order of the court committing the child to the care of a local authority under these Acts		

CHILDREN AND YOUNG PERSONS   ORDERS FOR SUPERVISION IN:

QUESTION	Criminal Proceedings	Care Proceedings	Matrimonial Proceedings	Divorce Proceedings	Wardship Proceedings	Guardianship Proceedings
Who is to be responsible for supervision?	A probation officer appointed for the petty sessions area named in the order—if (a) the supervised person is above a certain age—now (1975) 13, and (b) the probation officer is already exercising duties in relation to another member of the household, *and* the local authority has requested him to undertake supervision under the order *or* The local authority for the area in which the supervised person resides,* or a different authority if it agrees to be named, (ss. 11, 13. A "child" in s. 13(2) is as defined in s. 34(1) (a)—at present not over 13)	No	A probation officer for the petty sessions area in which the supervised person will reside, or a* specified local authority (s. 2(1) (f) as amended by Local Government Act 1972	A welfare officer—that is to say a probation officer selected under arrangements made by the Secretary of State, or a local authority selected by the court s. 44(2)	s. 7(4)	If an order under this Act is made in a magistrates' court, a probation officer for the Petty Sessions area in which the supervised person will reside,* or the local authority for that area
Is the consent of the supervised person required as in probation orders?	No, in criminal proceedings it is a sentence, and may therefore be the subject of an appeal. *But* if the person is over 14, his consent is required to the insertion of a requirement to undergo treatment under the Mental Health Act 1959 s. 12(4). Though consent is not in general required, Rules 11 and 21 of the Magistrates' Courts (C. and Y.P. Act) Rules 1970 provide for the court to allow representations to be made unless the court considers this either undesirable or impracticable on account of age and understanding	No	No, but when the court contemplates making the order, the parties to the case (parents) must be served with a notice setting out the powers which the court may invoke. See r. 3 of Magistrates Courts (Matrimonial Proceedings) Rules 1960	No	No	No

Supervision under these Acts makes no demands upon the children who are to be supervised

* Resides means "habitually resides" (s. 7) (1). This is of special importance when a supervision order is made in respect of a child or young person already subject to supervision by another local authority—residence is not necessarily at the place where he lives for the time being.

What is the purpose of the order?

Not stated, but by implication it creates opportunity for the supervisor to establish a personal relationship with the supervised person. (Guide, para. 120). The supervisor may then bring to bear influences which while not punitive will discourage further offences

Similarly, by implication to create a personal relationship which will provide care (including protection and guidance) or control (including discipline) which is unlikely to be provided without the order

Not stated, but it is to provide independent supervision for a minor who has been involved in domestic civil proceedings

It should be remembered that the order can only have been made in exceptional circumstances

11

What are the duties of the supervisor?

To advise assist and befriend the supervised person (s. 14). This provides the basis for the personal relationship referred to in 11 above. The relationship is primarily with the person to be supervised rather than with any other persons. (Probation officers in exercising their supervisory duties are subject to the Probation Rules 1965, which specify the records to be kept, explanation of the order, frequency of visiting and other contact, enquiry as to progress at school, use of voluntary and other facilities and reports to the case committee and the court. These may serve as a guide to local authority social workers undertaking supervision under orders pending the issue of Regulations)

The Probation Rules 1965 may be applied to any person under supervision, so far as is suitable to the circumstances of the case. Application is therefore discretionary, but the Rules of course apply only to probation officers.

12

Is the supervisor named in the order

No. The order names the area of the local authority (see 9 above), and the petty sessions area in which the supervised person will reside. *
S. 18(1)

No. (See under "Who is to be responsible for supervision?" above)

13

What provision may the order contain?

Any which will help the supervisor to assist, advise and befriend, including any prescribed under the Justices of the Peace Act 1949, s. 15. These are optional but may require the supervised person to inform the supervisor of any change of address or employment, and/or to keep in touch with the supervisor as instructed. Magistrates' Courts (Children and Young Persons) Rules 1970, r. 28(2).
It appears from s. 12(2) that if *these* provisions are included in the order by the court, the supervisor is not free to decide whether or not they should be complied with

* See note, *ante* on "resides"

None relating to supervision itself, but the whole order may contain other provisions relating to custody, access, maintenance and other such matters

14

CHILDREN AND YOUNG PERSONS | ORDERS FOR SUPERVISION IN:

QUESTION	Criminal Proceedings	Care Proceedings	Matrimonial Proceedings	Divorce Proceedings	Wardship Proceedings	Guardianship Proceedings
What other requirements may the order contain?	These are to be found in s. 12 1. A requirement to live with a specified *person*, who is agreeable to this, such as a relative. There is no power to make a requirement for unlimited residence at a specified *place*. This residence requirement may be overridden by the others, set out below: 2. A requirement to comply with directions of the supervisor to: (a) Live at a specified place for one period not exceeding ninety days within the first year; (b) live at specified places for specified periods not exceeding thirty days in all within each year (maximum ninety days in all); (c) present himself to a specified person when and where specified; (d) take part in activities when and where specified Requirement under (a), (b), (c) and (d) may not exceed ninety days in all during the period of supervision. No requirement under (a), (b), (c) or (d) may be included unless it is available under the regional plan approved by the Secretary of State. The supervisor may or may not give any directions under (a), (b), (c) or (d), but if he does, may give them orally or in writing (if orally, it is suggested that a note should be kept for record purposes). Costs under 2 (a), (b), (c) and (d) are to be met by the local authority (s. 18(4)). Costs under 1 (residence with a named person) may be met by the Probation Committee under r. 40, if a probation officer is the supervisor. If the court is satisfied by medical evidence that a person needs mental treatment, but not under a hospital order, the supervision order may contain a requirement that he shall undergo such treatment as is appropriate without time limit—but not beyond the 18th birthday. Such a requirement may only be made if the court is satisfied also that the treatment can be provided If the person to be supervised is over the age of 14, his consent to this requirement is necessary, s. 12 (4), (5)		—See previous page—	—As above—	

What is the duration of the order?	Not more than three years, and the period may extend beyond the 18th birthday	Not more than three years – not valid after the 18th birthday	Up to the age of 16	Up to the age of 18	If the parents are living together when the order is made, the court may direct that the order shall not be operative while they continue to live together, *or* the court may order that the supervision order shall cease to have effect if they are still living together three months after it was made, S. 3(2). Otherwise expires at age 16. (Mag. Ct.) or 18 (Higher Cts.)
	S. 17(a)	S. 17(b)	S. 3(9)		
	It is desirable that there should be a standard explanation of a supervision order for the information of the supervised person.				
Can an order be cancelled before it would otherwise expire?	Yes by a juvenile court only, if the supervised person is under 18. But if the supervised person is aged 17 but not yet 18, the juvenile court may discharge the order, *or* may decide to use the powers available to a magistrates court in dealing with the persons aged 18, s. 15(2). The above applies also when the supervision order was originally made on the discharge of a care order made in care or criminal proceedings. S. 15(2) If the supervised person is aged 18, discharge of the order can only be dealt with by a magistrates' court, s. 15 (3, 4)	If the Order was made in care proceedings, cancellations will be dealt with by a juvenile court which may, on cancelling the supervision order make a care order, s. 15(1). But in discharging a supervision order whether or not making a care order, the court must apply the care or control test, s. 16(6)	Yes, under ss. 8 and 10 (d, f)	Yes; it is rare for orders to be made after the age of 16 in the High Court, and therefore many orders can be considered for cancellation before or at, that age. In the Magistrates' courts, orders expire at 16, but may be cancelled before then	

QUESTION	Criminal Proceedings	Care Proceedings	Matrimonial Proceedings	Divorce Proceedings	Wardship Proceedings	Guardianship Proceedings
Who may apply for cancellation?	The supervisor or the supervised person s. 15(1) (3), or his parent or guardian if he is under 18, s. 70(2). If the supervised person is over 18 and has failed to comply with any requirements in the order, the application may only be made by the supervisor, s. 15(4)		The parties to the marriage, any parent, the supervisor, any person having or seeking the custody of the child	Either party to the marriage, a parent, or other person who has custody, an appointed and functioning guardian, the supervisor or a parent seeking custody		Either parent, or other person who has custody, any guardian appointed and functioning and the supervisor, s. 3(3)
			(The child under supervision under these Acts is not served with a copy of the order, and has no right of direct application for its discharge)			**18**
	General Note: The courts having jurisdiction to vary or discharge supervision orders under the 1969 Act are the juvenile or magistrates' courts acting for the petty sessions area which is named in the supervision order at the time of the application. Subject to 17 and 19 above the juvenile court has jurisdiction to deal with an application which is pending when the supervised person attains the age of either 17 or 18 as the case may be					
Can the order be varied while it is in force?	In dealing with persons under the age of 18, the juvenile court may: (a) amend the duration of supervision within the limits set out in 16 above; (b) name another local authority or petty sessions area and probation officer for supervision purposes; (c) cancel any requirement contained in the order; (d) insert or substitute provisions in the order. (Except that a new requirement of residence at a specified *place* may not be inserted later than twelve months from the date of the order. Nor may a new requirement to undergo treatment for mental disorder be inserted later than three months from the date of the order, and consent is required if the supervised person is over 14.		Yes, by adding or altering provisions as to custody	Yes, in the High Court, in any way thought necessary in the interests of the child		In magistrates' courts, s. 3(3) of the Guardianship Act 1973 applies

A requirement to undergo mental treatment may only be inserted or varied on receipt of a report from a medical practitioner)

Apart from minor variations, the court may only insert cancel or vary requirements in a supervision order or make a care order in place of it, if it is satisfied that as a result of the variation, the "care or control" test will be satisfied, ss. 15 and 16(6)

An adult (magistrates' court, or a juvenile court which has decided to use the powers of an adult court in dealing with a supervised person aged 17 but under 18 may:

(a) amend the duration of the order;

(b) vary the local authority and petty sessions area for supervision purposes;

(c) cancel any of the requirements in the order—but may not insert or vary any requirement. The "care or control" test does not apply. Usually, proceedings in respect of persons aged 17 and 18 will arise from a failure to comply with requirements, and the application will be made by the supervisor. In such cases, the court may impose a fine up to £20 or make an attendance order and may, or may not, vary or discharge the order. If the order is discharged, the court may deal with the case in the same way as a breach of probation would be dealt with in the magistrates court. (See note at 17 above)

Only the juvenile court may vary an order made in care proceedings

See above

CHILDREN AND YOUNG PERSONS   ORDERS FOR SUPERVISION IN:

QUESTION	Criminal Proceedings	Care Proceedings	Matrimonial Proceedings	Divorce Proceedings	Wardship Proceedings	Guardianship Proceedings	
Who may apply for variation?	The supervisor or the supervised person, s. 15(1)(3); or his parent or guardian if he is under 18, s. 70(2). If the supervised person is over 18 and has failed to comply with any requirements in the order, the application may only be made by the supervisor, s. 15(4)		The parties to the marriage, any parent, the supervisor, any person having or seeking the custody of the child (The child under supervision under these Acts is not served with a copy of the order, and has no right of direct application for its variation)	Either party to the marriage, a parent, or other person who has custody, an appointed and functioning guardian, the supervisor or a parent seeking custody		Either parent, or other person who has custody, any guardian appointed and functioning and the supervisor, s. 3(3)	20
Can a supervision order be made in the absence of the child or young person concerned?	No	Yes, if he is under 5 and the parents or guardian are in the court, or have been given adequate notice of the proceedings, s. 2(9). No, if he is over the age of 5	Yes	Yes	Yes	Yes	21a
Can a supervision order be discharged or varied in the absence of the child or young person concerned?	Yes, if the application is for discharge, cancelling or reducing the duration of any requirement or provision in the order, or for a change of supervisor or supervising area, s. 16(5). For other variation, the person must be present, s. 16(1)		Yes	Yes	Yes	Yes	21b
How can attendance at court, when required, be secured?	For a variation, the normal practice is for notice to be served, Rule 14 but a justice may issue a summons or warrant, s. 16(2). S. 16 also deals with procedure after arrest in pursuance of such a warrant.		There is no similar provision for orders under these Acts				22
Can any number of applications be made for the discharge of a supervision order?	Yes, but when such an application is dismissed no fresh application can be made within three months, unless the court consents, s. 16(9)						23
Can a child or young person subject to a supervision order be admitted to care under the Children Act 1948, s. 1?	Yes	Yes	Yes, but note that if so received into care, the only parent for the purposes of ss. 1–5 (admission, discharge and assumption of parental rights) is the person who has been awarded custody by the court (Children Act 1948, s. 6)				

Can the local authority pass a resolution in respect of him under s. 2?	Yes, s. 6	Yes, s. 6	Yes, subject to above—s. 6 In the High Court cases this might well be one of the situations in which the supervisor might seek the direction of the court. This should be done whenever there is any serious cause for concern regarding the welfare of the child
When is a supervision order cancelled automatically?	If a supervised person under the age of 18 appears before a juvenile court under s. 15(1), and the court makes a full care order, the existing supervision order is thereby discharged, s. 15(1). If a supervised person is aged 17 and the order was not made in care proceedings nor on the discharge of a care order, the juvenile court may decide to use the powers by an adult court acting in the case of a person aged 18, s. 15(2). If punishment is imposed under s. 15(4) (b) in respect of a person aged 17 or 18 the supervision order is discharged, (see Q. 19 above)	Apart from C. and Y.P. Act 1969, s. 15(2) and 15(4) (b) no supervision order is automatically cancelled. There may thus be a supervision order in force for a person who has been sent to a detention centre or to borstal under different legislation; supervision will also be provided under that other legislation and the original supervision order may be superfluous. (Application for a discharge should be made under s. 15(1))	Supervision orders under these Acts will not be cancelled automatically except by the expiration of the period of supervision according to age. Application for cancellation must be made to the appropriate court
Appeals (in the first instance)	To crown court on questions of law or fact, or—on point of law only—to Divisional Court of Appeal. The child, not the parent, is the appellant		From magistrates' courts, appeals lie to the Court of Appeal, Civil Division, which also hears appeals from county courts and the High Court, Family Division. In these cases the child is not the appellant
Legal aid	The child may make application for legal aid under the Legal Aid Act 1974		Application may be made for legal aid, but not by the child himself

26

27

28

Some of the difficulties and anomalies arising in the exercise of the various orders for supervision which are not made by a juvenile court, are examined in an article in *Social Work Today* of 4 September 1975. See "Supervision Orders in matrimonial and guardianship cases" by Edward Griew and Alastair Bissett-Johnson of Leicester University residence in a probation home or hostel and this has been regretted in some quarters.

In criminal proceedings a social report will be available to the court after it has decided the question of guilt. The report will have been compiled either by a probation officer or on behalf of a local authority and will indicate which of the various forms of treatment might be thought appropriate. (See para. 77 of the Guide.) If of all the alternatives the court chooses to make a supervision order, it may be thought that this most closely approximates to a probation order, although there are differences between the two.

In care proceedings, a supervision order may be made for a maximum period of three years, but is of no effect after the subject of it attains the age of 18. In these proceedings, of course, the order can only be made if the care or control test is satisfied, and it must therefore be assumed that in all cases (including those in which the offence condition is alleged) there has been a referral to the Social Services Department. Following this, either voluntary supervision, voluntary admission to care, or other suitable facilities would have been considered and offered to the individual concerned and his family; either they have not been accepted, or they have not been successful in providing the necessary care or control, and it has been thought essential for the person to be brought before a court so that a suitable order can be made.

It follows that the question of consent to the supervision order, in general, does not arise. Had there been co-operation there would have been no need to apply to the court.

As we have seen, before making an order, the court will itself have to apply the care or control test, and when it has decided that an order is necessary will consider reports provided by the probation officer, or the local authority, or perhaps both. Such reports in care cases will often be based on the information and insight gained during a period of voluntary supervision, or the attempt to provide it, and will indicate why an application is being made to the court, and what needs to be done to provide the individual concerned with

(a) the care, or

(b) the control, which he needs.

The court itself will then need to choose between the various orders which it may make under s. 1(3) and in particular perhaps between a care order, which may be used to remove a child from his home on a long-term basis, and a supervision order, which may not. There are of course other possible orders as set out in Chapter 8.

There may seem to be little difference between a care order if under it a child is allowed to live at home (s. 13 of the Children Act 1948, as amended) and a supervision order, except that the care order is effective until the age of 18 (or 19) while the supervision order is valid only for three years. There are however other differences to be borne in mind. The care order entrusts the care and control of the child to the local authority which has freedom to exercise its legal powers for the whole period of care, whereas the supervision order may contain requirements inserted by the court.

One of these is that the person to be supervised shall live with a person named in the order, with that person's consent. This could clearly be a valuable provision when it is considered that a child or young person would benefit from living, for instance, with a relative or friend rather than with his own parents for a time, but that it is not necessary to make a care order conferring parental rights on the authority. It must be assumed however, in care cases, that the local authority or other person taking the proceedings would have considered this possibility before bringing the case to court, but had met opposition from either the child or his parents. This suggests that a requirement of this kind is more likely to be imposed in orders arising from criminal proceedings.

It will be noted that there is no power to make a requirement that a supervised person shall live at a particular place, as under a probation order. If this is thought necessary it can be better achieved by the making of a care order (119).

The second requirement that a court may make is one relating to mental treatment —unlimited as to time within the span of the order except that it may not extend beyond the 18th birthday, and may be varied from time to time, subject always to the care or control test, which in this instance applies to the variation of orders made in criminal proceedings (117, 138–140). This requirement may be imposed on anyone under 14, but after that age his consent must be obtained (117–139). This will be valuable when there is an apparent need for mental treatment, but not such as to warrant the making of a hospital order. The requirement can only be made however if the court is satisfied that there are available facilities for treatment by a doctor, or as an outpatient or inpatient of a hospital and the treatment period is to be specified in the order. A court might find this a useful provision when dealing with a young person addicted to drugs, but again in care cases the requirement would not be necessary had there been co-operation on a voluntary basis before the proceedings were instituted.

The third requirement is that the supervised person shall comply with any directions given to him by his supervisor.

   a to live at a specified place for a period or periods not exceeding ninety days (123) and/or;

   b to live at a place or places specified for a series of shorter periods (124);

   c *or* to present himself to specified persons at places and times specified;

   d *or* to take part in specified activities at specified times.

Directions may be given in respect of **b** from time to time, and may be given in respect of all or any of the alternatives if they are specified in the order: **a** and **b** may be combined, but not so that the total period exceeds ninety days in all. The method of calculation is set out in paras 124 and 125. The local authority will be required to meet the expenditure (s. 18 (4)) whether one of its own social workers or a probation officer is the supervisor.

Here again, in non-criminal cases any of these arrangements could have been made on a voluntary basis during the period before the proceedings were instituted, and it must be assumed that the co-operation of the juvenile or his parents was not forthcoming. In orders arising from criminal proceedings in which requirement (**a**) or (**b**) is imposed the effect may be seen to have something in common with the detention centre or attendance centre order which it is designed ultimately to replace but so far the comparison has not been much in evidence.

It is to be noted that the supervision order itself will not direct the supervised person to *do* any of the things specified in the requirement. It will simply give the power to the supervisor to direct him to comply to the extent thought fit within the limits imposed in the order; whether the supervisor actually uses this power is a question for him to decide as indicated in Appendix C *to Children in Trouble*.

Supervision orders made in either criminal or care proceedings, have the effect of

a naming the area of the local authority and the petty sessional division in which the supervised person is to reside (109);

b laying upon the supervisor the duty to advise, assist and befriend (114);

c containing any provisions to be prescribed by Rules for assisting the supervisor in that duty. A rule may be made for instance requiring the supervised person to visit his supervisor;

d containing, where appropriate, a requirement that the supervised person shall live with a named individual (not at a particular place) or shall submit to mental treatment;

e containing any of the requirements inserted into the order to assist the supervisor. Before such requirements (loosely called intermediate treatment) are included in an order, the facilities for carrying them out must be contained in a regional plan and known to the court, except for those given general approval by the Secretary of State.

There is a body of opinion which considers that regional plans should have been directed towards these facilities in the first place, rather than to the establishment of a system of residential care in community homes. The requirement for up to ninety-days residential treatment (not necessarily all in one period) might for instance have prevented a number of admissions for much longer periods in community homes with education on the premises.

With a few exceptions, there are no specially provided places for the meeting of this requirement, and even when such a place exists, there seems to be some confusion as to the real purpose of the requirement, though it is agreed that both the staff and the boys concerned found the experience enjoyable.[1] A study of the experience of boys in eighteen approved schools, as they then were, suggests, among other things, that the new community homes might make available short-term experience and projects, even for weekends, and that they might act as bases from which boys could undertake community service work under supervision.[2] There would seem to be no reason why more local homes should not be used in a similar way for short placements, but something more than mere residence would be needed, and might not be readily provided.

The lack of the facilities for the ninety-day residence provision may well be one reason for the increase in the courts' use of the detention centre order; if this is to be diminished there must be viable alternatives in the regional plan.

There has been a great deal of interested discussion of intermediate treatment which at present seems to consist largely of non-residential arrangements. In the D.H.S.S. Development Group Report of 1973 some of the projects then in existence are described;[3] they consist of a camp, a day centre, holiday camps, various activity groups, and a children's club. The impression is that these were all arranged for groups of children and young persons known to the respective authorities (including some who had appeared before a juvenile court) and attendance was of course voluntary. There seems to be no mention of anyone attending in accordance with a requirement in a supervision order that he should "take part in specified activities", or "present himself to a specified person at specified times". Similarly in the Report on the Feltham-Hanworth Intermediate Treatment Group",[4] it appears that a number of adolescents in the group have been before the court, some being under statutory supervision and some being in care under orders but living at home. In assessing the effect of the group, the report points out that its involvement with the boys is for two hours weekly, and implies that there is a need for more help from other agencies such as the Youth Service. It is not suggested in this report that a greater impact might be made by short residential placements within the *local community*—but perhaps there are insuperable problems.

Apart from the book cited earlier, there is little mention of anything in the nature of community service being developed as a part of supervision even on a voluntary basis. There is, however, one reference to a county which would use the "presenting to a person" requirement in order to see that offenders made good damage they had caused.

"Intermediate treatment" is a phrase which is applied to a great deal of activity which is really preventive work and very valuable as such, but it seems to have little to do with supervision under the terms of an order of a court. When requirements are inserted into an order, they are meant to assist the supervisor, who should keep them under review and not hesitate to ask for changes if this seems necessary. In cases of adolescent offenders, if this is not done, and if the supervisor cannot bring himself to exercise direction, it would seem likely that in the event of a further offence, there may be a custodial sentence which directive supervision might have avoided.

The supervisor under supervision orders is to be a probation officer, or a local authority, normally that for the area of residence (110).

If the person to be supervised is under 13 years of age the local authority will be named, unless it asks that a probation officer should be named because he is concerned or has been concerned in exercising supervision under some statutory authority in respect of an adult or juvenile member of the household (111–112).

If the person to be supervised is 13 years old or more, either the probation officer or the local authority may be named, and courts will presumably make their decision in accordance with the circumstances of each case and the local conditions prevailing at the time.

The dividing line at the age of 13 is for the time being and may be raised when thought appropriate under s. 34. In the meantime local authorities are supervising some young people in the age group 13–17, and may feel the need to seek the advice and counsel of the probation service for some time to come. In particular they may need to draw upon the accumulated experience of probation officers in such questions as where, how often and when to see persons under supervision, how to make the arrangements for such meetings, and how to review progress in each case. Probation Rules govern these matters, and if these are applied by local authority social workers they will be of great assistance, pending Regulations to be made.

Supervision orders may be discharged or varied on application under s. 15; until the supervised person is 18. When a supervision order is discharged the court may make a care order, but only if the care or control test is applied. The care or control test is in fact to be applied in all applications for discharge or variation of supervision orders whether the result will be favourable or unfavourable to the supervised person. But when the result will be favourable to him, or when the variation is purely technical, the supervised person need not be brought before the court (140, 146).

After the age of 18, only supervision orders made in criminal proceedings can still be in force. The power to discharge or to make minor variations is thus confined to adult courts which are not required to consider the care or control test, and may impose the penalties for non-compliance set out at the beginning of this chapter.

There are cross-border arrangements to meet cases in which the supervised person moves lawfully from one part of the United Kingdom to another. See para. 247 of the "Guide" and the Social Work (Scotland) Act 1968, operative from April 1971.

2. THE COURTS

The Children and Young Persons Act 1933, did not make Children's Committees responsible for Part I of the Act (prevention of cruelty and exposure to moral and physical danger) or for Part II (regulation of employment). Prosecutions under these Parts of the Act were, therefore, left in the hands of the Police, the N.S.P.C.C. and the local Education Authority. It is now provided additionally that the local authority may institute proceedings in respect of offences under either Part I or Part II of the Act (*e.g.* neglect or cruelty, or offences against employment statute or by-laws).[5] Social workers may at times appear at the adult court either as a witness or to make a report. They may also appear in the magistrates' domestic court and in the county court and crown court, where procedures are not the same as in a juvenile court (see "The Social Worker and the Court").

3. THE JUVENILE COURT

Social workers will frequently represent their local authority in the juvenile courts in their own area and at times in other areas. They will often be expected to supply reports in proceedings and to recommend to courts the making of appropriate orders.

The institution of proceedings is however a rather different matter, as they are to be instituted by the authority, not by an individual. Unless the Director of Social Services has the delegated authority to institute proceedings, he would seek the authority of his committee, or at the very least the authority of his chairman subject to confirmation by the committee. This is a matter for each local authority to determine, but if a Director has delegated powers it makes possible the freedom of action which is sometimes essential in emergencies, and would be expected to lead to a situation where an individual officer could be authorised to institute proceedings under the authority of the Director.

An officer of a local authority who is not a solicitor may conduct proceedings if authorised to do so, under the Local Government Act 1972, s. 223, but there will be cases in which it is necessary for the case to be conducted by a solicitor on behalf of the authority, especially in view of the wider provisions for legal aid to be available for persons concerned in care and similar proceedings.

4. REPORTS TO COURTS

A social worker may be present in court for various reasons: to act as a supporter to someone who is appearing as a defendant, to act as advocate, to give evidence as a witness in proceedings, or to present a report. These functions must not be confused. A report is only put into the court after it is satisfied that the case has been made out, and is not in itself evidence. There are several other points of importance. In the juvenile court, proceedings are governed by the Magistrates' Court (Children and Young Persons) Rules 1970, but it will be found that practice varies from one court to another. For example, some courts expect a report to contain references to any police cautions which have been administered prior to the present case; others do not. Some courts follow the Rules precisely by disclosing to defendants and parents the salient points of a social report; others require a copy of the report to be handed to the parties; yet others read the report aloud but paraphrase it as they read. These are all ways of ensuring natural justice. No social report is entirely confidential. If parts of it are very delicate, they can be suitably marked to draw the attention of the court to those matters which would cause concern.

The writing of a social report is in itself a most important task, since it will often lead to a recommendation that a certain course should be followed. The actual content is not prescribed, but must include the basic facts clearly distinguished from opinion. The language used should be clear, concise and free from jargon, so that it can be understood by all concerned. A brief outline of the minimum content of a report is given in "The Social Worker in the Juvenile Court" along with other helpful suggestions for training in the task. Social workers will make reports to adult courts less frequently than to juvenile courts, and will find that the report itself will be handed to the parties, or their legal representatives. In the event of statements being challenged, the social worker may be called upon to give sworn evidence.

5. CONVEYING

A further responsibility undertaken by local authority social workers in the courts—and this may arise in adult and in higher courts—is that of conveying to and from courts children and young persons subject to a care order, interim order, supervision order, remand warrant or, in some cases, detained in a place of safety. This responsibility extends also to conveying children and young persons from one type of accommodation to another, and recovering those who abscond—officially to be known as absentees.

The main burden of all conveyals falls upon the local authority as the probation service is no longer concerned in it, but the police may be willing to assist by arrangement, such as that suggested in *Social Work Today* for 3 June 1971.

The police will still be responsible for conveying to and from courts those persons sent to detention centres, remand centres, borstals and prisons.

6. INVESTIGATIONS AND REPORTS

As we have seen, every part of the country has a Social Services Department and because of the excellent co-operation which usually exists it is possible for one department to obtain reports from another department in any part of the British Isles, or to exercise supervision over children through this agency service wherever they may be. A Social Service Department, therefore, receives a number of enquiries from other departments and it is essential that work carried out on behalf of other authorities or voluntary societies, which is considerable, should receive the same careful attention as is given to the authority's own duties towards the children in its care. It is frequently necessary for enquiries to be made or for supervision to be carried out in respect of children outside the British Isles and in such cases authorities often make use of International Social Service which, in turn, asks for the co-operation of English authorities in undertaking work on behalf of social agencies overseas. I.S.S. charge a fee of £10 for each enquiry and report.

A social worker today may thus be called upon to carry out duties not only for his own authority but for voluntary organisations, other local authorities and social workers in other countries. This work is carried out under the various Acts and Rules and is summarised at the end of this chapter.

7. ACCOMMODATION OF CHILDREN SUFFERING FROM MENTAL DISORDER

Such children, if otherwise eligible, may be received into care or committed to care.

It should be noted, however, that a local authority may also accommodate in its homes such a child under the age of 18 who is not in the authority's care under the Children Act. An arrangement of this kind will be readily made by the Social Services Department which is responsible for such children whether in care or not.

8. RELATIONSHIP BETWEEN LOCAL AUTHORITIES AND VOLUNTARY SOCIETIES

We have so far been concerned with local authority departments. It will be remembered that in addition to local authorities there are a number of voluntary societies which provide a separate child care service, either in part or in whole.

The best known of the national societies are Dr. Barnardo's, the National Children's Home, the Catholic Crusade of Rescue and the Church of England Children's Society, but there are others operating on a smaller scale and concentrating on a particular aspect of child care work, such as adoption, whereas the larger societies provide nurseries, children's homes, hostels and special schools and also arrange adoption and the boarding-out of children.

The Children Act 1948 recognised the importance of the voluntary bodies and empowered the Secretary of State to make grants to voluntary organisations for improving premises; it also empowered local authorities to make contributions to any voluntary organisation which has as its main object the promotion of the welfare of children.[6]

The great virtue of the voluntary organisation is that it is not governed by the Children Act in deciding which child to admit to care and it may, therefore, admit any child—usually at the request of a parent—and in some cases children may not be regarded as eligible to be received into the care of a local authority. It is now usual for a voluntary organisation to consult a local authority before offering care or other services.

A disadvantage from the point of view of the voluntary organisation is that it cannot enforce contributions from a parent and relies on the collection of money by agreement. Nor has it power to assume parental rights.

In recent years local authorities have increasingly sought the help of voluntary organisations in accommodating children in public care especially through the community homes system.

Because of the two parallel systems of child care, the statutory and the voluntary, there is a great need for continuing co-operation between the officers of local authorities and voluntary organisations. There is already a close link between the Secretary of State, local authorities and voluntary organisations, the main provisions of the Act and Regulations being as follows:

a CHILDREN'S HOMES

The Children and Young Persons Act 1969, s. 58 empowers the Secretary of State to "cause to be inspected" any premises where children in care are accommodated, including foster homes.

Since 1948 it has been necessary for every voluntary home (whether administered by one of the large voluntary societies or not) to be registered by the Secretary of State, who has power to remove any particular home from the register if it is not carried on properly, subject to the right of the home to appeal to a tribunal.[7] (This does not now apply to these homes which are community homes.)

The Secretary of State notifies the local authority of any voluntary home in its area which has been registered and the local authority then has a duty to cause the children in that home to be visited and to authorise its officers to enter the voluntary home for this purpose.

With regard to voluntary homes outside its own area, the local authority has the right to visit any of the children in its care who are accommodated in such a home, but may delegate the duty of visiting to the local authority for the area of the home.

Local authority officers are, therefore, required to visit voluntary homes in the discharge of their duties and should have a proper form of authority which they can produce if required; it is an offence for any person to obstruct the entry of a properly authorised officer, under a penalty of £5 for the first offence and £20 for the second.

In order to control the conditions in children's homes the Secretary of State issued the Administration of Children's Homes Regulations in 1951—these apply to voluntary homes which are not community homes within the regional plans.

b BOARDING-OUT

In arranging boarding-out the Regulations of 1955 require a considerable degree of co-operation between the local authority and the voluntary society. Before placing a child in a foster home the voluntary society must enquire of the local authority if there is any reason to suppose that the placing would be detrimental to the child. Fourteen days' notice is required for this enquiry and the local authority is not required to visit the home but merely to supply information from official sources. The local authority does not approve or disapprove of the home which it is proposed to use but must give the voluntary society any information it has on which they can make their own decision. When the placing has been arranged the voluntary society must inform the local authority of the name, sex, date of birth and religious persuasion of the child, full names and religious persuasion of each foster parent and their address and the date of placing. They must also state clearly what arrangements have been made for supervision and in the event of the child's removal must report the fact, together with the reasons.

All placings by voluntary societies within an authority's area are recorded by the authority in its boarding-out register along with details of its own children placed in the area.

A local authority has also a duty to enquire from time to time what staff and facilities a voluntary society has for carrying out its statutory duties and, if not satisfied that they are adequate, must itself take over the supervision and relieve the voluntary society of its duties.[8]

As we have seen, it is possible for a local authority to place children in its care with a voluntary society which may decide to place the child in a foster home. In such cases the society is required to notify the authority in whose care the child is and to keep it informed of the child's progress.

c AFTER-CARE

When a child over compulsory school age ceases to be in the care of a voluntary organisation, either in a home or otherwise, the organisation must inform the local authority for the area in which the child proposes to live and must state whether or not the organisation has the facilities for advising and befriending the child or whether it wishes the local authority to do so. This is the same provision as exists for children formerly in the care of a local authority under the Children Act 1948 and the after-care continues until the child is 18 or until it is felt that it is no longer necessary.[9]

d ADOPTION

It will be remembered that voluntary bodies acting as adoption agencies must make certain enquiries of the local authority before placing a child with prospective adopters, and must be registered with the authority in whose area their office is situated; they must supply details of their accounts for inspection at the end of each financial year.[10]

9. DUTIES OF LOCAL AUTHORITY SOCIAL WORKERS

The main duties may be summarised as follows so far as children's legislation is concerned:

1. INVESTIGATION OF:

a applications for admission to care;

b allegations that children are in need of care or control (involving consultation with police, education authority and N.S.P.C.C.);

c circumstances of children at request of divorce court;

d circumstances of children at request of magistrates' court: Such investigations are more frequently made by the probation service. They should be made at the request of the court, not at the request of solicitors or parties to a case. There is an agreed procedure by which probation officers (acting as Court Welfare Officers) and local authority officers should consult one another in such cases. For details consult "Memorandum of Guidance for Divorce Court Welfare Officers" (August 1968). This deals with consultation which children are known to the local authority.

e circumstances of children under 13 who are to appear before a court, of those over that age who are to be brought before the court by the local authority in care proceedings; of those over 13 appearing in criminal proceedings if requested to do so.[11]

f cases referred for advice, guidance and assistance;

g applications for approval as foster parents or prospective adopters or child-minders;

h applications for adoption order (guardian *ad litem*).

Such investigations may also be made at the request of other local authorities or voluntary societies.

2. SUPERVISION OF CHILDREN UNDER EIGHTEEN:

a boarded-out foster homes, including on request those placed by other authorities or voluntary societies;

b placed privately in foster homes;
c placed by third party for adoption with person who is not a parent, guardian or relative;[11]
d placed with prospective adopters who have given notice of intention to adopt;
e committed to care but under charge of parent guardian, relative or friend.
f under statutory supervision orders made by juvenile or higher courts (care, or control), High Court (Matrimonial Causes Act 1973 and Family Law Reform Act 1969, Guardianship Act 1973) and magistrates courts (Matrimonial Proceedings (Magistrates' Courts) Act 1960);
g discharged from the care of a local authority or voluntary society after school-leaving age;
h placed in voluntary homes within the authority's area;
i placed in voluntary homes outside the area.

Again, some of the foregoing duties may be undertaken at the request of another authority or organisation.

3. GENERAL DUTIES:

a case work with families whose children are in care, have been in care or are at risk;
b maintaining contact with children in residential care;
c attendance at juvenile and county courts and presentation of reports;
d conducting proceedings in juvenile courts in respect of children alleged to be in need of care or control;
e arrangement for provision of accommodation for children remanded to care or committed to care on interim orders;
f visitation of voluntary children's homes within the area, whether they are accommodating children in the care of the authority or not.
g assessment of family situations and of needs of individual children in cases arising under the 1969 Act, and applying the care or control test;
h assessment of those situations and needs when criminal proceedings are being considered;
i conveying children and young persons in care from one type of accommodation to another, recovering absentees, conveying persons to and from juvenile and adult courts;
k maintaining adequate case records of all work undertaken with families and children;
l taking part in six-monthly reviews of children in any form of care (ideally there should also be periodical reviews in respect of children under voluntary or statutory supervision, though this is not at present required);
m making reports to juvenile court justices on persons subject to

care or supervision orders, as advocated in para. 107 of the Guide to Part I of the Act;

n stimulating and encouraging community activity in the interests of families and children; promoting group work as a supplement to individual case work with children, parents, and prospective foster parents or adopters, or with other groups within the community.

(**Note:** Case records kept under the Boarding-Out of Children Regulations 1955 are statutory records, confidential and privileged. In *re D* (*infants*) January 1970 the Court of Appeal held that such records should not be produced in Wardship proceedings, and that there was no cause for an exception to be made to the privilege attaching to such records.)

The whole question of confidentiality, both personally, and in relation to records is one of great importance to a social worker, especially in a situation in which he becomes aware that an offence has been committed, and that criminal proceedings may be under consideration. The subject is complex, but some guidance may be found in the following publications by B.A.S.W.:

Confidentiality in Social Work; A Code of Ethics for Social Work; Advice to Members who are Questioned by the Police about Clients; Disclosure of Confidential Information.

NOTES

1. "Open Air Treatment", *Community Care*, 4 June 1975.
2. *After Grace—Teeth*, Millham Bullock and Cherrett, Human Context Books.
3. *Intermediate Treatment Project and Intermediate Treatment Guide* (*Appendix B*), D.H.S.S., H.M.S.O.
4. *Youth Social Work*, Vol. 2, No. 4, 1975.
5. Children and Young Persons Act 1963, s. 56, as amended.
6. Children Act 1948, s. 46 and C. and Y.P. Act 1969, s. 65(2).
7. Children Act 1948, ss. 29 and 30.
8. Boarding-Out Regulation 15.
9. Children Act 1948, s. 34.
10. See Chapter 15.
11. For an examination of time spent in this activity and the variations noted, see "Social Enquiry Reports and the Probation Service" of August 1973 (Home Office).

GENERAL NOTE

The contents of this chapter will be affected in due course by the Children Act 1975. It will be possible for parental rights to vest in a voluntary organisation. A local authority will not be involved in the supervision of children placed for adoption by an approved agency; appointment of a guardian *ad litem* will be at the discretion of a court. Social workers will however be involved in adoption and custodianship applications, and in supervision of other groups of children not at present subject to it. Chapter 17 contains some comment on several of these points.

Chapter 15

LEGAL ADOPTION

SUMMARY

PRELIMINARY ARRANGEMENTS

Legal adoption is effected by an order made by the High Court, a county court or a juvenile court.[1]

The effect of an adoption order is to bring the child into a relationship with the adopters such as he would have had if he had been born to them in marriage. It transfers parental rights and duties from the parents to the adopters.[2] See Schedule 1 of the Children Act 1975. There is, however, no need for complete severance of parental interest if this is the wish of the adoptees (J.P. 1972, p. 238).

Adoption orders once made are irrevocable, except those set aside on appeal or by legitimation, or by re-adoption.

Affiliation orders in respect of the child cease to have effect unless he is adopted by his mother and she is a single woman. The rights and powers of local authorities under care orders, except interim orders, and resolutions passed under s. 2 of the Children Act 1948, are extinguished.[3]

An adopted child who was not a citizen of the United Kingdom and Colonies prior to the adoption acquires such citizenship if the adopter, or male adopter is a citizen of the United Kingdom and Colonies.[4]

PLACING FOR ADOPTION

A child may be placed for adoption:

a by a registered adoption society;[5]
b by a local authority;[6]
c by a "third party" (Chapter 7);[7]
d by the parent or guardian direct.

When an adoption society or local authority places a child for adoption it is careful to see that legal and other requirements are met so that there may be a minimum of difficulty later when the matter goes to court. In placings by a third party or direct by the parent or guardian the same care is not always taken and such people are often unaware of the formalities which have to be complied with. A local authority or adoption society is now subject to ss. 3 and 13 of the Children Act 1975 which have important implications.

TYPES OF ORDER

The most common type of order is that made under s. 1 of the Adoption Act 1958, where the applicants are *resident and domiciled* in England or Wales.[8]

Section 12 of the Act permits the making of an adoption order (by the High Court or a County Court, but not a Juvenile Court) in the case of applicants who are domiciled in England or Wales but *not resident* there. This section meets the needs of colonial civil servants and others who spend tours of duty abroad but who regard England or Wales as their home and intend to return there after the completion of the period of duty, by some relaxation of the rules relating to the period of care and possession of the child, and the notification of the intention to adopt the child given to the local authority.

Section 1 of the Adoption Act 1968 authorises the High Court to make an adoption order in respect of adopters or children who are nationals of countries recognising the convention on the Adoption of Children.

Section 53 of the Act authorises the making of a "Provisional Order" in the case of applicants who are not domiciled in England or Wales. Such an order can only be made by the High Court or a

County Court (not a juvenile court) and permits the removal of the child to the country of domicile for adoption in accordance with the law of that country. The applicants must give *six months'* notice to the local authority of their intention to apply for a provisional order and must have the care and possession of the child for *at least six months* before the date of the order.

An interim order gives applicants the custody of the child for a probationary period of up to two years. It is not an adoption order within the meaning of the Act and has the effect of postponing the determination of the application if the court is not satisfied that an adoption order should be made immediately. In making an interim order a court may specify such terms as it thinks fit with regard to the maintenance, education and supervision of the child.[9]

Before the expiration of the interim order the court will fix a date for the hearing of the original application for an adoption order.[10]

NOTIFICATION TO LOCAL AUTHORITY

Unless the child is above compulsory school-leaving age or one of the applicants is the father or mother of the child, an adoption order may not be made until after the expiration of at least *three months* from the date on which the applicants notified the local authority, in writing, of their intention to adopt the child.[11] This requirement is relaxed in the case of applicants under s. 12 to the extent that the notice may be given by either of the applicants. Applicants for provisional orders under s. 53 must give *six months'* notice instead of three months.

One important effect of this notification is that the child becomes a "protected" child and therefore liable to supervision by the local authority (Chapter 7).[12]

Applicants desiring an early hearing should, therefore, understand the necessity for an early notification.

Applicants are sometimes under the impression that application to the court cannot be made until the three months has expired. This is not so, as the application can be made as soon as all the requisite court documents are completed[13] but the hearing will not take place until the three months' period has expired. The notification is to be made to the local authority within whose area the applicants are resident. If they change their address before the court hearing they must notify the local authority and if the new address is in the area of another local authority then the first-named local authority must inform the other local authority concerned.[14]

Notification is important also as, in the case of children who are in the care of the local authority, the contributions from the parents in respect of the maintenance of the infant cease to be payable, and a further point is that the local authority lose the right to require the child to be returned to their care under the Boarding-Out Regulations.[15]

ACTUAL CUSTODY

At the date of hearing the child must have been in the actual custody of the applicants for at least three months not counting any period during which the child was less than six weeks old.[16] In applications under s. 12 the child must have been in the care and possession of both applicants for one month and in the care of one of the applicants for three months. The corresponding period for provisional orders is six months for both applicants.[17] Care and possession is not disturbed by temporary absence, *e.g.* at boarding school. *Re B.(G.A.)*(1963).

CHILD

For the purpose of the Act a child is a person under 18 years of age who is not, and has not been, married.[18] (Persons under 18 may be described as "minors". Family Law Reform Act 1969, s. 12.)

CONSENTS

Subject to the court's powers to dispense with consents, every person who is a parent or guardian of a child must give consent to the making of an adoption order. In the case of an application by one of two spouses the other spouse must give consent.[19] Consent may be given on personal attendance at the court hearing but is in nearly all cases given on the appropriate court form, which is an integral part of the application for the order.[20]

The consent of a local authority, even if the authority hold parental rights and powers under a s. 2 resolution or a care order, is not required.[21]

"Parent" is not defined in the Adoption Act 1958, but "guardian" means a person appointed by deed or will in accordance with the provisions of the Guardianship of Infants and Minors Acts, or by a court of competent jurisdiction to be the guardian of the infant.[22] It now includes a natural father who has custody.

The term "parent" does not include the natural father of an illegitimate child (*Re M. An Infant*, 1955).

A consent must be to a *particular* application as evidenced either by the names of the applicants or by a serial number, but a consent once given cannot be withdrawn on the grounds that the identity of the applicants was not known.[23]

Consents on forms not bearing this information are invalid as also are consents to adoption "generally".

In giving consent to an application which is made under a serial number the parent or guardian has the right to make a stipulation with regard to the religious persuasion in which the child is to be brought up. If the names of the applicants are shown on the form of consent this right does not exist.

A form of consent is invalid if it is signed before the infant is 6 weeks old or not attested on the date of signature.[24]

Forms of consent must be attested in the manner set out in the Adoption Rules (usually by a Justice of the Peace, Clerk to Justices or an authorised County Court Officer), and in the case of at least one of the parents must be accompanied by a birth certificate of the infant similarly attested. Shortened forms of birth certificate are accepted for this purpose by some courts but it is usual for a full copy of the birth certificate to be used.

Difficulties sometimes arise where the mother of the child is a married woman who was married at the time of the conception of the child. In such a case the child is presumed to be the child of the marriage unless the contrary is proved and a consent would, therefore, be required from the husband. (But see Family Law Reform Act 1969, s. 26.) If the husband is unaware of the child's existence or is unwilling to sign the consent, courts will sometimes accept an affidavit from the mother with regard to the paternity of the infant.

The court has power to dispense with the consent of any person if it is satisfied:

a that the person has abandoned, neglected or persistently ill-treated the child; or

b cannot be found or is incapable of giving his consent or is withholding his consent unreasonably; "Cannot be found" must mean cannot be found by taking all reasonable steps (*F. (R) an infant* 1969); withholding consent "unreasonably". See the unanimous judgment of Court of Appeal in *Re W (an infant)* reported in J.P. 17 April 1971.

c has failed without reasonable cause to discharge the obligations of a parent or guardian.

The court may dispense with the consent of the spouse to an application if it is satisfied that the person cannot be found or is incapable of giving consent or that the spouses have separated and are living apart and that the separation is likely to be permanent.[25]

The consent may be withdrawn at any time before the date of hearing but the child may not be restored to the parents without the consent of the court once the application has been made.[26] The person withdrawing consent would normally attend the court hearing to explain his request to the court and unless the court dispenses with the consent the application for an adoption order would fail and the child would then return to the parent or guardian. It should be noted that a parent opposing an adoption application may now be given legal aid.

APPLICANTS

Applicants for adoption orders must fulfil certain conditions if they are to have an order granted to them:[27]

    a In a joint application the applicants must be married to each other.

    b Both applicants must be 21 or over; one of the applicants must be 25 years old or 21 and a relative of the child; if one of the applicants is the father or mother of the child there is no age limit.

    c The court will not allow a male applicant to adopt a female child unless there are special circumstances justifying the making of an adoption order as an exceptional measure.

COURT PROCEDURE

Applications for adoption orders are made by completing the appropriate court forms and delivering them or sending them to the court office.[28]

Once an application is lodged in the court a parent or guardian of the child who has consented to the application cannot remove the child from the care and possession of the applicants without the leave of the court.[26] This restriction also applies to local authorities and registered adoption societies who have arranged placings.[29]

The actual forms used in county courts are in the Appendix.[30] The forms should be very carefully completed and the explanatory notes given on the forms should be studied to ensure that the documents are in order. There is now a simplified form of application for persons living in England or Wales. This is also included in the Appendix.

NOTICES OF HEARING

Notices of hearing of the application must be served by the court on the following:[31]

    a Every person not being an applicant whose consent to the making of an order is required under the Act.

    b Any person having the rights and powers of a parent of the child.

    c Any person liable by an order or agreement to contribute to the maintenance of the child.

    d The local authority to whom notice of intention to adopt has been given.

    e The local authority or adoption society taking part in the arrangements for the adoption.

    f Any other person not being the child who in the opinion of the court should be served with notice of hearing.

SERIAL NUMBER

Applicants may obtain from the court a serial number which is inserted on the form of application and forms of consent in order to prevent the parents or guardians of the child from learning the applicants' identity.[32]

COURT ARRANGEMENTS

Applications to county courts are heard *in camera*[33] and to petty sessional courts in the juvenile court.

ATTENDANCE OF PARTIES

The court requires the personal attendance of the applicants before making an adoption order except that in the case of a joint application the court may dispense with the attendance of one spouse provided he has verified the application by affidavit.[34]

Where the guardian *ad litem* reports to the court that in his opinion the child is old enough to understand the nature of an adoption order, the court must serve a notice on the applicants requiring them to bring the child to the court hearing.[35]

APPOINTMENT OF GUARDIAN AD LITEM

The guardian *ad litem* of the child must be appointed by the court as soon as practicable after the application is made.[36]

DUTIES OF COURT

In making a decision relating to adoption, a court is now subject to s. 3 of the Children Act 1975 as regards the interests of the child. Before making an adoption order the court must be satisfied:[37]

a that all necessary consents have been obtained and that the persons concerned understand the nature and effect of an adoption order. In the case of a parent, he must understand that the effect of the adoption order will be permanently to deprive him of his parental rights;

b that the order, if made, will be for the welfare of the infant. "Welfare" means, *inter alia*, the health of the applicants as evidenced by medical certificates, and the wishes of the child having regard to his age and understanding;

c that the applicant has not received or agreed to receive and that no person has made or given or agreed to make or give to the applicants any payment or other reward in consideration of the adoption except such as the court may sanction (for "reward" see s. 50).

The court when making the order may impose such terms and conditions as the court may think fit and, in particular, may require the adopter to make provision for the child by bond or otherwise.

IDENTIFICATION OF CHILD

In the county court a child is sufficiently identified by the birth certificate attached to the form of consent[38] but in the juvenile court proof of identity may be made by affidavit and the court may still require the attendance of a witness in special circumstances.

PREVIOUS APPLICATIONS

If a previous application or applications to adopt the same child have been dismissed by any court on their merits the court will not proceed to hear a further application unless satisfied that there has been a substantial change in the circumstances since the date of the previous application.[39]

REFERRAL TO HIGH COURT

If the court considers that it would be more fit for an application to be dealt with in the High Court it may refuse to deal with the application.[40]

RESULT OF HEARING

The court must notify the result of the application to all parties who were not present at the hearing.[41]

INFORMATION

Information in connection with an application for an adoption order must be treated in confidence and must not be disclosed except as far as is necessary in the proper execution of business, or at the request of a court, or to a person engaged in research with the written authority of the Secretary of State.[42]

COMPLETION OF ADOPTION

RE-ADOPTIONS

An adopted child may be the subject of a second or further application, in which case the previous adopters are regarded as the parents of the child.[43]

LEGITIMATION FOLLOWING ADOPTION

An adoption order may be revoked when the person adopted has been legitimated by the marriage of his parents.[44]

BAPTISM

Section 25 of the Adoption Act 1958 dealing with baptism after adoption is now repealed.[45] New certificates of baptism may be obtained in respect of children who had been baptized before adoption.

FORM OF ORDER

The forms of adoption order and abridged adoption order are set out in the rules. A copy of the full order is sent by the court to the Registrar General and a copy of the abridged order is sent to the applicants, within seven days of the order being made.[46]

FAMILY ALLOWANCES

An adopted child is included in the family of the adopters for purposes of family allowances with effect from the date on which the local authority were given notification of intention to adopt.[47]

INCOME TAX

An adopter who proves that he has the custody of an adopted child whom he maintains at his own expense is entitled to income tax relief as if the child were his own, provided that no other person is receiving allowance for the same child.[48] If the child is received into the care of the adopters during the income tax year prior to that in which the adoption order is made then they may claim income tax allowance for the previous year.

APPEALS

Appeals against decisions in magistrates' courts[49] lie to the High Court and from county courts to the Court of Appeal.[50]

COSTS

The court may make orders as to costs and in particular may direct the applicant to pay the out-of-pocket expenses of the guardian *ad litem* and the expenses incurred by a respondent in attending the hearing.[51] Local authorities do not usually claim expenses in respect of their duties as guardian *ad litem* and orders in favour of respondents for other costs are rare.

ADOPTION RULES

The references are to the Adoption (County Court) Rules 1959 and 1965. The Adoption (Juvenile Court) Rules 1959 and 1965, and the Adoption (High Court) Rules 1959, are very similar to the County Court Rules, but for the sake of simplicity the references have not been triplicated. All Rules concerning adoption have been amended in 1965 and 1973.

SCOTLAND, IRELAND, ISLE OF MAN, AND CHANNEL ISLANDS

The Adoption Act 1958, applies to Scotland but the provisions of the Act relating to Scottish law have not been dealt with in this chapter. For most purposes of English law adoption orders made in Scotland or Northern Ireland have the same effect as orders made in England, as do orders made in the Isle of Man or in the Channel Islands (Adoption Act 1964).

ADOPTION ORDERS MADE OVERSEAS

The Adoption Act of 1968 provides *inter alia* for the recognition in the United Kingdom of orders previously made in certain overseas countries whose adoption laws are similar to our own. This provision will make it unnecessary for new adoption applications to be made in such cases of children already adopted elsewhere.

REGISTERED ADOPTION AGENCIES

POWER TO ARRANGE ADOPTIONS

Local authorities (*i.e.* the councils of counties and county boroughs acting through their social service committees) have power to arrange adoptions whether the children concerned are in the care of the local authority or not.[52]

The only other *body* of persons empowered to arrange adoptions is a registered adoption society.[53] The arrangement of adoptions by any other body of persons is unlawful and anyone taking part in such arrangements becomes liable to a fine of not more than £100 and/or six months' imprisonment.

REGISTRATION OF ADOPTION SOCIETIES

Adoption Societies wishing to be registered under the Adoption Act 1958, must apply to the local authority for the area in which their administrative centre is situated, enclosing the statutory fee of £1 and a completed form giving details of the society as required by the Act and Regulations.[54]

The local authority may refuse to register an adoption society if it does not consider it to be a charitable association, or for other reasons defined in the Act relating to the unsuitability of members or staff of the society.

APPEAL

An adoption Society may appeal to the Crown Court against a refusal to carry out registration or against a cancellation of registration.[55]

REGULATIONS

Acting under the power given to him by the Adoption Act, the Secretary of State for Home Affairs made regulations governing the conduct of registered adoption societies and local authorities in making arrangements for adoption. The regulations concerned are the Adoption Agencies Regulations 1959, the Adoption Agencies Regulations 1961, and the Adoption Agencies Regulations 1965.

ANNUAL RETURN

Registered adoption societies are required to provide the appropriate local authority with an annual return containing accounts, statistics and a copy of their annual report.[56]

BEFORE PLACING

Before a child is made available for adoption the society or local authority must provide the parent, or parents, with a memorandum in the form set out in the Regulations, and the parent must sign an acknowledgment to the effect that he, or she, has read and understood the memorandum.[57] Registered adoption societies before placing a child for adoption are required by the Regulations:[58]

a to obtain details of the proposed adopters in a form prescribed by the Regulations, to interview the adopters and inspect their home;

b to obtain a medical report on the child in a form prescribed by the Regulations, including blood tests for syphilis for babies more than 6 weeks old and a test for phenylalanine for children between the ages of 6 days and 2 years;

c to enquire of the local authority for the area where the applicants reside whether there is any reason to believe that it would be detrimental to the child to be kept by the applicants in the particular premises.

After considering all the information relating to the applicants and the child the case committee of the society must approve the particular placing.

AFTER PLACING

After the child is placed the society must make adequate arrangements for supervision until such time as the applicants notify the local authority of their intention to adopt the child.[59] When this notification is received the responsibility for visitation passes to the local authority as the child becomes a "protected" child within the meaning of the Act.

All information received by adoption societies and local authorities in connection with adoption must be treated as confidential and documents must be preserved for at least twenty-five years.[60]

DUTIES OF THE GUARDIAN *AD LITEM*

These are set out in the Adoption Act 1958, s. 9, sub-ss. (7) and (8), Adoption (County Court) Rules 1959, as amended Adoption (Juvenile Court) Rules 1959, as amended, and Adoption (High Court) Rules 1973.

Where an application is made for an adoption order, the court must appoint a person to act as guardian *ad litem* of the child to safeguard the interests of the child before the court. Except in High Court cases, the person so appointed may be an officer of the local authority (*i.e.* county or metropolitan district councils acting through their Directors of Social Services), provided the local authority agree, or a probation officer, or in the event of the court considering the appointment of either of these two persons undesirable in the circumstances, some other person to be appointed by the court. An officer of a local authority may not be appointed guardian *ad litem* if the authority holds parental rights and powers over the child or has taken part in the arrangements for the adoption.

The Director of Social Services may carry out guardian *ad litem* duties personally or may appoint a member of his staff for the purpose.

The function of the guardian *ad litem* is to represent the child "in the ordinary course of the proceedings"; he does not act in a custodial capacity. The duties of the guardian *ad litem* are to investigate all circumstances relevant to the proposed adoption, including the verification of the information contained in the application and the detailed list of which is set out in a Schedule to the Rules and which is reprinted below.

Where the guardian *ad litem* informs the court that the child to be adopted is able to understand the nature of an adoption order the court must notify the applicants that the child must attend the hearing.

The work of guardian *ad litem* requires great care and accuracy, and the reports to the court must be carefully prepared. A practice direction is printed in the Appendix;[61] it serves as a guide to officers in one local authority in connection with the preparation of reports to the court. The list of matters set out in this memorandum is not necessarily exhaustive but contains all the relevant points to be covered in the majority of applications.

The court may authorise a local authority to incur any expenditure necessary to the prosecution of its officer's enquiries as guardian *ad litem*.

The particular duties of the guardian *ad litem* are set out in the second Schedule to the Adoption (County Court) Rules 1959 as amended by r. 7 of the Adoption (County Court) (Amendment) Rules 1965.

They are as follows:

1. The guardian *ad litem* shall interview the applicant and shall ascertain:

   a   particulars of all members of the applicant's household and their relationship (if any) to the applicant;

   b   particulars of the accommodation in the applicant's home and the condition of the home;

   c   the means of the applicant;

   d   whether the applicant suffers or has suffered from any serious illness and whether there is any history of tuberculosis, epilepsy or mental illness in the applicant's family;

   e   in the case of an application by one only of the two spouses, why the other spouse does not join in the application;

   f   whether any person specified in the application as a person to whom reference may be made is a responsible person and whether he recommends the applicants with or without reservations;

   g   whether the applicant understands the nature of an Adoption Order and, in particular, that the Order, if made, will render him responsible for the maintenance and upbringing of the child.

   h   why the applicant wishes to adopt the infant;

   i   *such other information, including an assessment of the applicant's personality and, where appropriate, that of the child, as has a bearing on the mutual suitability of the applicant and the child and on the ability of the applicant to bring up the child;*

   j   *the applicant's religious persuasion, if any.*[62]

2. The guardian *ad litem* shall ascertain and inform the applicant:

   a   whether the child has been baptised and, if so, the date and place of baptism;

   b   what treatment the child has received with a view to immunising him against disease;

   c   whether the child has any right to, or interest in, any property;

   d   whether an insurance policy for the payment on the death of the child of money for funeral expenses has been effected.

3(1) The guardian *ad litem* shall, as soon as is reasonably practicable, ascertain whether the child is able to understand the nature of an adoption order.

 (2) If, in the guardian's opinion, the child is able to understand the nature of an adoption order, the guardian shall forthwith inform the court and ascertain whether the child wishes to be adopted by the applicant.

4. The guardian *ad litem* shall interview either in person or by an agent appointed by him for the purpose every individual who is a respondent or who appears to him to have taken part in the arrangements for the adoption of the child.

5(1) The guardian *ad litem* shall obtain from every respondent, not being an individual, such information concerning the child as they have in their possession and which they consider might assist the court in deciding whether or not the child should be adopted by the applicant.

(2) Where such information is given in the form of a written report, the guardian *ad litem* shall append it to his own report to the court.

6. The guardian *ad litem* shall ascertain when the mother of the child ceased to have the care and possession of the child and to whom the care and possession was transferred.

7. The guardian *ad litem* shall ascertain that every consent to the making of an adoption order in pursuance of the application is freely given and with full understanding of the nature and effect of an adoption order.

8. Where either parent of the child is dead, the guardian *ad litem* shall forthwith inform the court if he learns of any relation of the deceased parent who wishes to be heard by the court on the question whether an adoption order should be made.

9. Where the child is illegitimate but no-one is liable as the putative father to contribute to the maintenance of the child by virtue of any order or agreement, the guardian *ad litem* shall forthwith inform the court if he learns of any person, claiming to be the father, who wishes to be heard by the court on the question whether an adoption order should be made.[63]

10. The guardian *ad litem* shall forthwith inform the court if he learns of any other person or body who wishes or ought in his opinion to be heard by the court on the question whether an adoption order should be made.

11. Where the applicant is not ordinarily resident in Great Britain, the guardian *ad litem* shall endeavour to obtain a report on the applicant's home and living conditions from a suitable agency in the country in which he is ordinarily resident.

12. The guardian *ad litem* shall draw the attention of the court to the difference in age between the applicant and the child if it is less than the normal difference in age between parents and their children.

PROPOSED CHANGES IN LAW AND PROCEDURE

This chapter relates to procedure at January 1976. The Children Act 1975 will ultimately bring about considerable changes some of which are mentioned in Chapter 17. Attention is drawn to s.10(3) which deals with applications by divorced and re-married parents for adoption orders. In such cases, the alternative to adoption (variation of a custody order made under s. 42 of the Matrimonial Causes Act 1973) would appear to be available now, before s. 10(3) comes into operation.

NOTES

1. Adoption Act 1958, ss. 1 and 9.
2. *Ibid.*, s. 13 and Children Act 1975, Schedule 1.
3. Adoption Act 1958, s. 15.
4. *Ibid.*, s. 19.
5. *Ibid.*, s. 29.
6. *Ibid.*, s. 28.
7. *Ibid.*, s. 37.
8. *Ibid.*, s. 1.
9. Adoption Act 1958, s. 8.
10. Adoption (County Court) Rules 1959, r. 19.
11. Adoption Act 1958, s. 3.

12. *Ibid.*, s. 37 (1)(b).
13. Adoption (County Court) Rules 1959, r. 1.
14. Adoption Act 1958, s. 40(4).
15. Adoption Act 1958, s. 36.
16. *Ibid.*, s. 3.
17. *Ibid.*, s. 53.
18. Adoption Act 1958, s. 57, as amended.
19. *Ibid.*, s. 4.
20. Adoption (County Court) Rules 1959, r. 5.
21. Adoption Act 1958, s. 4.
22. *Ibid.*, s. 57.
23. Adoption (County Court) Rules 1959, ss. 2 and 5.
24. Adoption Act 1958, s. 6.
25. Adoption Act 1958, s. 5.
26. *Ibid.*, s. 34.
27. Adoption Act 1958, s. 2.
28. Adoption (County Court) Rules 1959, r. 1.
29. Adoption Act 1958, ss 35 and 36.
30. Adoption (County Court) Rules 1959, rr. 1 to 5, *post*.
31. *Ibid.*, r. 10.
32. Adoption (County Court) Rules 1959, r. 2.
33. *Ibid.*, r. 16.
34. *Ibid.*, r. 12.
35. *Ibid.*, r. 11.
36. *Ibid.*, r. 8.
37. Adoption Act 1958, s. 7.
38. Adoption (County Court) Rules 1959, r. 15.
39. *Ibid.*, r. 6.
40. *Ibid.*, r. 7.
41. Adoption (County Court) Rules 1959, r. 23.
42. *Ibid.*, r. 27 as amended by the Adoption (County Court) (Amendment) Rules 1965, r. 3. See also Adoption Act 1958, s. 20(5) for information to adopted person.
43. Adoption Act 1958, s. 1(4).
44. Adoption Act 1958, s. 26 and Adoption Act 1960, s. 1.
45. For information regarding children baptised before adoption, see letter addressed to clergy by Archbishops in 1966.
46. Adoption (County Court) Rules 1959, r. 20.
47. Adoption Act 1958, s. 36.
48. Income Tax Act 1952, s. 212.
49. Adoption Act 1958, s. 10.
50. County Courts Act 1934, s. 105.
51. Adoption (County Court) Rules 1959, r. 24.
52. Adoption Act 1958, s. 28.
53. *Ibid.*, s. 29.
54. *Ibid.*, s. 30.
55. Adoption Act 1958, s. 31.
56. Adoption Agencies Regulations 1959, r. 3.
57. *Ibid.*, r. 4. See Appendix, *post*.
58. *Ibid.*, r. 5.
59. Adoption Agencies Regulations 1959, r. 6.
60. *Ibid.*, r. 8.
61. Appendix, *post*.
62. Particular difficulties may arise if the adoptive parents are of the Jewish faith. They should be advised to consult the Beth Din (Jewish Ecclesiastical Court) before adopting a child.
63. A Practice Direction states that the guardian *ad litem* has no *duty* to seek out the natural father; literal compliance with this Rule is sufficient. (*Re W (an infant)*, [1963] 3 All E.R. 459, Wilberforce, J.)

Chapter 16

MANAGEMENT

In view of the many activities listed in Chapter 14, it is not surprising that members of social work teams say that they spend most of their time on child care rather than on other aspects of the team's work. Estimates vary but probably average about 65%. By child care they usually mean all those cases in which there are children, whether in care or under supervision and also those in which a family has been offered social work support on a voluntary basis under s. 1 of the 1963 Act, possibly coupled with material assistance of some kind. Such cases seem to constitute a good deal of the child care caseload, and tend to be suddenly closed when a social worker leaves a department or team.

There is reason to suppose that child care in this broad sense is more attractive than other forms of social work, so that under the generic concept it receives possibly more attention than it should. The effect of this on the work of one department can be seen in a report of a study of the integration of services, which was carried out in 1972.)[1] This report also reveals the attitudes of some social workers to specialisation and their attitudes to the many problems brought about by the Seebohm changes. It questions assumptions lying behind the concept of "casework" and "caseloads", and the ways in which work is allocated, kept under review, and terminated; and it calls for more clearly defined aims and a better use by social workers of manpower resources other than themselves.

These points merit even more attention now, in a climate of economic restraint, when it is obvious that there can be no big influx of additional manpower, even if it were available. If the pressures on social workers are to be reduced, the only option lies in better management of present resources. To bring this about, there must be a re-appraisal of attitudes towards volunteers', social work assistants and unqualified social workers who far outnumber the qualified. There must also be a recognition of residential social workers, especially in child care, as partners who can be relied upon to maintain and strengthen family ties which, as we have seen, are weak in too many cases. And there must be a willingness on the part of social workers to accept that clerical and administrative duties are important in their own right, not to be regarded with hostility as irrelevant and bureaucratic.

This latter point was touched upon in an earlier chapter. The failure to recognise that social work and administration can be distinguished from each other has led very often to an ineffective use of social workers' time and skills. As Andrew Leigh has pointed out, whenever anything goes wrong—as in several well-publicised cases—the effectiveness of administrative and clerical procedures is the first thing to be put under the microscope.[2] The failure of some simple clerical process can have tragic consequences.

In a well-known case of many years ago it was rumoured that a report calling for urgent attention did not receive it because the report itself was accidentally attached to other papers in a paper clip and filed away. Whether or not this was true, simple errors of the kind do occur, but even these are more understandable than a failure to make and record statutory visits, or to arrange for a medical examination at the right time, to quote only two examples of bad practice. Clearly such matters have implications for the training of all staff, not only social workers. But they are primarily the concern of management, and especially of the management of a social work team.

It has been said that every qualified social worker is a manager and should be capable of using time and skill to the best advantage. While this may be true, the burden in present organisations falls most heavily on the team leader, as is evident from the kind of job description which is currently in vogue. This usually refers to the "management of a team, including social workers, clerical staff and staff such as occupational therapists, the allocation of referrals and work, case consultation, control and oversight of visits and report writing, preparation of statistics" and to more generalised administrative or community duties.

Descriptions of this kind, which may vary in detail from one authority to another certainly seem to make the team leader "accountable" in the management sense of the word; he cannot escape the responsibility for what each and every member of the team does, or fails to do. The supervisory element—though it may be unwelcome—is ineluctable. This is even more the case now that the Social Work Service has modified its inspectorial role, while Social Services Departments in general have not yet introduced inspectorates of their own.

Because of the wide range and complexity of social work, quite apart from child care, it seems likely that local inspection must come. It might well result in the removal of several layers of control, leaving the individual social worker as personally accountable, and the team leader free to advise and support rather than to supervise and direct.

The present dilemmas of management in social work are not new, though they now concern a wider field of operation. In essence they were all present in the former separate departments. So far as child care was concerned, the growth of the old children's departments and the setting up of area teams had focused attention on the changed position of the many social workers who had become managers, almost by accident. In 1965, a special course was mounted for senior child care officers, and some of the papers were published under the title *Administration and Staff Supervision in the Child Care Service*.[3] This booklet contains much that is relevant in the context of the work of a team in a Social Services Department.

RESEARCH

Social workers in teams are probably aware that in their departments there are research staff, and may wonder what they do, or whether their work has any connection with the problems "in the field". Generally speaking research is concerned at present with what the Seebohm Report called "good housekeeping". As there has been little research into social work until recently, there has been a great interest in what has in fact been happening and a great deal has been learned. Inevitably, research staff have been involved in the corporate management approach to the use of resources by the authority as a whole, and are in a position to relate the practice of social work to objectives as set out in programmes such as that in Appendix A.

In previous chapters there have been several references to fact-finding reports of recent years. These illustrate the extent of general ignorance of the facts until they are properly examined, and if the reports are read it will be found that they quote a number of references to previous work on the topics concerned. There are a number of bodies now conducting research on a national scale, while locally most Social Services Departments are looking at various areas of work and sharing the results through the clearing house set up for the purpose at Birmingham.

Research in a sense is something which all social workers should share with research staff. Almost all the information comes from social workers, and it is to be hoped and expected that a great deal of helpful work can be done within the teams, perhaps under the general guidance of research staff. There is perhaps no area of work which does not need scrutiny, and it is encouraging to see that social workers themselves are either suggesting subjects for research, or are carrying it out themselves. What could be more interesting and startling, for instance, than interviewing a number of children in residential care, and their parents to find out how they see the situation?[4] Many other similar down to earth topics come to mind. The scope for learning is enormous, and knowledge personally gained is likely to result in better practice among the very many pressures which surround the social worker of today.

NOTES

1. "Reactions to Integration", Research Unit of the National Institute for Social Work, *Social Work Today*, 1 November 1973.
2. "The Great Paper Chase", *Observer*, 24 February 1971.
3. *Association of Child Care Officers*, Monograph No. 2.
4. Meg Keyte, "Caring", *Social Work Today*, 4 April 1974.

Chapter 17

THE CHILDREN ACT 1975

SUMMARY

This Act is intended primarily to implement the report of the Houghton Committee,[1] but does not do so in all respects. It does not, for instance, provide for Family Courts, but it will transfer magisterial adoption from the juvenile court to the domestic court (s. 100). It also contains some sections arising from the Report of the Committee of Inquiry into the care and supervision of Maria Colwell.[2]

Part I concerns the setting up of an improved adoption service, Part II introduces a new concept of custodianship, Part III deals with proposed changes in relation to children in the care of a local authority or voluntary society, and Parts IV and V are concerned with ancillary provisions.

The Bill during debate aroused a great deal of controversy; on the one hand, there are those who consider that everything possible should be done to strengthen family life by putting in support of all kinds to enable parents, including single parents, to bring up their own children satisfactorily without recourse to care or adoption or other substitutes for family care. On the other hand are those who, while recognising the need for supporting natural families, consider that children have needs and rights of their own, and that not all parents are fitted for the upbringing of children however much support they may be given. There is thus a conflict between the upholders of parental rights, and the advocates of parental duties, and (failing their fulfilment) of a child's *rights* to benefit from love and care from someone other than the parent.

ADVANTAGES AND DISADVANTAGES

There are many points of detail in the Act, but the *main* points of dissension are commented upon below; it will be seen that the "pros" and "cons" broadly follow the two schools of thought set out in the previous paragraph.

Pro

SECTIONS 1 AND 2 AND 4–7
These sections provide for a nation-wide adoption service, including the counselling of children, their parents and actual or prospective adopters.

SECTION 3
This section seeks to ensure that in adoption matters, the first consideration is to be the promotion of the welfare of the child *throughout his childhood* i.e. up to age of 18, and provides that as far as possible the child's views shall be taken into account. (This proposal is included again in s. 59 where it relates to a child in the care of a local authority.) "First consideration" does not make the child's welfare paramount, but makes it weightier than any other consideration.

SECTIONS 14–16
These sections set out a procedure by which a parent may relinquish parental rights to a local authority or adoption agency, and a court may declare a child "free for adoption". This procedure is meant to be used as an alternative to the practice of agreeing to adoption by specified persons, as at present carried out. The sections contain certain safeguards for the parents who choose this method.

Con

It is necessary for adoption services to be provided, but there is a danger that adoption may still be seen as something apart from the main stream of child care alternatives.

The best way of providing for a child throughout childhood is by enabling his family to bring him up. "Rescuing" a child from his family is not by any means always the right answer. Adoption is not an unqualified success, foster home breakdowns are all too frequent, and residential care rarely provides a child with satisfying personal relationships. Adoption in particular extinguishes the parent–child relationship for ever, and in the case of babies the child's point of view is ignored.

This change will benefit prospective adopters, but the Act makes no provision for new services which would help a natural parent to maintain his or her own child adequately, without feeling the need, for the child's sake, to seek adoption arrangements.

Pro   *Con*

SECTION 12

If a child has not been declared "free for adoption" and the parent's consent to adoption is required, the grounds for dispensing with it are widened to include serious ill-treatment, but only if the rehabilitation of the child with the parent is "unlikely".

The other grounds for dispensing with consent are not subject to the proviso about rehabilitation being "unlikely". How is the decision as to whether it is likely or not to be made? The failure to make this decision in respect of children in long-term but indeterminate care is possibly the nub of the whole present problem of "Children who Wait". Will the Act make it any easier for the decision to be made?

These provisions are thought to be helpful in cases of children who have languished for years in care because parents will neither agree to adoption, nor make their own plans for rehabilitation.

It is doubtful whether children who are no longer babies will benefit from this provision. Languishing in care is probably due to low priority which social workers give to the maintenance of contact between parents and children in care, and also to the failure to use s. 2 resolutions in all appropriate cases. There is nothing in theory now to prevent the placing of such children in long-stay foster homes, where adoption or custodianship might well follow later.

SECTION 29

This section empowers a person, including a foster parent, who has cared for a child for *5 years* to apply for an adoption order, and to retain the child against any claim by a parent until the application is made, or 3 months have elapsed since notification to the local authority of intention to adopt.

This appears to apply to children who are in the care of a local authority or voluntary agency and are boarded out with foster parents. The application may be made without the consent of the parent. "Private" foster parents who have cared for a child for 5 years may use this power.

SECTIONS 33 TO 46

These sections set out the new concept of custodianship. A court may give legal custody to a relative or other person (in-

Custodianship falls short of guardianship and if the child concerned were in the care of a local authority or voluntary

Pro

cluding a foster parent, but excluding a parent or a natural father); if the child has been living with the applicant for 3 years, the consent of the parent is not required. A custody order does not convey parental rights to the custodians, and they may apply to be relieved of their powers. Custodianship is designed to give a child long-term protection without adoption, and without depriving parents of their right to apply for access or of their liability to maintain the child if an order is made for that purpose.

Con

agency, the order might create a very difficult situation.

The objection to this provision is that if the child has lived with the prospective custodian for three years, the application can be made without the consent of either the parent or the local authority (if the child is in fact in care).

SECTION 56

If a child has been in the care of a local authority for 6 months under the Act of 1948 (that is, voluntary care) the authority may require a parent to give 28 days' notice of intention to take the child's discharge, instead of—as at present—simply asking for discharge without notice. This power is meant to be used in situations where sudden and unprepared removal from care, specially from a foster home, might be harmful or damaging. The section applies in the same way to a child in the care of a voluntary organisation.

Provision of this kind, though it might be used in a small number of cases, ought not to be necessary, and would not be necessary if:

(a) social workers devoted more time to working with the parents of children in care in a partnership for the benefit of the child, or

(b) where that is not feasible, or is not successful, took steps to protect the child from removal either by obtaining a section 2 resolution or possibly a care order.

From a practical point of view, the 28-day notice may be difficult to enforce in face of opposition from a parent, and if enforced would make further support impossible after the child's discharge.

Enforcement could attract the penalties laid down in s. 3(8) of the Children Act 1948 (now

Pro   *Con*

increased to a fine of £400 or
3 months' imprisonment).

SECTION 57

This section enables a local
authority to pass a section 2
resolution in two new situations:

(a) where there is a resolution in force in respect of one
parent, who is, or may become,
a member of the same household as the other parent and the
child, the authority may pass a
resolution assuming joint rights
with the latter parent;

(b) when a child has been in
care continuously for three years
the care being either that of a
local authority, or partly that of
a local authority and partly that
of a voluntary organisation.

(a) This has merit but would
often be impossible to operate;
it would be better for all
resolutions to be passed against
both parents, though this would
have to be explained in order to
avoid apparent injustice.

(b) This does not seem necessary. In such cases there must be
evidence for the passing of a
resolution under existing
grounds, especially if it is
remembered that a parent may
agree to a resolution voluntarily.

SECTION 60

This section enables a local
authority to pass a resolution
under s. 2 of the Children Act
1948, vesting parental rights and
duties in a voluntary organisation which has a child in care.

It would be preferable for
voluntary organisations to have
the power to pass resolutions on
the same ground as local
authorities.

The effect of these sections,
taken together, is to introduce
time as a factor in diminishing
the rights of parents whose
children are in the care of a
local authority, or a voluntary
organisation, or a person. The
time limits introduced are however to be subject to review.

Time limits in themselves are
not good in principle in matters
such as this, but if there are to
be any they should vary according to the age of the child, and
his own wishes. The various
ways in which the parents'
position may be weakened may
deter them from seeking help
when it is needed.

There should be a duty on the
part of the local authority or
voluntary organisation to provide a clear written statement of
the possible effects of admission
to care on a voluntary basis.

INITIAL IMPLEMENTATION FROM
1 JANUARY 1976

The Act which has emerged from these conflicts cannot be brought fully into operation without considerable additional resources of finance and staff; in the light of the criticism which has been directed at the working of the Children and Young Persons Act 1969, it is understood that this new Act of 1975 will only be brought into effect as and when the necessary resources are made available by, and to, local authorities. (See DHSS Local Authority Circular (75)21, December 1975.)

There will therefore be a period—perhaps of several years— during which the Act will be partly of non-effect; confusion may arise for social workers unless they clearly recognise that, for the most part, this present edition of this Manual represents the child-care situation as at January 1976, and as it may remain for some little time. The following provisions have effect from *1 January 1976*, and where applicable have been noted in the text in the appropriate chapter. They are further explained in Annex B to Circular (75)21.

GENERAL PRINCIPLES

Section 3. "In reaching any decision relating to the adoption of a child a court or adoption agency shall have regard to all the circumstances, first consideration being given to the need to safeguard and promote the welfare of the child throughout his childhood; and shall so far as practicable ascertain the wishes and feelings of the child regarding the decision and give due consideration to them, having regard to his age and understanding."

Section 59. This places a similar duty on a local authority with regard to any decision relating to a child in its care; but authorises the authority to exercise its powers in a manner inconsistent with the duty if this is necessary for the purpose of protecting members of the public (new s. 12 of the Children Act 1948).

Section 13. "An adoption agency shall in placing a child for adoption have regard (so far as is practicable) to any wishes of the child's parents and guardians as to religious upbringing of the child".

POWER OF SECRETARY OF STATE TO MAKE REGULATIONS

Regulations may be made as to (a) the exercise by a local authority of its powers under a supervision order made under the Children and Young Persons Act 1969, and (b) the establishment of a panel of persons from whom guardians *ad litem* and reporting officers may be appointed for the purpose of this and other Acts for which such appointments may be required.

CONCEPTS

Section 85 sets out a number of concepts contained in this Act. *Parental rights and duties* relate to a child and his property, and include a right of access *inter alia*. They cannot normally be transferred. They may be exercised jointly or by one parent without the other, unless there is a signified disapproval. Other points relate to the death of a parent, and the exclusive rights and duties of the mother of an illegitimate child.

Section 86 defines "legal custody", as rights affecting the person of a child, but not his property; s. 87 "actual custody", meaning the actual possession of the child, whether or not shared with others. Section 88 provides that if a voluntary organisation has actual custody of a child he is in its care. Section 89 provides for the meaning of some of these expressions in any future legislation.

Sections 90 and 91 deal with the making of reports to a magistrates' court in guardianship and matrimonial proceedings, and with the procedure to be followed when the reports are in writing.

GENERAL

Section 98 empowers the Secretary of State to cause inquiries to be held into specified matters relating to children; s. 100 defines the phrase "authorised court". Section 107 establishes that the area covered by a magistrate's court is the commission area, i.e. the whole county. Section 107 also contains other definitions, such as "child", "guardian" and "relative".

STATUS CONFERRED BY ADOPTION

Part II of Schedule 1 sets out the implications of adoption and creates a "vocabulary" relating to the adoptive relationship, and "adoptive" parents and relatives. Definitions of "parent" such as that set out in s. 59 (1) of the Children Act 1948 are revised accordingly.

MINOR AND CONSEQUENTIAL AMENDMENTS

A number of paragraphs in Schedule 3 came into operation on 1 January 1976. Some deal with increased fines for offences under protective legislation, and these are noted in the text.

Other amendments made by this Schedule have an effect on practice and are listed as follows:

SCHEDULE 3

Adoption Act 1958

Para. 21   Substitutes "child" for infant and "actual custody" for care and possession.

Para. 39   Natural father who has obtained custody of his child is a guardian whose consent to adoption must be sought.

Children and Young Persons Act 1969

Para. 67 Inserts new primary condition "bb" in s. 1(2).

Para. 69 Applies care or control test to cases in which an application is made under s. 21(2) for discharge of a care order.

Para. 70 Care order to cease to have effect on making of an adoption order, or other orders not yet in force, under this Act.

Matrimonial Causes Act 1973

Para. 78 Amends s. 44 so that a supervision order may be made when *care* (not custody) of a child has been committed to a person.

(These amendments have been incorporated in the text of the appropriate chapter.)

Schedule 4, Parts I, II, and III (only) come into effect on 1 January 1976; they repeal a number of sections of earlier Acts consequent on the passing of the Children Act 1975.

FUTURE IMPLEMENTATION OF THE ACT

Relevant chapters

Much of the Act will not be implemented immediately, but the following sections will be of interest to social workers. A note on the implementation of these sections appears at the end of the chapter.

ADOPTION

Section 8 contains a new definition of an adoption order. — 15

Section 9 provides that applicants for an adoption order must have had the child in their home at all times for a period of 12 months before the order can be made, unless they are related to the child, or the child was placed by an adoption agency (*i.e.* a local authority, or adoption society). — 10, 11, 15

Section 10 and 11 lay down new qualifications of age domicile and status for applicants for an adoption order. They contain provisions which will have the effect of greatly reducing the number of adoptions made in favour of parent and step-parent, or of step-parent or relative. — 15

Section 12 introduces "agreement" rather than "consent" to adoption, and widens the grounds on which agreement may be dispensed with. — 15

Sections 14–16 set out a new procedure known as "freeing a child for adoption" which may be used as an alternative, in agency cases, to the present pro- — 10, 11, 15

cedure. In certain conditions, such a procedure may
be used without parental consent but only if the child
is already in the care of the agency.

Section 17 enables a court on refusing an adoption   9, 14, 15
order to make a supervision or care order.

Section 18 brings about changes with regard to   7, 15
notification (to a local authority) of intention to
adopt, and relieves the local authority of "welfare
supervision" if the child has been placed by an
adoption agency.

Section 20 provides for the appointment of guard-   15
ians *ad litem* and reporting officers who will witness
agreement to adoption.

Section 26 enables an adopted person aged 18 to   15
obtain information about his birth record, and provides that counselling for such persons shall be
available.

Section 28 prohibits "third-party" placings, except   7, 15
under a High Court order, or when the proposed
adopter is a relative of the child.

Section 29 and 30 deal with restrictions on the   15
removal of a child from prospective adopters and the
action to be taken if a child is so removed.

Section 32 makes it possible for a scheme to be   15
prepared for the payment of money to adopters in
respect of children with special needs.

CUSTODY

Section 33 enables a court to make a custodianship   7, 9, 10, 11
order, vesting legal custody of a child in the applicant,
who may be a relative, step-parent or foster parent
(see note on s. 10 and 11 above).

Section 34 deals with supplementary orders for   7, 9, 10, 11
access and maintenance in respect of children under
custody orders, and empowers a local authority to
make payments to a custodian, except if he or she is a
step-parent.

Section 36–40 deal further with custodianship   7, 9, 10, 11
orders and the involvement of the local authority in
the procedures.

CARE

Section 56 gives a local authority power to require   9, 10, 11, 13
notice of removal from care of a child who has been

Relevant
chapters

in care for six months, and applies the same principle
to children in the care of voluntary organisations.

Section 57 extends the power of a local authority   9, 10, 11
to pass a resolution under s. 2 of the Children Act;
s. 60–63 provide a similar safeguard for children in
the care of a voluntary organisation. Section 58
provides for an appeal to High Court from a juvenile
court order confirming or terminating such resolutions.

Section 64 introduces a new procedure to safeguard   8, 9, 13, 14
the interests of a child before the court in care proceedings, by making it possible to order that a parent
shall not act on the child's behalf in the proceedings,
and to consider the appointment of a guardian *ad
litem* for the child. In such a situation the parent
would be entitled to apply for legal aid.

Section 67 deals with the recovery of children who   12, 13
have absconded from care, and

Section 68 gives powers of arrest (by a constable)   7, 12
in respect of children or young persons who have
absconded, or been taken, from any place of safety.

Section 95 empowers the Secretary of State to make   7
regulations as to the visiting of privately placed
foster children.

Section 96 empowers the Secretary of State to make   7
regulations requiring *parents* to give information to a
local authority about proposed fostering arrangements.

Section 97 authorises the making of regulations   7
prohibiting parents from advertising for private foster
parents.

Para. 71 of Schedule 3 enables the Secretary of   11
State to make regulations as to the way in which local
authorities are to conduct periodical reviews under
s. 27 of the Children and Young Persons Act 1969.

Schedules 3 and 4 contain a number of minor   Most
amendments and repeals which do not become   chapters
operative from 1 January 1976.

One such amendment, para. 74 of Schedule 3, will   1–5
amend the Schedule of the Local Authority Social
Services Act 1970 by adding to the list of functions
"counselling services for adopted persons", and the
contents of Parts I and II of the Children Act 1975.

Sections 8–12, 17, 20, 26, 29, 30, 56, 57, 64, 67 and
68 are likely to be implemented during the financial
year 1976/77. Note that pending the operation of
Section 12, the additional ground for dispensing with

consent is brought into effect by s. 108(6). No date has
yet been specified for the implementation of ss. 14–16,
18, 28, 32–34, 36–40, 95–97, Schedule 3, para. 71 and
the minor amendments and repeats contained in
Schedules 3 and 4.

NOTES

1. Report of the Departmental Committee on the Adoption of Children, Cmnd.
   5107, 1972.
2. Report of the Committe of Inquiry into the care and supervision provided in
   relation to Maria Colwell, 1974, Department of Health and Social Security.

APPENDIX

SUMMARY

A. SPECIMEN COMMUNITY CARE PROGRAMME AREAS AND OBJECTIVES

This outline structure consists of an overall objective which states the philosophy, five first-level objectives which serve the overall objective, and a number of separate activities which are undertaken to achieve the stated objectives. Where activities are actually carried out within another programme area, and by another local authority department, there is a note in the margin to that effect. Probation activities, though not strictly local authority services, have been included because expenditure on them serves the community care objectives. Similarly, Area Health Authority activities are included in those activities which serve the objectives of this programme.

The word "care" where it is used means accommodation and maintenance, and is thus separated from "support". It will be noticed that short-term care of various types is included in Programme C, among those activities which are used to minimise the prospect of long-term dependence on care or treatment of different kinds.

Very simply, the concept is that everything should be done to promote an environment which is helpful (A), but that there will be those who will nevertheless be at risk of long-term care; there must be ways of detecting them (B) and of providing ways of supporting them in the community (C), but finally there will be some who need long-term care or treatment, which is provided under (D), but with the intention of rehabilitation into the community wherever this is possible. All activities in support of these objectives, such as travelling, and clerical work, are deemed to be part of the actual activities themselves. Other administrative activities, which should be minimal, are provided for in (E).

OVERALL OBJECTIVE

To build up a community of families and individuals able to lead a full personal life, supported, when required, by appropriate social measures.

FIRST-LEVEL OBJECTIVES

A. To contribute towards the creation of a physical and social environment favourable to human development.
B. To detect those families and individuals who are at risk of becoming dependent upon the community.
C. To provide, and deploy, resources to minimise long-term dependence on community care.
D. To provide long-term care or treatment for those families and individuals who need it.
E. To provide general administration and support services.

Note: Headings in the left-hand margins refer to other major programmes served by the activity on the right.

	A	To contribute towards the creation of a physical and social environment favourable to human development
PLANNING	1	By influencing the physical environment in the light of social factors, through:
and		(a) Social element of allied County plans
TRANSPORTATION		(b) District councils
		(c) Voluntary housing provision
DISTRICT COUNCILS	2	(a) By liaising with the housing authorities for the provision of suitable and sufficient housing especially for the handicapped and homeless
		(b) By providing grants for special housing schemes

<table>
<tr><td></td><td colspan="2">3 By encouraging the community to involve itself in the construction of a healthy social environment, through:</td></tr>
</table>

EDUCATION	3 By encouraging the community to involve itself in the construction of a healthy social environment, through:
	(a) Education in personal relationships and in citizenship
EDUCATION	(b) Training in domestic skills
DISTRICT	(c) Community relations
COUNCILS	(d) Community centres, adventure playgrounds, etc.
	(e) Involvement of local interest in homes and other establishments provided by the authority
	(f) Village or area community schemes and street warden schemes
POLICE, EDUCATION and PROBATION PROBATION D.H.S.S.	4 By providing an advisory service:
	(a) General advice and guidance
	(b) Information about rights
	(c) Information about services
	5 By research:
	(a) Research into personal and community factors causing problems
	(b) Devising and executing surveys
	(c) Processing routine flows of information
	(d) Circulation of research findings
	6 By interpretation and reappraisal of social policy in the light of research findings

---

B To detect those families and individuals who are at risk of becoming dependent upon the community

---

	1 By encouraging self-referral:
	(a) Publicity to encourage referral
	(b) Accessible facilities in areas
AREA HEALTH AUTHORITY	(c) Accessible facilities in hospitals
	(d) Provision of an on-call system
PROBATION, POLICE	2 By establishment of early warning systems:
	(a) Police and courts: Police; probation service; juvenile courts; divorce courts; magistrates courts; county courts; crown courts; prisons
PROBATION, POLICE AREA HEALTH AUTHORITY	(b) Juvenile bureau
	(c) Medical; area health authority; general practitioners and health visitors

EDUCATION
DISTRICT
COUNCILS,
ETC.

(d) Education:
    Schools; education welfare officer
(e) Financial need:
    Housing authorities and building societies; Department of Health and Social Security; Department of Employment and Productivity; electricity and gas boards
(f) Community services:
    Citizens advice bureau; clergy; home helps; volunteers—meals service, W.R.V.S., village or area community scheme; voluntary agencies—children, elderly, mental health, handicapped children

---

C To provide, and deploy, resources to minimise long-term dependence on community care

---

PROBATION/
EDUCATION

1 By initial assessment of need:
    (a) Reports to courts

    (b) Reports on all other cases detected under Programme B

2 By periodical reviews of all cases receiving supervision or support so that:
    (a) Any unmet need can be identified
    (b) Support is given only as long as it is necessary

EDUCATION

EDUCATION/
PROBATION
PROBATION

PROBATION
PROBATION

AREA HEALTH
AUTHORITY

3 By counselling:
    (a) Consultation with nuclear and extended family
    (b) Provision of individual casework support/supervision
    (c) Group therapy
    (d) Legal supervision of persons under court orders
        (i) Persons under 17
        (ii) Persons over 17
    (e) Supervision of children placed for adoption
    (f) Supervision of private foster homes, etc.
    (g) Counselling in hospital

DISTRICT
COUNCILS

4 By counselling plus material and financial assistance:
    (a) Homelessness prevention
    (b) Assistance in cash or kind to diminish need for care (for children)

PROBATION   (c)   Minimising long-term dependence or community care through financial assistance

EDUCATION   (d)   School meals and clothing

5   By counselling plus support services including voluntary services, in managing the home:

    (a)   Training in domestic management within the home

DISTRICT
COUNCILS

    (b)   Meals on wheels
    (c)   Home helps
    (d)   Family aids and night sitters
    (e)   Aids and equipment to improve mobility
    (f)   Adaptation of property
    (g)   Telephones
    (h)   Television and radio
    (i)   Use of young volunteers
    (j)   Car badges

6   By counselling plus personal support services:

EDUCATION   (a)   Social counselling in child guidance
    (b)   Home tuition
    (c)   Services for the blind:
        teaching, talking books, mobility teaching, vocational guidance, etc.
    (d)   Services for the deaf and hard of hearing:
        teaching, communication, vocational guidance, etc.
    (e)   Services for the handicapped:
        occupational therapy, instruction, vocational guidance, etc.

7   By counselling plus support services outside the home:

PLANNING and
TRANSPORTATION, HEALTH

    (a)   Transport

    (b)   Child-minders
EDUCATION   (c)   Playgroups
EDUCATION   (d)   Day nurseries
EDUCATION   (e)   Nursery schools
EDUCATION   (f)   Adventure playgrounds
EDUCATION   (g)   Youth clubs and organisations
    (h)   Day care
    (i)   Day centres and clubs
    (j)   Luncheon clubs
    (k)   Social clubs and activities
    (l)   Provision of holidays
PROBATION   (m)   Community training centres (Probation)

8   By counselling and facilities for employment or training:

EDUCATION   (a)   Special day schools

(b) Workshops
(c) Industrial out-work
(d) Adult training centres

9 By counselling and the provision of temporary care:

EDUCATION
    (a) Residential assessment of social need
      (i) Community homes (for children and young persons)
      (ii) Homes for the elderly
      (iii) Homes for the handicapped
    (b) Short-stay foster homes
    (c) Mother and baby homes
    (d) Training units for mothers and children
    (e) Intermediate treatment under Children and Young Persons Act 1969

EDUCATION
    (f) Residential special schools

EDUCATION
    (g) Boarding school education
    (h) Short-stay accommodation
    (i) Temporary accommodation (Part III)

PROBATION
    (j) Probation and voluntary hostels
    (k) Rehabilitation units
      (i) Blind
      (ii) Families
      (iii) Handicapped

HEALTH
    (l) Admission to hospital

PUBLIC PROTECTION
10 By providing community care during and after civil emergencies

---

D To provide long-term care for those families and individuals who need it

---

1 By the provision of long-term care:
    (a) Long stay foster homes
    (b) Voluntary homes
      (i) Children
      (ii) Others
    (c) Training establishments

EDUCATION
    (d) Community homes (for children and young persons)
    (e) Homes for the aged
    (f) Hostel homes:
      (i) Young people up to the age of 21
      (ii) Mentally ill
      (iii) Mentally handicapped

2 By the enforcement of care and/or treatment where necessary, failing voluntary agreement:

EDUCATION
    (a) Children/young people

PROBATION   (b)   Offenders in breach of probation orders and statutory licences
       (c)   Elderly
       (d)   Mentally disordered

3   By the provision of support services:
       (a)   Development of foster care for children, elderly and mentally handicapped
       (b)   Development of adoption service (children)
       (c)   Homes services
       (i)   Casework

            (i)   Casework
            (ii)   Local community interests

HEALTH   (iii)   Medical services
HEALTH   (iv)   Dental services
            (v)   Spiritual guidance
            (vi)   Leisure activities/holidays
            (vii)   Occupational therapy
            (viii)   Property protection
            (ix)   Receiverships

PROBATION   (d)   Prison welfare
PROTECTION   (e)   Registration and inspection of or advice to homes
       (f)   Visiting voluntary children's homes
       (g)   Providing official visitor for certain children
AREA HEALTH AUTHORITY   (h)   Liaison arrangements with hospital service

4   By encouraging rehabilitation:
       (a)   Using powers to allow children in care under Orders or Resolutions to live at home under supervision
       (b)   Acting as Guardian *ad litem* in adoption cases
       (c)   Allocating social work support to each client or family in long-term care
PROBATION   (d)   Group work (probation)
       (e)   Making and maintaining contact with the wider family
       (f)   Periodically reviewing each case with a view to ensuring that care is not continued longer than essential for the client's well-being
       (g)   Providing support services (as in Programme C) as required after discharge from care
PROBATION   (h)   Providing after care support for persons released from prisons, borstals and detention centres
PROBATION   (i)   After care support (probation)

E General administration and Support Services

1 Training and development of staff, through:
    (a) Training
        (i)   Induction training
        (ii) Post-entry training and trainees
        (iii) Refresher training

PERSONNEL
        (iv) Management training
        (v) Training or personnel placed for practical experience

PROBATION
        (vi) Training of volunteers (probation)
    (b) Staff development

PROBATION

2 Maintaining contact with voluntary agencies and training of individual volunteers, in order to provide voluntary support and assistance to probation officers and other social workers.
3 Liaison at all levels with area health authority.
4 General administration and support services.

B. PLACE OF SAFETY ORDER

The order is set out in due form, which should be completed, stating precisely what the grounds for the application are in accordance with the Act, so that the Justice of the Peace can see what is the basis of the informant's "reasonable cause to believe that . . .".

The name of the Petty Sessional Division, and the name and office address of the informant should also be completed. The form of order should then be taken personally to a Justice of the Peace, and the informant should be prepared if asked to show that he is an officer of the local authority and authorised to make the application.

As the application is *ex parte*, the parent or guardian has no legal right to be present, but may attend if so desired.

The informant should be prepared to give details of his cause for concern about the child, and should be prepared to answer questions arising from his statement.

If the Justice of the Peace is satisfied that the application is well founded, he will sign the order authorising detention for a period not exceeding twenty-eight days. The period for each case may be suggested, within that limit.

The informant is then authorised to remove the child to whatever place of safety has been arranged, and must inform the parent or guardian (if not present at the application) of the reason for the detention.

It will then be necessary to take action to ensure that a decision as to the next stage is reached with as little delay as possible.

AUTHORITY TO REMOVE TO A PLACE OF SAFETY
CHILDREN AND YOUNG PERSONS ACT 1969 (SECTION 28(1))

In the County of

Petty Sessional Division of: ....

(Name of Officer applying for Place of Safety Order): ....

of (Office address): ....

....
(hereinafter called the Applicant) has this day applied under section 28(1)
of the Children and Young Persons Act 1969 for authority to detain and
take to a Place of Safety

(Name of relevant Infant) ....

of (address of relevant Infant) ....
a child or young person (hereinafter called the relevant Infant).

AND I, the undersigned Justice of the Peace, am satisfied that the
Applicant has reasonable cause to believe that (specify belief in terms of
section 28(1) (a), (b) or (c)).

and hereby grant the said Application.

AND the relevant Infant may be detained in a Place of Safety by virtue
of this authorisation for a period of .... days beginning
with the date hereof.

Dated this ....day of 197

....J.P.

Justice of the Peace for the County aforesaid

C. A SUGGESTED PROCEDURE FOR PRELIMINARY INVESTIGATION OF PROSPECTIVE ADOPTERS, PRIVATE AND LOCAL AUTHORITY FOSTER PARENTS, AND CHILD-MINDERS

Anyone undertaking the care of a child, or children, in one of these ways is providing a service; in all, this represents a considerable resource to the department which is specially valuable because the service is offered within private homes, and within a defined locality, which may be identical with the place in which the need for the service arises.

This opens up the possibility of using these services, or some of them, for different purposes at different times. A person registered as a child-minder may be willing to act as a short-term foster parent for instance, or someone who has adopted a child may be willing to provide day care to a child living near by. Not everyone of course will be willing to assist in more than one capacity, but the possibility can be encouraged.

One apparent difficulty is the slightly different criteria for "approval" as between registered child-minders and local authority foster parents. In addition there are no regulations laying down precisely what enquiries should be made in the cases of people intending to act as private foster parents, or to have children placed with them with a view to adoption. But in the last two situations, there is a duty to notify the local authority under the Children Act 1958 and the Adoption Act 1958 respectively; the authority has power to prohibit the placing and could only do this if it had made enquiries as to the suitability of the persons making the notification. Similarly, if there is a failure to notify before placing, enquiries should be made after the placing becomes known, as the authority has the power to apply for an order for the removal of the child; here again enquiries would have to be made to justify this action.

The procedure for enquiry in the case of a child-minder is laid down in an old Circular, Ministry of Health 36/68, and surprisingly seems rather better than the procedure for foster parents under the Boarding-Out Regulations 1955.

The recommended procedure is for a general discussion of the position first, with explanation of what is entailed; this is followed by an application completed by the person wishing to be registered, with a declaration containing a number of statements all of which can be verified, and a declaration of health. The Circular recommends verification by means of enquiries to various sources, including the police and probation services. No visit by a member of staff is needed until all this preliminary work has been carried out and the ground has then been cleared for a real assessment of the personal qualities of the applicant.

There seem to be advantages in using the application method in all four types of case set out above, but only as a means of establishing certain *facts* before the assessment, which is a matter of *opinion*, takes place.

In this way everyone would first apply, or enquire, and be given advice or counselling, which can be done individually or—probably better—in groups. After this, those who still wish to continue would be invited to complete a simple form of application (A and B) and the statements in it would be verified by a series of form letters to the persons mentioned at the head of form C. When all the replies have been received, and marked off, the social worker concerned could begin the necessary detailed enquiry knowing that there was no basic objection to acceptance on *personal grounds.* If the replies disclosed any adverse facts, such as a conviction, the weight of this could be considered, but need not necessarily lead to rejection; if it does there would be some good reason. (The likelihood of rejection would be greatly minimised by the initial discussion before the application is made, as in the course of it applicants would be told of the *kind* of enquiries which would be instituted in the event of an application being received. Self-rejection would be specially likely if the preliminary discussion took place in a group.)

The requirements for registration as a child-minder are more detailed and more precise than those for a foster parent, local authority or otherwise, so that given the basic information, two different assessments of *opinion* may be required, form C or D being used as appropriate.

In using this method, the department would treat in the same way everyone who wishes to offer a home for a child whether for two hours a day, or for life, and the basic facts would be established before the particular kind of personal assessment was embarked upon. This would make a later "change of use" possible without a repetition of enquiries already made. A further advantage is that the basic work, after initial counselling, would be purely an administrative matter until such time as the way was clear for fuller social work investigation. The suggested Forms A, B, C and D are set out in the following pages; the form letters at present used for foster parents would be suitable, after slight amendment to take in the whole of the suggested scope of enquiry.

FORM A

COUNCIL

SOCIAL SERVICES DEPARTMENT

Information given by persons wishing to care, in their
own home, for a child or children under the age of 18

	Wife (or lady householder)	Husband (or other householder)
1. Full Name		
2. Maiden or former Name		
3. Date of Birth		
4. Married/Single/Widowed Divorced/Separated		
5. If married date of marriage		
6. Address and Tel. No.		
7. How long here		
8. If less than two years previous address		
9. Any qualifications (Child Care, Nursery etc.)		
10. Religion		
11. Occupation		
12. Approx. Income per week		
13. Name and address of G.P. Telephone Number		

14. Family and Household
    (1) Other persons *over 16* living here   All members of the family (*under 16*)

Full Name	*Age*	*Full Name*	*Address*

(2) The following persons would assist in the care of the children:

Name	Address	Age
Name	Address	Age
Name	Address	Age

15. Brief description of home—owned or rented, from landlord or
    Council, how many rooms, main Services, whether there is a
    garden, etc.

I DECLARE that neither I nor any of the persons named overleaf has had made against him or her an order under any of the following enactments:

(a) Part 1 of the Children Act 1958 removing a child from his or her care.

(b) The Children and Young Persons Acts 1933–1969 or the Social Work (Scotland) Act 1968 in respect of any child found to be in need of compulsory care, being an order by virtue of which the child was removed from his or her care.

(c) Section 1(4) of the Nurseries and Child-Minders Regulation Act 1948 refusing his or her registration under that Act or an order under Section 5 of that Act cancelling his or her registration under that Act or the registration under that Act of any premises occupied by him or her.

(d) Section 43 of the Adoption Act 1958, (removal of protected children from unsuitable surroundings) for the removal of a child from his or her care.

I FURTHER DECLARE that neither I nor any of the persons named overleaf have been convicted of any of the following offences:

(a) The murder or manslaughter of a child or young person, also aiding, abetting, counselling or procuring the suicide of a child or young person.

(b) Infanticide.

(c) Any offence under section 27 or 56 of the Offences against the Persons Act 1861, and any offence against a child or young person under section 5, 42 or 43 of that Act.

(d) Any offence under sections 1, 3, 4, 11 or 23 of the Children and Young Persons Act 1933.

(e) Any offence against a child or young persons under any of the following sections of the Sexual Offences Act 1956, that is to say sections 2 to 7, 10 to 16, 19, 20, 22 to 26 and 28, and any attempt to commit against a child or young person an offence under sections 2, 5, 6, 7, 10, 11, 12, 22 or 23 of that Act.

(f) Any offence specified in the First Schedule to the Children and Young Persons (Scotland) Act 1937.

(g) Any other offence involving bodily injury to a child or young person.

I FURTHER DECLARE that neither my rights and powers nor any of the rights and powers of the persons named with respect to a child have been vested in a local authority under section 2 of the Children Act 1948.

I understand that the   Council has a duty to make enquiries about the members of a household in which children may be cared for away from their parents. I therefore authorise the Council to verify any of the information I have given above.

I also authorise the Council to make enquiries of the following persons who are willing to act as referees in this application:

(1) *Name and Address*

(2) *Name and Address*

Signed...................... Date........................

Signed...................... Date........................

FORM B

.... COUNCIL SOCIAL SERVICES DEPARTMENT

BOARDING-OUT OF CHILDREN REGULATIONS 1955

CHILDREN ACT 1958

as amended by the

CHILDREN'S AND YOUNG PERSONS ACT 1969

ADOPTION AGENCIES REGULATIONS 1959

NURSERIES AND CHILD-MINDERS REGULATION ACT 1948

as amended by the

HEALTH SERVICES AND PUBLIC HEALTH ACT 1968

DECLARATION OF HEALTH

Name ....

Address ....

Date of
.... Birth ....

Are you in good health at present? ....

Are you at present attending the doctor
for any reason? (If so, state reason) ....

Do you have any treatment prescribed
regularly by the Doctor? (If so, give details) ....

Have you ever suffered from nervous or other
similar illness and, if so, what age were
you when this happened? ....

Have you ever suffered from epilepsy or fits? ....

Have you ever suffered from tuberculosis or
have you been in close contact with a known
case of tuberculosis? (If yes, please give details) ....

When did you last have a chest X-ray and with
what result? ....

Is everyone else living in your household
(including lodgers) as far as you know in
good health? ....

I agree that an authorised Medical Officer of the Area Health Authority may seek medical information from any doctor who has at any time attended me and I authorise the giving of such information.

My general practitioner is: Name ....

Address ....

....

I certify that the above statements are true.

Signature ....

Date ....

FORM C
ASSESSMENT OF APPLICATION TO CARE FOR A CHILD

1. Enquiries regarding ....

	Date sent	Date Reply		Date sent	Date Reply
Police			Personal Ref. (1)		
Probation			Personal Ref. (2)		
Education			A.H.A. (T.B.)		
G.P. (1)			Health Care team		
G.P. (2)			Shire Hall Record		
			Area Record		

2. *Accommodation*: Type of house, neighbourhood, number of rooms, material condition, play facilities, fire precautions, sanitation, water supply, heating, space, etc.

3. *Assessment*: Family background and relationships, special skills and interests, attitude to natural parents, temperament, age of children to be cared for, motivation (including infertility investigations when appropriate)

3. *Assessment* (Cont'd/......)

4. Date of group meetings attended

   Date of personal interviews

5. Recommendation, including restrictions on number of children to be cared for, and any special provisions to be made.

Signed .... Social Worker   Date..........

Approved/Not approved/Deferred..............   Date..........
                            Area Director

Registered as approved or not approved ....

If refused, date   notified for Committee Report ....

           To file.......................... Date............
                        Signed

FORM D

NURSERIES AND CHILD-MINDERS REGULATION ACT 1948
Assessment of application to care for a child (Child-Minders)

	Date Sent	Date Reply		Date Sent	Date Reply
Police			Personal Ref. (1)		
Probation			Personal Ref. (2)		
Education			A.H.A. (T.B.)		
G.P. (1)			Health Care team		
G.P. (2)			Shire Hall Record		
			Area Record		

1. Name of Occupier ....

2. Address of Premises ....

....

3. Number and description of rooms, and floor area:

    (i) .... (iv) ....

    (ii) .... (v) ....

    (iii) .... (vi) ....

4. Water supply............... (5) W.C. accommodation........

6. Lavatory basins............. (7) Drainage ....

8. How are premises heated ...... (9) Fire/Radiator guards ....

10. Any person suffering from tuberculosis or any other infectious disease? ....

11. General condition of premises ....

....

....

....

12. Other remarks...

....

....

....

....

Date............. Signature of Officer........................

Recommendation as to number of children permitted................

Recommendation—Approved/Disapproved/Deferred

If not approved state reason.....................................
....
....
....

Reported to Committee .... Result ....

Certificate issued ....
     or   Entered in Register ....

Notice of Refusal sent ....

Subsequent action ....
....
....
....
....
....
....
....
....
....
....

Regulations 20, 23 and 27
D. FORM OF UNDERTAKING TO BE SIGNED BY FOSTER PARENTS[1]

We/I, A.B. [and B.B.], of
having on the   day of   , 19   , received
from [the council of the county/county borough of
(hereinafter called "The council")] [*name of voluntary organisation*
(hereinafter called "The organisation")] C.D., who was born on the
                    day of   19   , and whose religious persuasion
is   , into our/my home as a member of our/my family
undertake that—

1. We/I will care for C.D. and bring him/her up as we/I would a child of our/my own.

2. He/she will be brought up in, and will be encouraged to practise, his/her religion.

3. We/I will look after his/her health and consult a doctor whenever he/she is ill and will allow him/her to be medically examined at such times and places as [the council] [the organisation] may require.

4. We/I will inform [the council] [the organisation] immediately of any serious occurrence affecting the child.

5. We/I will at all times permit any person so authorised by the Secretary of State or by [the council] [the organisation] [or by the council of the county/county borough where we/I live] to see him/her and visit our/my home.

6. We/I will allow him/her to be removed from our/my home when so requested by a person authorised by [the council] [the organisation] [or by the council of the county/county borough where we/I live].

7. If we/I decide to move, we/I will notify the new address to [the council] [the organisation] before we/I go.

(Sgd.) ....

(Sgd.) ....

Dated...

Note: The Adoption Forms which follow are those for the County Court. There are similar separate forms for use in applications to the High Court and the juvenile court. "Infant" means "minor" (to be replaced by "child").

Rule 1 (1)

E. ORIGINATING APPLICATION FOR AN ADOPTION ORDER OR A PROVISIONAL ADOPTION ORDER[2]

In the .... County Court

No. ....

In The Matter of the Adoption Act 1958
and

In The Matter of .... [1] an infant.

[This Form must be filed in duplicate, but duplicates of the attached documents need not be filed. Every paragraph must be completed or deleted, as the case may be.]

I, the undersigned .... /We the undersigned ...., being desirous of adopting [or obtaining a provisional adoption order in respect of] .... [1], an infant, under the Adoption Act 1958, hereby give the following particulars in support of my/our application.

Part I
Particulars of the applicant[s]

1. Name of [first] applicant in full ....
   Address [2] ....
   Occupation ....
   Date of birth ....
   Relationship (if any) to the infant ....
[2. Name of second applicant in full ....

   Address [2] ....
   Occupation ....
   Date of birth ....
   Relationship (if any) to the infant ....]

3. I am/We are resident and domiciled in England or Wales/Scotland [or I am/We are domiciled in England or Wales/Scotland but not ordinarily resident in Great Britain] [or I am/We are not domiciled in England or Wales or Scotland].

4. I am unmarried/a widow/widower/I am married to .... of .... /We are married to each other and are the persons to whom the attached marriage certificate (or other evidence of marriage) relates.

[5. The consent of my husband/wife to the making of an adoption order/a provisional adoption order in pursuance of my application is attached [or I request the judge to dispense with the consent of my husband/wife on the ground that .... [3]].] [4]

[6. A certificate as to my/our health, signed by a fully registered medical practitioner, is attached.] [5]

PART II
Particulars of the infant

7. The infant is of the .... sex and is not and has not been married. He/She was born on the .... day of ...., 19....., and is the person to whom the attached birth/adoption certificate [6] relates [or was born on or about the .... day of ...., 19....., in ....] [7]

[8. A report on the health of the infant [8], made by a fully registered medical practitioner on the .... day of ...., 19....., [9] is attached.]

9. The infant is the child/adopted child [10] of .... [11] whose last known address was .... [or deceased] and .... [12] whose last known address was .... [or deceased].

[10. The guardian[s] of the infant is/are .... of ....
[and .... of ....]] [13]

11. I/We attach a document/documents signifying the consent of the said .... [14] to the making of an adoption order/a provisional adoption order in pursuance of my/our application.

[12. I/We request the judge to dispense with the consent of ....
on the ground that .... [15].]

[13. The .... Council [or ....] of ....
has/have the rights and powers of a parent of the infant.] [16]

[14. .... of .... is liable by virtue of an order made by the .... court at .... on the .... day of ...., 19....., [or by an agreement dated the .... day of ...., 19.....,] to contribute to the maintenance of the infant.] [17]

15. If an adoption order/a provisional adoption order is made in pursuance of this application, the infant is to be known by the following names:—

Surname ....

Other names ....

Part III
General

16. The infant was received into my/our care and possession on the .... day of ...., 19......, and has been continuously in my/our care and possession since that date.

[17. I/We notified the .... Council on the .... day of ...., 19......, of my/our intention to apply for an adoption order/ a provisional adoption order in respect of the infant.] [18]

18. I have not made/Neither of us has made a previous application for an adoption order/a provisional adoption order in respect of the infant [except an application No. .... made to the .... court at .... which was heard on the .... day of ...., 19......, and was dealt with as follows ....] [19]

19. I/We have not received or given any reward or payment for, or in consideration of, the adoption of the infant or for giving consent to the making of the adoption order/provisional adoption order [except as follows ....] [20]

20. As far as I/we know, no person or body has taken part in the arrangements for placing the infant in my/our care and possession [except ....] [21]

[21. For the purposes of this application reference may be made to .... of ....] [22]

[22. I/We desire that my/our identity should be kept confidential and the serial number of this application is ....] [23]

[23. I/We intend to adopt the infant under the law of or within .... [24] and for that purpose I/we desire to remove the infant from Great Britain.] [25]

I/We accordingly apply for an adoption order/a provisional adoption order in respect of the infant.

Dated this .... day of ...., 19......

Signature(s) ....

....

Notes:

[1] Enter the first name[s] and surname as shown in any certificate referred to in entry No. 7; otherwise enter the first name[s] and surname by which the infant was known before being placed for adoption.

[2] Insert the applicant's address and, where he is not ordinarily resident in Great Britain, the place abroad where he ordinarily resides.

[3] The consent of the applicant's spouse may be dispensed with if the court is satisfied that he or she cannot be found or is incapable of giving his or her consent or that the spouses have separated and are living apart and the separation is likely to be permanent.

[4] This entry should be deleted if the application is made jointly by husband and wife or the applicant is unmarried.

[5] A separate medical certificate is required in respect of each applicant. There is an official form (Form No. 3) which may be used for this purpose. No certificate, however, need be supplied if the applicant, or one of the applicants, is the father, or mother of the infant or the infant has reached the upper limit of the compulsory school age.

[6] If the infant has previously been adopted, a certified copy of the entry in the Adopted Children Register should be attached and not a certified copy of the original entry in the Registers of Births.

[7] Where a certificate is not attached, enter the place (including country) of birth, if known.

[8] As the court may require up-to-date information as to the health of the infant, a medical report should be attached unless the applicant, or one of the applicants, is a parent or relative of the infant or the infant has reached the upper limit of the compulsory school age. There is an official form (Form No. 4) which may be used for this purpose.

[9] If the infant is less than one year old on the date of the application, the report should have been made not more than one month before that date. If the infant is one year old or more on that date, the report should have been made not more than six months before that date.

[10] If the infant has previously been adopted, give the names of his adoptive parents and not those of his natural parents.

[11] Enter mother's name.

[12] Enter name of father, if known.

[13] Guardian means a person appointed by deed or will in accordance with the provisions of the Guardianship of Infants Acts 1886 and 1925, or by a court of competent jurisdiction, to be a guardian.

[14] Enter the names of the persons mentioned in entries No. 9 and 10 except, in the case of an illegitimate infant, his father.

[15] The consent of a parent or guardian may be dispensed with if the court is satisfied that the person whose consent is required has abandoned, neglected or persistently ill-treated the infant, or has persistently failed without reasonable cause to discharge the obligations of a parent or guardian, or cannot be found, or is incapable of giving his consent or is withholding his consent unreasonably (statement of facts to be attached).

[16] This entry should be deleted except where some person or body has the rights and powers of a parent of the infant by virtue of section 75 of the Children and Young Persons Act 1933, or paragraph 12 (1) of the Fourth Schedule to that Act, or section 3 of the Children Act 1948.

[17] This entry should be deleted except where some person or body is liable to maintain the infant under a court order or agreement.

[18] Notice does not have to be given if the applicant or one of the applicants is a parent of the infant or if at the time of the hearing the infant will have reached the upper limit of the compulsory school age.

[19] The court cannot proceed with the application if a previous application made by the same applicant in respect of the same infant has been heard and dismissed on its merits, unless there has been a substantial change in the circumstances since the previous application.

[20] Any such payment or reward is illegal except payment to an adoption society or local authority in respect of their expenses incurred in connection with the adoption.

[21] Enter the name of any local authority, adoption society or indi-

vidual who has taken part in the arrangements for placing the infant in the care and possession of the applicant with a view to his adoption.

[22] Where the applicant, or one of the applicants, is a parent of the infant or a relative as defined by section 57 (1) of the Adoption Act 1958, no referee need be named.

[23] If the applicant wishes his identity to be kept confidential, the serial number obtained under Rule 2 of the Adoption (County Court) Rules 1959, should be given; otherwise this entry should be deleted.

[24] Where the application is for a provisional adoption order, insert the country in which the applicant is domiciled. The applicant must provide evidence of the law of adoption in that country. For this purpose an affidavit as to that law, sworn by a person who is conversant with it and who practises, or has practised, as a barrister or advocate in that country or is a duly accredited representative of the Government of that country in the United Kingdom, will be admissible if filed with the application.

[25] This entry should be deleted except when the application is for a provisional adoption order.

F. SIMPLIFIED ADOPTION APPLICATION FORM
EX. 113. (Rule 1(1) of the Adoption (County Court) Rules 1959)

In the .... County Court

No. ....

In The Matter of the Adoption Act, 1958
and
In The Matter of(a) .... an Infant

We, the undersigned .... and

.....................................being desirous of adopting

.....................................(a) an infant, under the Adoption Act 1958, hereby give the following particulars in support of our application.

Part I
Particulars of the applicant(s)
1. Name of first applicant in full................................

Address (b)...

Occupation ....

Date of Birth..

Relationship (if any) to the infant..............................

2. Name of second applicant in full..............................

Address (b)...

Occupation ....

Date of Birth..

Relationship (if any) to the infant..............................

3. We are resident and domiciled in England or Wales.

4. We are married to each other and are the persons to whom the attached marriage certificate (or other evidence of marriage) relates.

[5. A certificate as to our health, signed by a fully registered medical practitioner is attached.] (c)

PART II
Particulars of the Infant

6. The infant is of the........................sex and is not and has not been married. He/She was born on the....................day of........................19...., and is the person to whom the attached birth certificate relates [or was born on or about the.......... day of.................19...., in........................]. (d)

[7. A report on the health of the infant (e), made by a fully registered medical practitioner on the.................day of............... 19...., (f) is attached.]

8. The infant is the child of................................(g) [whose last known address was..................................

....] [or deceased] and (h)... [whose last known address was..................................

....] [or deceased].

9. We attach a document/documents signifying the consent of the said:

.... (i) to the making of an adoption order in pursuance of our application.

[10. We request the judge to dispense with the consent of:

....
on the ground that...
....
....(j( ]

[11. The......................Council [or....................]
of..............................has/have the rights and powers of a parent of the infant.] (k)

[12...................... of................................
is liable by virtue of an order made by the........................
court........................... at..........................
on the.................day of........................19....,
[or by an agreement dated the...........day of.................
19....,] to contribute to the maintenance of the infant.] (l)

13. If an adoption order is made in pursuance of this application, the infant is to be known by the following names:

Surname ....

Other names ....

PART III
General

14. The infant was received into our care and possession on the
................day of....................................19...., and has been continuously in our care and possession since that date.

[15. We notified the....................................Council

on the....................day of........................19...., of our intention to apply for an adoption order in respect of the infant. (m)]

16. Neither of us has made a previous application for an adoption order in respect of the infant.

17. We have not received or given any reward or payment for, or in consideration of, the adoption of the infant or for giving consent to the making of the adoption order [except as follows:

....

....] (n)

18. As far as we know no person or body has taken part in the arrangements for placing the infant in our care and possession [except........

....] (o)

19. For the purposes of this application reference may be made to

.... of........................] (p)

[20. We desire that our identity should be kept confidential, and the

serial number of this application is...........................] (q)

We accordingly apply for an adoption order in respect of the infant.

Dated this.................day of.......................19....

Signature(s)...........................

....

[This Form must be filed in duplicate, but duplicates of the attached documents need not be filed. Every paragraph must be completed or deleted, as the case may be.]

Notes:

(a) Enter the first name(s) and surname as shown in any certificate referred to in entry No. 6; otherwise enter the first name(s) and surname by which the infant was known before being placed for adoption.

(b) Insert the applicant's present address.

(c) A separate medical certificate is required in respect of each applicant. There is an official form (Form No. A.C.A.3) which may be used for this purpose. No certificate, however, need be supplied if the applicant is the father or mother of the infant or the infant has reached the upper limit of the compulsory school age.

(d) Where a certificate is not attached, enter the place (including country) of birth if known.

(e) As the court may require up-to-date information as to the health of the infant, a medical report should be attached unless the applicants, or one of the applicants, is a parent or relative of the infant or the infant has reached the upper limit of the compulsory school age. There is an official form (Form No. A.C.A.4) which may be used for the purpose.

(f) If the infant is less than one year old on the date of the application, the report should have been made not more than one month before that date. If the infant is one year old or more on that date, the report should have been made not more than six months before that date.

(g) Enter mother's name.

(h) Enter name of father, if known.

(i) Enter the names of the persons mentioned in entry No. 8 except, in the case of an illegitimate infant, his father.

(j) The consent of a parent or guardian may be dispensed with if the court is satisfied that the person whose consent is required has abandoned, neglected or persistently ill-treated the infant, or has persistently failed without reasonable cause to discharge the obligations of a parent or guardian, or cannot be found, or is incapable of giving his consent or is withholding his consent unreasonably.

(k) This entry should be deleted except where some person or body has the rights and powers of a parent of the infant by virtue of section 75 of the Children and Young Persons Act 1933 or paragraph 12(1) of the Fourth Schedule to that Act, or section 3 of the Children Act 1948.

(l) This entry should be deleted except where some person or body is liable to maintain the infant under a court order or agreement.

(m) Notice does not have to be given if the applicant or one of the applicants is a parent of the infant or if at the time of the hearing the infant will have reached the upper limit of the compulsory school age.

(n) Any such payment or reward is illegal except payment to an adoption society or local authority in respect of their expenses incurred in connection with the adoption.

(o) Enter the name of any local authority, adoption society or individual who has taken part in the arrangements for placing the infant in the care and possession of the applicant with a view to his adoption.

(p) Where the applicant, or one of the applicants, is a parent of the infant or a relative as defined by section 57(1) of the Adoption Act 1958, no referee need be named.

(q) If the applicants wish their identity to be kept confidential, the serial number obtained under Rule 2 of the Adoption (County Court) Rules 1959 should be given; otherwise this entry should be deleted.

Rule 1 (4)

G. NOTICE OF AN APPLICATION FOR AN ADOPTION ORDER OR A PROVISIONAL ADOPTION ORDER[3]

IN THE MATTER OF the Adoption Act 1958
and
IN THE MATTER OF .... [1] an infant

(Seal)

To .... of ....

Whereas an application for an adoption order/a provisional adoption order in respect of .... [1], an infant of the .... sex born on the .... day of ...., 19....., has been made [by .... and ....] [2] *or* [under the serial number ....];

And whereas .... of .... has been appointed guardian *ad litem* of the said infant:

Take notice:

A. [3] [that the said application will be heard at the .... County Court at .... on the .... day of ...., 19....., at .... o'clock, and that you may then appear and be heard on the question whether an adoption order/a provisional adoption order should be made.]

B. [3] [That if you wish to appear and be heard on the question whether an adoption order/a provisional adoption order should be made, you should give notice to the court on or before the .... day of ...., 19....., in order that a time may be fixed for your appearance.]

[And further take notice that while the said application is pending, a parent or guardian of the infant who has already signified his consent to the making of the adoption order must not, except with the leave of the judge, remove the infant from the care and possession of the applicant[s]. Application for such leave may be made personally to the judge.] [4]

It would assist the court if you would complete the attached form and return it to me.

Dated the .... day of ...., 19.....

Registrar.

Notes:

[1] Enter the name[s] and surname of the infant.

[2] The name of the applicant must not be given where a serial number is specified in the originating application (entry No. 22) and the notice is addressed to an individual other than the spouse of the applicant. In that case complete the second entry in square brackets.

[3] Paragraph A should be completed and paragraph B struck out where the notice is addressed to a local authority, an adoption society, any other body of persons or the spouse of the applicant, or where the applicant does not desire his identity to be kept confidential (see the originating application, entry No. 22). Where a serial number is specified in that entry and the notice is addressed to an individual respondent other than the spouse

of the applicant, paragraph A must be struck out and paragraph B completed.

[4] Delete words in square brackets except where the notice is addressed to a parent or guardian of the infant.

.... Perforation ....

To the Registrar of the .... County Court.

No. ....

I have received notice of the application for an adoption order/a provisional adoption order in respect of .... an infant.

I *do/do not wish to oppose the application.

I *do/do not wish to appear and be heard on the question whether an adoption order/a provisional adoption order should be made.

....

(*Signature*)

....

(*Date*)

....

(*Address*)

H. MEDICAL CERTIFICATE AS TO HEALTH OF APPLICANT[5]

Rule 3

I examined .... on .... and have formed the opinion that he is physically, mentally and emotionally suitable to adopt a child.

Signature ....   *Date* ....

Qualifications ....

Address ....

---

* Delete one or other alternatives.

Rule 4

I. MEDICAL REPORT ON HEALTH OF INFANT[4]

Note:

This form is for a medical report on a child who may be adopted. The report is for the benefit of the adopters and the court. In order that the adopters may benefit fully from the report, it is important that the certifying doctor should explain to the adopters the nature and extent of any disability or abnormality disclosed by the examination which might affect their decision whether or not to adopt the child.

Child's name .... Date of birth ....

Sex .... Weight .... Height ....

A   General condition

Skin

Eyes (including vision)

Ears (including hearing)

Nose and throat

Speech

Cardio-vascular system

Respiratory system

Alimentary system

Genito-urinary system (including examination of urine for albumen and sugar)

Skeletal and articular system (including examination for congenital dislocation of hip)

Nervous system (including fits)

Lymphatic system

Any other comments

Is the child physically normal having regard to his age?

B   Are there any items in the child's history or examination which suggest that he may be mentally abnormal having regard to his age?

C   Particulars of any illness from which the child has suffered.

D   If known,
Weight at birth (if child is under one year of age)

Details of birth, including result of mother's serological tests for syphilis.

Particulars, with dates, of vaccination or immunisation against—
Tuberculosis (state result of Mantoux test or whether child has been successfully vaccinated with B.C.G. vaccine)

Smallpox

Diphtheria

Whooping cough

Poliomyelitis

Tetanus (active)

Any other diseases.

E (i) (To be completed in the case of a child at least six weeks old at the time of the test—either test (a) or tests (b) (i) and (ii)may be carried out except where test (b) (i) or (ii) is positive, when test (a) must also be carried out)

    (a) Result of a suitable serological test of the child's blood for syphilis (please specify test) ....

    (b) Result of suitable serological tests of the mother's blood for syphilis
       (i) reagin (please specify test)
       ....
       (ii) verification (please specify test)
       ....

(ii) (To be completed in the case of a child over six complete days (excluding the day of his birth) and under two years old at the time of the test)

Result of test of the child's blood for the purpose of estimating the level of phenylalanine therein ....

F I examined the child on the .... day of ...., 19.....,
and I have informed the adopters of the state of health of the child disclosed by the examination.

Signature ....   *Date* ....

Qualifications ....

Address ....

Rule 5
J. CONSENT TO AN ADOPTION ORDER OR A PROVISIONAL ADOPTION ORDER[5]

IN THE MATTER OF the Adoption Act 1958
and
IN THE MATTER OF .... [1] an infant.

Whereas an application is to be/has been made by .... /and .... [*or* under the serial number] [2] for an adoption order/a provisional adoption order in respect of .... [1], an infant;

[And whereas the infant is the person to whom the birth certificate [3] now produced and shown to me marked "A" relates] [4]:

I, the undersigned .... of ...., being [5] the mother [6]/father [7]/guardian [8] of the infant, hereby state as follows:—

1. I understand that the effect of an adoption order will be to deprive me permanently of my rights as a parent/guardian and to transfer them to the applicant[s] [*or* I understand that the effect of a provisional adoption order will be to enable the applicant[s] to remove the infant from Great Britain for the purpose of adopting him/her abroad and to give the applicant[s] custody of the infant pending his/her adoption]; and in particular I understand that, if an order is made, I shall have no right to see or get in touch with the infant or to have him/her returned to me.

2. I further understand that the court cannot make an adoption order without the consent of each parent or guardian of the infant unless the court dispenses with a consent on the ground that the person concerned has abandoned, neglected or persistently ill-treated the infant, or cannot be found, or is incapable of giving consent, or is unreasonably withholding consent or has persistently failed without reasonable cause to discharge the obligations of a parent or guardian.

3. I further understand that, when the application for an adoption order is heard, this document may be used as evidence of my consent to the making of the order unless I inform the court that I no longer consent [9].

4. I hereby consent to the making of an adoption order/a provisional adoption order in pursuance of the application [on condition that the religious persuasion in which the infant is proposed to be brought up is ....] [10].

5. As far as I know, no other person or body has taken part in the arrangements for placing the infant in the care and possession of the applicant[s] [except .... of ....] [11].

....
(*Signature*)

This form, duly completed, was signed by the said .... before me [12] at .... on the .... day of ....19......

Signature ....

Address ....

Description ....

Warning. It is an offence to receive or give any reward or payment for, or in consideration of, the adoption of the infant or for giving consent to the making of an adoption order, other than a payment to a local authority society for their expenses incurred in connection with the adoption.

Notes:

[1] Insert the name[s] and surname as known to the consenting party.

[2] Insert either the name of the applicant or the serial number assigned to the applicant for the purpose of the application.

[3] If the infant has previously been adopted, a certified copy of the entry in the Adopted Children Register should be attached and not a certified copy of the original entry in the Registers of Births; and the description of the consenting party should include the words "by adoption" where appropriate.

[4] Delete the words in square brackets except where the consenting party is the mother or father of the infant and the birth certificate has not already been identified by the other parent.

[5] Delete all but one of the descriptions which follow.

[6] The mother's consent cannot be given before the infant is six weeks old.

[7] "Father" does not include the natural father of an illegitimate child.

[8] "Guardian" means a person appointed by deed or will in accordance with the provisions of the Guardianship of Minors Act 1971, or by a court of competent jurisdiction, to be guardian of the infant.

[9] Notice will be given of the making of the application and of the court by which it is to be heard. After the making of the application the consenting parent or guardian cannot remove the infant from the care and possession of the applicant except with the leave of the court.

[10] Delete the words in square brackets if the applicant is named or if, although the applicant is not named, the consenting party does not desire to impose a condition as to religious upbringing.

[11] Enter the name of any local authority, adoption society or person who is known to have arranged, or to have taken part in the arrangements, for the infant to be placed in the care and possession of the applicant.

[12] In England or Wales the document should be signed before a justice of the peace, a duly authorised county court officer or a justices' clerk and in Scotland before a justice of the peace or a sheriff. In Northern Ireland it should be signed before a justice of the peace. Outside the United Kingdom it should be signed before a person authorised to administer an oath for any judicial or legal purpose, a British consular officer, a notary public or, if the person signing it is serving in the armed forces, a commissioned officer.

Appendix to Home Office letter H.O. 53/59 dated March 25, 1959

K. EXPLANATORY MEMORANDUM TO BE GIVEN TO APPLICANTS FOR ADOPTION ORDERS[6]

1. When the court considers your application for an adoption order, it will want to know whether the child is old enough to understand about adoption and, if so, whether you have told him about your application. If

the court thinks the child is old enough to understand, you must tell him before the order can be granted.

2. If the child is still too young, it is best to decide to tell him as soon as he can begin to understand, or as soon as he begins to ask questions, which is normally at the age of four or five. You can then gradually tell him more as he grows older. You may prefer not to tell him anything; but that would be unwise, because he would be likely to find out for himself sooner or later and if you had not told him the discovery might be a great shock. If you find it difficult to tell him, the local children's officer or the adoption society, if a society arranged the adoption, may be able to help you, but he ought to be told by you.

3. When the court makes an adoption order, all the rights, duties, obligations and liabilities of the natural parents with regard to the child will be transferred to you.

4. After the adoption order is made, if you die (or anyone in your family dies) without leaving a will the child will be eligible to inherit just as he would if he had been a legitimate child born to you. If you or any of your relatives have already made wills and want to include the child as if he had been born into the family it would be well to seek legal advice.

5. When a married couple adopt a child jointly and the husband is a citizen of the United Kingdom and Colonies, the adoption order makes the child a citizen of the United Kingdom and Colonies (if he is not one already). When one person alone adopts a child and he or she is a citizen of the United Kingdom and Colonies, the granting of the adoption order has the same effect.

6. If the court makes an adoption order, you will be given, or sent within seven days, an abridged copy of the order. You are also entitled to receive, if you ask for it, a full copy of the order which includes particulars of the child's original parentage (thus disclosing illegitimacy if he is illegitimate). The abridged copy omits these particulars but it is headed "Adoption order" and you may prefer to use the abridged copy to show to anyone who needs to see the adoption order but whom you do not want to know all the particulars.

7. When an adoption order is made, the court directs the Registrar General to enter in the Adopted Children Register particulars of the adoption (quoting only the child's new name if his name has been changed). The Registrar General will send you, soon after he has received the copy of the order from the court, a short certificate of the entry in the Register; this will be issued free of charge but the fee for any additional short certificate will be 3s (15p) and a full certified copy of the entry 8s (40p). These certificates are generally acceptable for most purposes where a birth certificate is required.

8. If the child is under five years of age and you have not received a welfare milk token book for him, you should apply to the local office of the Ministry of Pensions and National Insurance producing, if you have one, the note handed to you by the adoption society or local authority about the previous token books.

9. If the court makes an adoption order and you wish the child to be registered with a doctor under the National Health Service, you should fill in the form opposite and take it to the doctor of your choice as soon as

possible after the order is made. When the doctor accepts the child for inclusion in his list arrangements will be made to send you a medical card in the child's new name (if there is a change of name) with a new National Health Service number which cannot be linked in any way with the child's previous identity. If you have the child's old medical card you should destroy it.

It is important in the child's future interests that you should use the form whether or not the adoption involves any change of name or change of doctor.

E.C. 58 C.

NATIONAL HEALTH SERVICE

To be completed by parent

Child's surname...

Child's forenames ....

Date of birth ....

Home address ....

....

Application to be placed on the list of Dr. ....

Signature of parent .... Date................................

To be completed by doctor
I accept the child named above for inclusion in my list.

Signed .... Date................................

Enter D here if supplying drugs   ☐

Enter distance here if claiming mileage   ☐

Home Office Circular No. 205/1965   *Dated* 9th *September,* 1965

L. REGISTRATION UNDER THE NATIONAL HEALTH SERVICE OF CHILDREN AWAITING ADOPTION

1. Paragraph 9 of the explanatory memorandum included as the Appendix to Home Office Circular No. 53/1959 of 25th March, 1959, about the Adoption Rules described a procedure for the registration of a child who is to be adopted with a doctor under the National Health Service.

The arrangement by which the appropriate form, which is part of the explanatory memorandum, is given by the courts to applicants for adoption orders does not provide for the situation of prospective adopters who may wish to have the child registered or re-registered with their doctor under the name by which the child is to be known as soon as he is received into their care and possession. The purpose of this letter is to invite the help of local authorities in remedying this position.

2. Most prospective adopters have an obligation under section 3 (2) of the Adoption Act 1958 to notify the local authority of their intention to adopt. In the ordinary course, they give notice as soon as they receive the child and this may be some time before they apply for an adoption order. Once notice has been given the local authority has an obligation under section 38 to secure that the child is visited from time to time by officers of the authority who shall satisfy themselves as to his well-being and give such advice as to his care and maintenance as may appear to be needed. Your authority may be willing to agree that the officers carrying out these duties could conveniently draw the attention of prospective adopters to the arrangements for registration by handing them a copy of the enclosed form. Where the local authority have themselves arranged the placing of the child or have received notice of the placing of the child under section 40, they will no doubt arrange for the prospective adopters to be given the form at the earliest possible stage. The use of this specially numbered form, although it does not mention adoption, sets in train a procedure whereby the child's previous medical history is transferred to his record in his new name whilst avoiding unnecessary disclosure of his new name.

3. A supply of the forms is enclosed. More can be obtained from the local executive council of the National Health Service who will be willing to answer any questions about registration arrangements.

4. In a few instances, prospective adopters who have applied for an adoption order will not be granted one and under the new arrangements they may have already registered the child with a doctor in his intended new name. If the local authority knows that an adoption order has not been granted, it would assist the Ministry of Health if the authority would notify the National Health Service Central Register, Smedley Hydro, Southport, Lancashire, so that Health Service records can be corrected as necessary. Preferably the child's medical card should be sent but if it is not available, the information which should be given to the Central Register is the name by which the child was to have been known, his date of birth, and the National Health Service number (if the local authority know it).

5. Records kept by local authorities—for example, health visiting record cards—sometimes link the child's old and new identities. Local authorities will no doubt wish to ensure that any records they keep (apart from confidential adoption records) should not disclose an adopted child's previous identity: when an adoption is known to have taken place new records in the new name should be substituted for those in the old, which should be destroyed.

6. Extra copies of this circular and its enclosure are sent for the information of the Children's Officer and Medical Officer of Health. Copies have also been sent to the Clerk and Medical Officers of Health of authorities exercising delegated health and welfare functions.

E.C. 58B.

(For issue to a person who
intends to adopt a child)

NATIONAL HEALTH SERVICE

If you have in your care a child whom you intend to adopt, and wish to register or re-register the child with a doctor under the National Health Service, you should fill in the form below and take it to the doctor of your choice. When the doctor accepts the child as a patient, arrangements will be made for you to receive a medical card in the child's new name (if there is a change of name) and with a new National Health Service number which cannot be linked in any way with the child's previous records.

You will notice that there is no reference to adoption in the form itself; please detach it from these notes and use it on its own.

You may have registered the child already with your doctor, using a form provided by the doctor or the Executive Council. If so, you should re-register the child, using the form below if you want to ensure that the special arrangements are made for keeping the adoption confidential.

You may also have received from the Court to which you have applied for an adoption order a form like the one below. If so, and if you have used it, there is no need to fill in the form below. If the Court gives you a form after you have used this one, do not complete it.

If you have the old medical card, you should destroy it when you receive the new one.

E.C. 58B

NATIONAL HEALTH SERVICE

To be completed on behalf of the child

Names by which ⎫ Surname ....
the child is   ⎬
to be known   ⎭ Forenames ....

Date of Birth ....

Home Address ....

....

Application to be placed on the list of Dr. ....

Signature of Applicant on behalf of the child ....

Date ....

Doctor's Code No. ....

To be completed by doctor

I accept the child named above for inclusion in my list

Signed .... Date..

	If Claiming a Rural Practice Payment	
If Supplying Drugs Enter D here	Enter distance from main surgery to patient's residence and inform Executive Council if claiming for other than ordinary distance	

Regulation 4

M. ADOPTION OF CHILDREN

Explanatory Memorandum[7]

This memorandum is addressed to the parent (a term which does not include the natural father of an illegitimate child) or guardian of a child who is about to be legally adopted.

A person proposing to adopt your child has to apply to a court for an adoption order. Before making an order, the court will have inquiries made by a person called the guardian *ad litem* to see whether it would be in the interests of the child that he should be adopted by the proposed adopters. The court will also require to know whether you (and any other parent or guardian of the child) consent. The court cannot make an adoption order without your consent unless it dispenses with your consent on the ground that you have abandoned, neglected or persistently ill-treated the child, or that you have failed without reasonable cause to discharge your obligations as a parent or guardian, or on the ground that you have unreasonably withheld your consent. The court may also dispense with consent on the ground that the parent or guardian cannot be found or is incapable of giving consent (for instance by reason of being insane).

You will be asked to sign a form of consent which can be shown to the court as evidence of your consent. This form will either give the names of the persons wishing to adopt the child or, if they wish to conceal their identity, will refer to them by a number. If you want to know what sort of people they are, you can ask the adoption society or local authority that is arranging the adoption.

Do not sign the form of consent unless you are quite sure that you are willing that your child should be adopted by these persons. If the court makes an adoption order, your rights as a parent or guardian will be transferred to the adopters and they will become in law the child's parents. You will then have no further right to see the child or to have the child returned to you. If the adopters live abroad, they will probably take the child abroad with them after obtaining an order.

If you do not know the names of the proposed adopters, but wish your child to be brought up in a particular religious faith, you may give your consent on condition that they propose to bring up your child in that faith.

If you sign the form of consent and then, before the adoption order is made, you wish to withdraw your consent, you should inform the court. But the proposed adopters are entitled to refuse to hand back your child to you unless you obtain the permission of the court.

You are not allowed to receive any money for giving your consent.

CERTIFICATE

To (name of adoption society or local authority)

I hereby certify that I have received from you a memorandum headed "Adoption of Children. Explanatory Memorandum", from which I have detached this certificate of acknowledgment; and I further certify that I have read the memorandum and understand it.

Signature ....

Address ....

....

Date ....

N. GUARDIAN *AD LITEM* REPORT

(*Suggested Form*)

....Juvenile Court   County Court ref: ....
County

Serial No. ....

....(date of hearing)

Report of Guardian *ad litem* on the application of .... and
.... to adopt ....

Infant:

existing name;
whether legitimate;
sex;
date of birth;
place of birth;
movements before being
placed with applicants;
which may need to be
proved by affidavits
religion;
previously adopted;

whether old enough to understand
nature of adoption order;
if so, wishes with regard to adoption
and whether interviewed;
whether any right to or interest in
property;
whether insured (details);
name by which to be known after
adoption;
health;
medical certificate;

(*cont'd*)

in care;
coloured;

whether related to either applicant;
report from local authority or adoption society attached;

Mother:
  full name;
  date of birth;
  address;
  nationality;
  occupation;
  income;
  religion;
  wishes with regard to child's religion;
  single, married, separated or divorced;
  if separated or divorced, court and date;

whether order seen;
any custody previously;
whether consent given freely and with full understanding of nature of adoption order;
reason for consenting to adoption;
whether consent and birth certificate verified;
interviewed by;
whether proposes to attend hearing;
whether supplied with memorandum;
medical history;
other children;
circumstances generally;

Father:
  full name;
  date of birth;
  address;
  occupation;
  income;
  nationality;
  religion;
  wishes with regard to child's religion;
  marital state;
  medical history;

whether consent required;
given freely and with full understanding of nature of adoption order;
verified;
whether liable to contribute by order or agreement;
if so, particulars of order and whether complied with;
interviewed by;
other children;
circumstances generally;

Applicants:
  Male:
    full name;
    date of birth;
    nationality;

occupation;
income;
religion (practising, confirmed);

  Female:
    full name;
    maiden name;
    date of birth;
    nationality;

occupation;
income;
religion (practising, confirmed);

Married:
  place and date, and whether certificate seen;

Children:
  details of children of marriage;

Nature of Order:
    whether applicants understand nature of order and that, in particular, it is irrevocable and will render them responsible for maintenance and upbringing of infant;

Health:
    whether applicants have suffered from any serious illness and whether there is any history of tuberculosis, epilepsy or mental illness in their families. Whether medical certificates satisfactory;

Reason:
    why do applicants wish to adopt;

Address:

address;	mortgage repayments;
brief description;	amount of rates;
whether rented;	number of rooms;
amount of rent;	garden;
or own property;	whether clean;
amount of mortgage	nature of furnishings;
outstanding;	where child sleeps;
	any other person living at this address;

Referee: whether responsible person and whether recommends applicants;

Interviewed by:

Memorandum: whether supplied;

Third Party: name, address, circumstances in which arrangements were made;

Reward: whether made; given; agreed; offered;
    date of notification (if applicable);

Supervision by:

Welfare Authority: date of notification; whether supervised and by whom; whether reports satisfactory; *assessment of suitability;*

Verification of Application: whether statements in application have been verified, including request for dispensing with consent of parent;

Information to Applicants: have the applicants been informed regarding:
    (a) infant's baptism
    (b) any immunisation treatment given to infant
    (c) the infant's right to property
    (d) any insurance policy on the child for funeral expenses;

Interim Order: whether recommended.

....
for Director of Social Services
.... Council
Guardian *ad litem*

...., 19......

NOTES

1. By reg. 20 of the Boarding-out of Children Regulations 1955, a foster parent is required to sign an undertaking in the form set out in Appendix D.
2. By rule 1(1) of the Adoption (County Court) Rules 1959 the proposed adopter must file a copy of the above form in the office of the appropriate court, but see also separate simplified forms for applicants resident in England or Wales reproduced in Appendix F.
3. By reg. 10 of the Adoption (County Court) Rules 1959, the above notice must be served on the respondents to the application and a copy served on the guardian *ad litem*.
4. By rule 4 of the Adoption (County Court) Rules 1959, a copy of the above report or a similar report shall be filed with the application for an adoption order.
5. By rule 5 of the Adoption (County Court) Rules 1959, the above form must be filed with the originating application.
6. Home Office letter HO 53/59 recommended that juvenile courts provide applicants with statements about the effect of an adoption order. The above memorandum was appended by the letter as a form which might serve this purpose.
7. By reg. 4 of the Adoption Agencies Regulations 1959 an adoption society must see that a parent or guardian proposing to place an infant at the disposition of a registered adoption agency is supplied with a copy of the above memorandum. This also applies to a local authority arranging adoptions.

INDEX